Deseret Industries
52

AF531090

A Thoughtful Faith

Essays on Belief by Mormon Scholars

Be ready always to give an answer to every man that asketh you a reason of the hope that is in you with meekness and fear.

(1 Peter 3:15)

A Thoughtful Faith

Essays on Belief by Mormon Scholars

Thomas G. Alexander · *Richard L. Anderson*
Leonard J. Arrington · *Allen R. Barlow*
Philip L. Barlow · *Francine R. Bennion*
Mary L. Bradford · *Carlfred B. Broderick*
Richard L. Bushman · *Victor B. Cline*
Richard H. Cracroft · *Eugene England*
Robert C. Fletcher · *Kenneth W. Godfrey*
John T. Kesler · *William Clayton Kimball*
Richard D. Poll · *Noel B. Reynolds*
E. Gary Smith · *Emma Lou Thayne*
Laurel Thatcher Ulrich · *Bruce W. Young*

Compiled and Edited by
Philip L. Barlow

Library of Congress Catalog Card Number:
86-71882

ISBN 0-939651-00-9

First Printing September 1986

Canon Press P.O. Box 213
Centerville, Utah 84014-0213

Printed in the United States of America

For...

Lowell L. Bennion

Contents

Preface

One day my friend Reuben decided to leave the Church. "I no longer consider myself a Latter-day Saint," he said. No more home teaching. No more temple attendance. No more faith.

I was troubled, just like his own thoroughly Mormon family. How was it that a man whom I so admired, a man whose heritage included bishops and stake presidents, whom I numbered among the most intelligent and morally sensitive of persons, and after whom I had, in fact, tried to pattern some of my own behavior—how was it that such a man could leave the Church that we both had loved for so long?

"Simple," he told me (though his pain was obvious), "I no longer believe that it is true."

Reuben and I spent weeks and months exploring what he meant by that statement. I knew him well enough to recognize that this was a case of genuine, irreducibly intellectual disbelief. His now dominant doubts, we both concurred, could not be facilely ascribed to sin, no matter what others might sometimes say about such matters. And Reuben was certainly not another tragicomic example of exaggerated evangelical zealotry; he was not a Christian fundamentalist who was leaving the Church in favor of the opportunity to misuse the name of Jesus in an endless series of quasi-magical incantations. Rather, during the course of his higher education and his growing awareness of what he called the underside of Mormon history, and as he became acquainted with the conflicting faiths of diverse peoples and the complex sufferings of an agonized world, Reuben's faith had failed—and thus far neither prayers nor tears nor friends had been able to revive it.

In the years since Reuben first openly declared his doubts (years in which I have experienced my own struggles of faith) I have spoken with dozens of people with concerns similar to his. Indeed, as an instructor of bright and probing college students at the LDS Institute of Religion in Cambridge, Massachusetts, I came to see clearly just how torturous the quest for authentic faith can be.

Lengthy conversations with students at the Institute eventually convinced me that a great many people would be blessed if a sampling of unusually thoughtful Latter-day Saints, persons who not only possessed enduring faith but who also appreciated philosophy and history and science, could be induced to publicly articulate the reasons for their steadfast belief in Joseph Smith's prophetic role and in the restored gospel of Jesus Christ.

However, before I had gone very far with this project I learned that I was not the only one with such ideas. At about the same time, another member of the Church had begun to assemble statements of faith primarily by Mormons in the sciences. When I learned this, I decided to restrict my anthology (with one or two exceptions) to essays by authors whose professional fields were in the social sciences and humanities. I felt these people would have something distinctive to tell us.

When I first solicited the papers during the spring and summer of 1985, most of the authors were (as evidenced by their inclusion herein) sufficiently convinced of the importance of the project to find time to write their contributions. In many cases, finding the time to write them was itself a significant accomplishment. In several other instances I was graciously allowed to reprint important articles which had been previously published.

Despite the authors' basic enthusiasm, however, there were also a few reservations. Some were inhibited by modesty: Do I have anything so distinctive to say that I should say it in print? Others were concerned lest the public candor demanded by the enterprise render them vulnerable to those who seem unwilling or unable to understand them, or to those who do understand but are intolerant of perspectives that differ from their own. More than one author wrote with self-described trepidation, wishing to avoid being categorized, anxious not to seem arrogant, yet wanting to be of help. In short, the essays were offered in a spirit of modest and constructive generosity.

It should be obvious that each author is solely responsible for his or her own words. None of these writers represents in any official way The Church of Jesus Christ of Latter-day Saints. Indeed, few will agree with everything they read in these pages, since the book is based on a broad range of human experience and highly personal feelings.

Yet I hope that the essays will serve as symbols of the enriching diversity that exists among thoughtful and believing Mormons. I trust that they will provide a wider angle of vision for those who are struggling (as we all should be) to enlarge and refine and better understand their own religious commitments.

Many individuals who are not Latter-day Saints have discovered that they admire Mormon ways; but, because of their reflective natures or their education, they have thus far been unable to take the Church itself seriously. Perhaps the essays will suggest to these people that there are others, also reflective and educated, to whom the gospel has proved a blessing. The essays should be equally instructive to those who misunderstand all questioning as apostasy, as well as those who think that the acceptance of any traditional view is intellectual compromise. Finally, I hope the book may serve to remind both intellectuals and those suspicious of the intellect that, though they may often remain in tension, the Spirit and the informed mind need not be perpetually at war.

Philip L. Barlow

1

Richard D. Poll

What The Church Means To People Like Me

Richard Poll gave the following sermon in a Palo Alto (California) Ward sacrament meeting in August 1967. Since then, his images of the "Iron Rod Saint" and the "Liahona Saint" have become classic symbols of broad identification for thousands of believing Mormons. Brother Poll is Professor Emeritus of history at Western Illinois University and currently lectures on American History at Brigham Young University. He is a co-editor of Utah's History *and, with Eugene E. Campbell, is the co-author of* Hugh B. Brown: His Life and Thought. *He has served in the Church as a branch president and high councilman. He and his wife Emogene are the parents of three children and seven grandchildren. His sermon was originally published in* Dialogue: A Journal of Mormon Thought, *and is reprinted here by permission.*

A natural reaction to my title—since this is not a testimony meeting in which each speaker is his own subject—might be, "Who cares?" For who in this congregation, with the possible exception of my brother, Carl, are "people like me"? I have a wife and daughter present who find me in some respects unique. And I am sure there are students at Brigham Young University who hope that I am unique. By the time I have finished there may be some among you who will share that hope.

Yet I have chosen the topic because I believe that in some important respects I represent a type of Latter-day Saint which is found in almost every ward and branch in the Church. By characterizing myself and explaining the nature of my commitment to the gospel, I hope to contribute a little something of value to each of you, whether it turns out that you are "people like me" or not.

My thesis is that there are two distinct types of active and dedicated Latter-day Saints. I am not talking about "good Mormons" and "Jack Mormons," or about Saints in white hats and pseudo-Saints in black. No, I am talking about two types of *involved* Church members who are here tonight, each deeply committed to the gospel but also prone toward misgivings about the legitimacy, adequacy, or serviceability of the commitment of the other.

The purpose of my inquiry is not to support either set of misgivings, but to describe each type as dispassionately as I can, to identify myself with one of the types, and then to bear witness concerning some of the blessings which the Church offers to the type I identify with. My prayer is that this effort will help us all to look beyond the things which obviously differentiate us toward that "unity of the faith" which Christ set as our common goal.

For convenience of reference, let me propose symbols for my two types of Mormons. They have necessarily to be affirmative images, because I am talking only about "good" members. I found them in the Book of Mormon, a natural place for a Latter-day Saint to find good symbols as well as good counsel.

The figure for the first type comes from Lehi's dream—

the Iron Rod. The figure for the second comes also from Lehi's experience—the Liahona. So similar they are as manifestations of God's concern for his children, yet just different enough to suit my purposes tonight.

The Iron Rod, as the hymn reminds us, was the Word of God. To the person with his hand on the rod, each step of the journey to the tree of life was plainly defined; he had only to hold on as he moved forward. In Lehi's dream the way was *not easy*, but it was *clear*.

The Liahona, in contrast, was a compass. It pointed to the destination but did not fully mark the path; indeed, the clarity of its directions varied with the circumstances of the user. For Lehi's family the sacred instrument was a reminder of their temporal and eternal goals, but it was no infallible delineator of their course.

Even as the Iron Rod and the Liahona were both approaches to the word of God and to the kingdom of God, so our two types of members seek the word and the kingdom. The fundamental difference between them lies in their concept of the relation of man to the "word of God." Put another way, it is a difference in the meaning assigned to the concept "the fulness of the gospel." Do the revelations of our Heavenly Father give us a handrail to the Kingdom, or a compass only?

The Iron Rod Saint does not look for questions, but for answers, and in the gospel—as he understands it—he finds or is confident that he can find the answer to every important question. The Liahona Saint, on the other hand, is preoccupied with questions and skeptical of answers; he finds in the gospel—as he understands it—answers to enough important questions so that he can function purposefully without answers to the rest. This last sentence holds the key to the question posed by my title, but before pursuing its implications let us explore our scheme of classification more fully.

As I suggested at the outset, I find Iron Rods and Liahonas in almost every LDS congregation, discernible by the kinds of comments they make in gospel doctrine classes and the very language in which they phrase their testimonies. What gives them their original bent is difficult to identify. The Iron Rods may be somewhat more common among converts, but many nowadays are attracted to the Church by those reasons more appropriate to Liahonas which I will mention later on. Liahona testimonies may be more prevalent among born members who have not had an emotional conversion experience, but many such have developed Iron Rod commitments in the home, the Sunday School, the mission field, or some other conditioning environment. Social and economic status appear to have nothing to do with type, and the rather widely-held notion that education tends to produce Liahonas has so many exceptions that one may plausibly argue that education only makes Liahonas more articulate. Parenthetically, some of the most prominent Iron Rods in the Church are on the BYU faculty.

Pre-existence may, I suppose, have something to do with placement in this classification, even as it may account for other life circumstances, but heredity obviously does not. The irritation of the Iron Rod father confronted by an iconoclastic son is about as commonplace as the embarrassment of the Liahona parent who discovers that his teen-age daughter has found comfortable answers in seminary to some of the questions that have perplexed him all his life.

The picture is complicated by the fact that changes of type do occur, often in response to profoundly unsettling personal experiences. The Liahona member who, in a context of despair or repentance, makes the "leap of faith" to Iron Rod commitment is rather rare, I think, but the investigator of Liahona temperament who becomes an Iron Rod convert is almost typical. The Iron Rod member who responds to personal tragedy or intellectual shock by becoming a Liahona is known to us all; this transition may be, but is not necessarily, a stage in a migration toward inactivity or even apostasy.

My present opinion is that one's identification with the Iron Rods or the Liahonas is more a function of basic temperament and of accidents than of premortal accomplishments or mortal choices, but that opinion—like many other views expressed in this sermon—has neither scriptural nor scientific validation.

A point to underscore in terms of our objective of "unity of the faith" is that Iron Rods and Liahonas have great difficulty understanding each other—not at the level of intellectual acceptance of the right to peaceful co-existence, but at the level of personal communion, of empathy. To the Iron Rod a questioning attitude suggests an imperfect faith; to the Liahona an unquestioning spirit betokens a closed mind. Neither frequent association nor even prior personal involvement with the other group guarantees empathy. Indeed, the person who has crossed the line is likely to be least sympathetic and tolerant toward his erstwhile kindred spirits.

I have suggested that the essential difference between the Liahonas and the Iron Rods is in their approach to the concept "the word of God." Let us investigate that now a little.

The Iron Rod is confident that, on any question, the mind and will of the Lord may be obtained. His sources are threefold: Scripture, Prophetic Authority, and the Holy Spirit.

In the standard works of the Church the Iron Rod member finds far more answers than does his Liahona brother, because he accepts them as God's word in a far more literal sense. In them he finds answers to questions as diverse as the age and origin of the earth, the justification for capital punishment, the proper diet, the proper role of government, the nature and functions of sex, and the nature of man. To the Liahona, he sometimes seems to be reading things into the printed words, but to himself the meaning is clear.

In the pronouncements of the general authorities, living and dead, the Iron Rod finds many answers, because he accepts and gives comprehensive application to that language of the Doctrine and Covenants which declares: "And whatsoever they shall speak when moved upon by the Holy Ghost shall be scripture, shall be the will of the Lord, shall be the mind of the Lord, shall be the word of the Lord, shall be the voice of the Lord, and the power of God unto salvation" (68:4). This reliance extends to every facet of life. On birth control and family planning, labor relations and race relations, the meaning of the Constitution and prospects for the United Nations, the laws of health and the signs of the times, the counsel of the "living oracles" suffices. Where answers are not found in the published record, they are sought in correspondence and interviews, and once received, they are accepted as definitive.

Third among the sources for the Iron Rod member is the Holy Spirit. As Joseph Smith found answers in the counsel of James, "If any of you lack wisdom, let him ask of God...," so any Latter-day Saint may do so. Whether it be the choice of a vocation or the choice of a mate, help on a college examination or in finding "Golden Prospects" in the mission field, healing the sick or averting a divorce—in prayer is the answer. The response may not be what was expected, but it *will* come, and it will be a manifestation of the Holy Spirit.

Implicit in all this is the confidence of the Iron Rod Latter-day Saint that our Heavenly Father is intimately involved in the day-to-day business of His children. As no sparrow falls without the Father, so nothing befalls man without His will. God knows the answers to all questions and has the solutions to all problems, and the only thing which denies man access to this reservoir is his own stubbornness. Truly, then, the person who opens his mind and heart to the channels of revelation, past and present, has the Iron Rod which leads unerringly to the Kingdom.

The Liahona Latter-day Saint lacks this certain confidence. Not that he rejects the concepts upon which it rests—that God lives, that He loves His children, that His knowledge and power are efficacious for salvation, and that He does reveal His will as the Ninth Article of Faith affirms. Nor does he reserve the right of selective obedience to the will of God as he understands it. No, the problem for the Liahona involves the adequacy of the *sources* on which the Iron Rod testimony depends.

The problem is in perceiving the will of God when it is mediated—as it is for almost all mortals—by "the arm of flesh." The Liahona is convinced by logic and experience that no human instrument, even a prophet, is capable of transmitting the word of God so clearly and comprehensively that it can be universally understood and easily appropriated by man.

Because the Liahona finds it impossible to accept the literal verbal inspiration of the standard works, the sufficience of scriptural answers to questions automatically comes into question. If Eve was not made from Adam's rib, how much of the Bible is historic truth? If geology and anthropology have undermined Bishop Ussher's chronology, which places creation at 4000 B.C., how much of the Bible is scientific truth? And if our latter-day scriptures have been significantly revised since their original publication, can it be assumed that they are now infallibly authoritative? To the Liahona these volumes are sources of inspiration and moral truth, but they leave many specific questions unanswered, or uncertainly answered.

As for the authority of the latter-day prophets, the Liahona Saint finds consensus among them on gospel fundamentals but far-ranging diversity on many important issues. The record shows error, as in Brigham Young's statements about the continuation of slavery, and it shows change of counsel, as in the matter of gathering to Zion. It shows differences of opinion—Heber J. Grant and Reed Smoot on the League of Nations, and David O. McKay and Joseph Fielding Smith on the process of creation. To the Liahona, the "living oracles" are God's special witnesses of the gospel of Christ and his agents in directing the affairs of the Church, but like the scriptures, they leave many important questions unanswered, or uncertainly answered.

The Iron Rod proposition that the Spirit will supply what the prophets have not, gives difficulty on both philosophical and experimental grounds. Claims that prayer is an infallible, almost contractual, link between God and man through the Holy Spirit find Liahona Mormons perplexed by the nature of the evidence. As a method of confirming truth, the witness of the Spirit demonstrably has not produced uniformity of gospel interpretation even among Iron Rod Saints, and it is allegedly by the witness of that same Spirit—by the burning within—that many apostates pronounce the whole Church in error. As a method of influencing the course of events, it seems unpredictable and some of the miracles claimed for it seem almost whimsical. By the prayer of faith one man recovers his lost eyeglasses; in spite of such prayer, another man goes blind.

All of which leaves the Liahona Mormon with a somewhat tenuous connection with the Holy Spirit. He may take comfort in his imperfect knowledge from the portion of the

Article of Faith which says that "God will yet reveal many great and important things...." And he may reconcile his conviction of God's love and his observation of the uncertain earthly outcomes of faith by emphasizing the divine commitment to the principle of free agency, as I shall presently do. In any case, it seems to the Liahona Mormon that God's involvement in day-to-day affairs must be less active and intimate than the Iron Rod Mormon believes, because there are so many unsolved problems and unanswered prayers.

Is the Iron Rod member unaware of these considerations which loom so large in the Liahona member's definition of his relationship to the word of God? In some instances, I believe, the answer is yes. For in our activity-centered Church it is quite possible to be deeply and satisfyingly involved without looking seriously at the philosophical implications of some gospel propositions which are professed.

In many instances, however, the Iron Rod Saint has found sufficient answers to the Liahona questions. He sees so much basic consistency in the scriptures and the teachings of the latter-day prophets that the apparent errors and incongruities can be handled by interpretation. He finds so much evidence of the immanence of God in human affairs that the apparently pointless evil and injustice in the world can be handled by the valid assertion that God's ways are not man's ways. He is likely to credit his Liahona contemporaries with becoming so preoccupied with certain problems that they cannot see the gospel forest for the trees, and he may even attribute that preoccupation to an insufficiency of faith.

As a Liahona, I must resist the attribution, though I cannot deny the preoccupation.

Both kinds of Mormons have problems. Not just the ordinary personal problems to which all flesh is heir, but problems growing out of the nature of their Church commitment.

The Iron Rod has a natural tendency to develop answers where none may, in fact, have been revealed. He may find arguments against social security in the Book of Mormon; he may discover in esoteric prophetic utterances a timetable for the Second Coming of which "that day and hour knoweth no man...." His dogmatism may become offensive to his peers in the Church and a barrier to communication with his own family; his confidence in his own insights may make him impatient with those whom he publicly sustains. He may also cling to cherished answers in the face of new revelation, or be so shaken by innovation that he forms new "fundamentalist" sects. The Iron Rod concept holds many firm in the Church, but it leads some out.

The Liahona, on the other hand, has the temptation to broaden the scope of his questioning until even the most clearly defined Church doctrines and policies are included. His resistance to statistics on principle may deteriorate into a carping criticism of programs and leaders. His ties to the Church may become so nebulous that he cannot communicate them to his children. His testimony may become so selective as to exclude him from some forms of Church activity or to make him a hypocrite in his own eyes as he participates in them. His persistence in doubting may alienate his brethren and eventually destroy the substance of his gospel commitment. Then he, too, is out—without fireworks, but not without pain.

Both kinds of Latter-day Saints serve the Church. They talk differently and apparently think and feel differently about the gospel, but as long as they avoid the extremes just mentioned, they share a love for and commitment to the Church. They cannot therefore be distinguished on the basis of attendance at meetings, or participation on welfare projects, or contributions, or faithfulness in the performance of callings. They may or may not be "hundred percenters," but the degree of their activity is not a function of type, insofar as I have been able to observe. It may be that Iron Rods are a little more faithful in genealogical work, but even this is not certain.

Both kinds of members are found at every level of Church responsibility—in bishoprics and Relief Society presidencies, in stake presidencies and high councils, and even among the general authorities. But whatever their private orientation, the public deportment of the general authorities seems to me to represent a compromise, which would be natural in the circumstances. They satisfy the Iron Rod by emphasizing the solid core of revealed truth and discouraging speculative inquiry into matters of faith and morals, and they comfort the Liahonas by reminding the Saints that God has not revealed the answer to every question or defined the response to every prayer.

As I have suggested, the Iron Rods and the Liahonas have some difficulty understanding each other. Lacking the patience, wisdom, breadth of experience, or depth of institutional commitment of the general authorities, we sometimes criticize and judge each other. But usually we live and let live—each finding in the Church what meets his needs and all sharing the gospel blessings which do not depend on identity of testimony.

Which brings me to the second part of my remarks—the part which gives my talk its title: "What the Church Means to People Like Me."

Although I have tried to characterize two types of Latter-day Saints with objectivity, I can speak with conviction only about one example from one group. In suggesting—briefly—what the Church offers to a Liahona like me, I hope to provoke all of us to re-examine the nature of our own commitments and to grow in understanding and love for those whose testimonies are defined in different terms.

By my initial characterization of types, I am the kind of Mormon who is preoccupied with questions and skeptical of answers. I find in the gospel—as I understand it—answers to enough important questions so that I can function purposefully, and I hope effectively, without present answers to the rest.

The primary question of this generation, it seems to me, is the question of meaning. Does life really add up to anything at all? At least at the popular level, the philosophy of existentialism asks, and tries to answer, the question of how to function significantly in a world which apparently has no meaning. When the philosophy is given a religious context, it becomes an effort to salvage some of the values of traditional religion for support in this meaningless world.

To the extent that existence is seen as meaningless—even absurd—human experiences have only immediate significance. A psychedelic trip stands on a par with a visit to the Sistine

Chapel or a concert of the Tabernacle Choir. What the individual does with himself—or other "freely consenting adults"—is nobody's business, whether it involves pot, perversion, or "making love, not war."

For me, the gospel answers this question of meaning, and the answer is grandly challenging. It lies in three revealed propositions: (1) Man is eternal. (2) Man is free. (3) God's work and glory is to exalt this eternal free agent-man.

The central conception is freedom. With a belief in the doctrine of free agency I can cope with some of the riddles and tragedies which are cited in support of the philosophy of the absurd. In the nature of human freedom—as I understand it—is to be found the reconciliation of the concept of a loving God and the facts of an unlovely world.

The restored gospel teaches that the essential stuff of man is eternal, that man is a child of God, and that it is man's destiny to become like his Father. But this destiny can only be achieved as man voluntarily gains the knowledge, the experience, and the discipline which godhood requires and represents. This was the crucial question resolved in the council in heaven—whether man should come into an environment of genuine risk, where he would walk by faith.

To me, this prerequisite for exaltation explains the apparent remoteness of God from many aspects of the human predicament—my predicament. My range of freedom is left large, and arbitrary divine interference with that freedom is kept minimal, in order that I may grow. Were God's hand always upon my shoulder, or his Iron Rod always in my grasp, my range of free choice would be constricted, and my growth as well.

This view does not rule out miraculous interventions by our Heavenly Father, but it does not permit their being commonplace. What is seen as miracle by the Iron Rod Saints, my type tends to interpret as coincidence, or psychosomatic manifestation, or inaccurately remembered or reported event. The same attitude is even more likely with regard to the Satanic role in human affairs. The conflict between good and evil—with its happy and unhappy outcomes—is seen more often as a derivative of man's nature and environment than as a contest between titanic powers for the capture of human pawns. If God cannot, in the ultimate sense, coerce the eternal intelligences which are embodied in His children, then how much less is Lucifer able to do so. We may yield to the promptings of good or evil, but we are not puppets.

There is another aspect of the matter. If, with or without prayer, man is arbitrarily spared the consequences of his own fallibility and the natural consequences of the kind of hazardous world in which he lives, then freedom becomes meaningless and God capricious. If the law that fire burns, that bullets kill, that age deteriorates, and that the rain falls on the just and the unjust is sporadically suspended upon petition of faith, what happens to that reliable connection between cause and consequence which is a condition of knowledge; and what a peril to faith lies in the idea that God can break the causal chain, that He frequently does break it, but that in my individual case He may not choose to do so. This is the dilemma of theodicy, reconciling God's omnipotence with evil and suffering, which is so dramatically phrased: "If God is good, He is not God; if God is God, He is not good."

From what has been said, it must be apparent that Liahonas like me do not see prayer as a form of spiritual mechanics, in spite of such scriptural language as "Prove me now herewith...," and "I, the Lord, am bound...." Prayer is rarely for miracles, or even for new answers. It is—or ought to be—an intensely personal exercise in sorting out and weighing the relevant factors in our problems, and looking to God as we consider the alternative solutions. (Many of our problems would solve themselves if we would consider only options on which we could honestly ask God's benediction.) We might pray for a miracle, especially in time of deep personal frustration or tragedy, but we would think it presumptuous to command God and would not suspend the future on the outcome of the petition.

This is not to say that Liahonas cannot verbalize prayer as proficiently as their Iron Rod contemporaries. One cannot be significantly involved in the Church without mastering the conventional prayer forms and learning to fit the petition to the proportions of the occasion. But even in the public prayers it is possible, I believe, for the attentive ear to detect those differences which I have tried to describe. To oppose evil as we can, to bear adversity as we must, and to do our jobs well—these are the petitions in Liahona prayers. They invoke God's blessings, but they require man's answering.

To this Liahona Latter-day Saint, God is powerful to save. He is pledged to keep the way of salvation open to man and to do, through the example and sacrifice of His Son and the ordinances and teachings of His Church, what man cannot do for himself. But beyond this, He has left things pretty much up to me—a free agent, a god in embryo who must learn by experience as well as direction how to be like God.

In this circumstance the Church of Jesus Christ performs three special functions for me. Without them, my freedom might well become unbearable:

In the first place, the Church reminds me—almost incessantly—that what I do makes a difference. It matters to my fellow men because most of what I do or fail to do affects their progress toward salvation. And it matters to me, even if it has no discernible influence upon others. I reject the "hippie" stance, not because there is something intrinsically wrong with beards and sandals, but with estrangement and aimlessness. Even though life is eternal, time is short and I have none to waste.

In the second place, the Church suggests and sometimes prescribes guidelines for the use of freedom. The deportment standards of the Ten Commandments and the Sermon on the Mount, the rules for mental and physical well-being in the Doctrine and Covenants, the reminders and challenges in the temple ceremony—these are examples, and they harmonize with free agency because even those which are prescribed are not coerced.

There is a difference here, I think, between the way Iron Rods and Liahonas look at the guidelines. Answer-oriented, the Iron Rods tend to spell things out; Sabbath observance becomes no TV or movies, or TV but no movies, or uplifting TV and no other, or no studying, or studying for religion classes but no others. For Liahonas like me, the Sabbath commandment is a reminder of the kinship of free men and a concerned and loving Father. What is fitting, not what is conventional, becomes the question. On a lovely autumn evening I may even, with quiet conscience, pass up an M.I.A. fireside for a drive in the canyon. But the thankfulness for guidelines is nonetheless strong.

In final place comes the contribution of the Church in giving me something to relate to—to belong to—to *feel* a part of.

Contemporary psychology has much to say about the awful predicament of alienation. "The Lonely Crowd" is the way one expert describes it. Ex-Mormons often feel it; a good friend who somehow migrated out of the Church put it this way the other day: "I don't belong anywhere."

For the active Latter-day Saint such alienation is impossible. The Church is an association of kindred spirits, a subculture, a "folk"—and this is the tie which binds Iron Rods and Liahonas together as strongly as the shared testimony of Joseph Smith. It is as fundamental to the solidarity of LDS families—almost—as the doctrine of eternal marriage itself. It makes brothers and sisters of the convert and the Daughter of the Utah Pioneers, of the Hong Kong branch president and the missionary from Cedar City. It unites this congregation—the genealogists and the procrastinators, the old-fashioned patriarchs and the family planners, the eggheads and the doubters of "the wisdom of men."

This sense of belonging is what makes me feel at home in the Palo Alto Ward. Liahonas and Iron Rods together, we are products of a great historic experience, laborers in a great enterprise, and sharers of a commitment to the proposition that life is important because God is real and we are His children—free agents with the opportunity to become heirs of His kingdom.

This is the witness of the Spirit to this Liahona Latter-day Saint. When the returning missionary warms his homecoming with a narrative of a remarkable conversion, I may note the inconsistency or naiveté of some of his analysis, but I am moved nevertheless by the picture of lives transformed—made meaningful—by the gospel. When the home teachers call, I am sometimes self-conscious about the "role playing" in which we all seem to be engaged, yet I ask my wife often—in our times of deepest concern and warmest parental satisfaction—what might our daughters have become without the Church. When a dear friend passes, an accident victim, I may recoil from the well-meant suggestion that God's need for him was greater than his family's, but my lamentation is sweetened by the realization of what the temporal support of the Saints and the eternal promises of the Lord mean to those who mourn.

For this testimony, the Church which inspires and feeds it, and fellowship in the Church with the Iron Rods and Liahonas who share it, I express my thanks to my Heavenly Father in the name of His Son, Jesus Christ, Amen.

2

Richard L. Bushman

My Belief

In the essay that follows, one of the Church's finest intellects argues for the final irrelevance of the intellect in matters of faith. Richard Bushman first achieved national stature as a historian with his path-breaking study From Puritan to Yankee: Character and the Social Order in Connecticut, 1690-1760. *Widely published since, in both Mormon and non-Mormon journals, his reputation has been more recently enhanced by two books:* Joseph Smith and the Beginnings of Mormonism *and* The King and People in Provincial Massachusetts. *He is the H. Rodney Sharp Professor of History at the University of Delaware. Brother Bushman has been a bishop and a stake president. He and his wife Claudia are the parents of six children.*

When I was growing up in Portland, Oregon, in the 1930s and 1940s I always thought of myself as a believing Latter-day Saint. My parents were believers; even when they were not attending church regularly, they still believed. All of my relatives were Latter-day Saints, and so far as I could tell they accepted the gospel as a given of life, like food and drink. In Sunday School I tried to be good. I answered the teachers' questions and gave talks that brought compliments from the congregation. From the outside my behavior probably looked like the conventional compliance of a good boy. But it went deeper than mere appearance. I prayed faithfully every night, and whenever there was a crisis I immediately thought of God. I relied on my religion to redeem me. I often felt silly or weak, and it was through praying and religious meditation that I mustered my forces to keep on trying. In high school I was a thoroughgoing wallflower, at least as I remember it now, with no close friends. At lunchtime I often ate all by myself because no one noticed me, and I had no idea how to insinuate myself into a circle of people. At the end of my junior year, a Mormon friend in the class above me said it was my obligation, for the honor of the Church, to run for student body president. One thing I had learned in Church was to speak, and a good speech could win an election. I prayed that for the sake of the Church, God would help me get my speech together, and was elected. That made redemption very real.

Partly because of the responsibilities student government gave me I was admitted to Harvard, and left my family and Portland for Cambridge in the fall of 1949. I loved everything about Harvard—the people, the studies, the atmosphere. I was more myself there than I had ever been in my whole life. Harvard helped redeem me too, but it also eroded my faith in God. I went to Church regularly and made good friends with Latter-day Saint graduate students, a faculty member or two, and the small circle of Mormon undergraduates. The undergraduates met Sunday afternoons to discuss the scriptures. We debated everything about religion, but we were all believers. I do not know why it was that by the end of my sophomore year my faith had drained away. Logical positivism was at high tide in those days, trying to persuade us that sensory evidence was the only trustworthy foundation for belief. At the end of my freshman year I wrote a paper comparing Freud and Nietzsche and confronted the assertion that Christian morality was the ideology of servile personalities who feared to express their own deepest urges. Until then I had prided myself on being a servant of God; was I also servile? These ideas, and perhaps the constant strain of being on the defensive for believing at all, must have eaten away at my belief. The issues in my mind never had anything to do with Latter-day Saint doctrine specifically. I was not bothered by the arguments against the institutional Church which so trouble people today, or by the problems of Mormon history, another current sore spot. I was not debating Mormonism versus some other religion; the only question for me was God. Did He exist in any form or not? I was not worried about evil in the world, as some agnostics are. I suppose Mormon theology had made the existence of evil perfectly plausible. I simply wondered if there was any reason to believe. Was all of religion a fantasy? Were we all fooling ourselves?

These doubts came on strongest in the spring of my sophomore year. During the preceding Christmas holiday I had been interviewed for a mission and received a call to New England, to serve under the mission president who attended the same Sacrament meeting as the students in Cambridge. Did I have enough faith to go on a mission? I debated the question through the spring, wondering if I were a hypocrite and if fear of displeasing my parents was all that carried me along. And yet I never really considered not going. As I look back, I think that my agnosticism was perhaps a little bit of a pose, a touch of stylish undergraduate angst. It was true enough that my bosom did not burn with faith; on the other hand, I was quite willing to pledge two years to a mission. So I went.

The mission president was J. Howard Maughan, an agricultural professor from Utah State and a former stake president. In our opening interview in the mission home in Cambridge, he asked if I had a testimony of the gospel. I said I did not. He was not at all rattled. He asked if I would read a book, and said that if I found a better explanation for it than the book itself gave, he wanted me to report it to him. He handed me the Book of Mormon. The next day I left North Station in Boston for Halifax, Nova Scotia. For the next three months as I tried to learn the lessons and the usual missionary discipline, I wrestled with the book and wrote long entries in my journal. I thought a lot about the three witnesses: were they liars, had they been hypnotized, were they pressured? I believe it was at that time I read Hugh Nibley's *Lehi in the Desert*. I also read the Book of Mormon and prayed, sometimes in agnostic form—"if you are God...." After three months the mission president came up to Nova Scotia for a conference, and when it was my turn to speak I said with conviction that I knew the Book of Mormon was right. The reasons for belief that I had concocted were not what made the difference—though Nibley made a great impression; it was more the simple feeling that the book was right.

The mission left me with another impression. At Harvard in those days we talked a lot about the masses, envisioning a sea of workers' faces marching into a factory. In Halifax we missionaries met the masses every day as we tracted, and they did not exist. Instead there were a great number of individual persons, quite idiosyncratic, perverse, and interesting. They were no more a mass than the Harvard faculty or the United States Congress.

That realization planted a seed of doubt about formal conceptions. Did they conform to the reality of actual experience? After the mission, I never again felt that the issues debated in the academy were necessarily the issues of real life. This skepticism grew, especially after I entered graduate school in history and learned how formulations of the past had continually altered, as each generation of historians overturned the conceptions of its predecessors and made new ones for itself. Rational discourse came more and more to seem like a kind of play, always a little capricious and unreal, and in the end, compared to the experience of life itself, not serious. To confuse intellectual constructions with reality, or to govern one's life by philosophy or an abstract system, came to seem more and more foolhardy. My attitude as it developed was not precisely anti-intellectual. Ideas did not strike me as dangerous; they were too weak to be dangerous. I was depreciating intellectual activity rather than decrying it. But whatever the proper label for this attitude, it put distance between me and the intellectuals whom I so admired and whom, as it later turned out, I would aspire to emulate.

Paradoxically, in my own intellectual endeavors I have benefited from this skepticism engendered in the mission field, for it has led me to trust my own perceptions and experience over the convictions of my fellow historians, considered individually or *en masse*. I have always thought it possible that virtually anything taught and believed in the academy could be wrong. Repudiation of God by every intellectual in creation did not mean He was non-existent. By the same token, any of the certainties of historical interpretation could be perfect errors. However fallible I might be myself, however much I was subject to influences and illusions, I had to trust my own perceptions above everything else.

After I returned from the mission field I no longer had doubts, but I did have questions. They were not specific questions about the meaning or validity of specific doctrines, wholesome questions that enlarge understanding. They were the questions of some unknown interlocutor who asked me to justify my faith. "Why do you believe?" the masked stranger asked. This was the old question of my sophomore year, asked now, however, of one who did believe, who had faith, and was being called upon to justify it. I suppose there was nothing complicated about the questioning. At Harvard I studied in the midst of people who made a business of defending their convictions. It was an unwritten rule that you must explain why you took a position or supported a proposition. "Why do you believe in God?" was a question that the trees in Harvard Yard whispered in one's ears without prompting from any skeptical inquisitors. In fact, when I returned to Harvard in 1953 the religious atmosphere was much more favorable to believers. The president, Nathan Pusey, was himself a believing person, and he had hired Paul Tillich as a University Professor and seen to the rejuvenation of the Divinity School. Even the agnostics listened respectfully to Tillich, and undergraduates talked more freely of their religious convictions. In my senior year I headed a committee sponsored by the student council on "Religion at Harvard," and our poll of undergraduates turned up a majority who said they had a religious orientation toward life. Even so, the mood did not quiet my faceless questioner. I still wanted to justify my convictions.

How those questionings came to an end is beyond my powers of explanation. For an undergraduate reader today, still fired by fierce doubts and desperate need to know for sure, one word may seem to explain all—complacency. But I myself do not feel that way. My questions have not simply grown dim over the years, nor have I answered them; instead I have come to understand questions and answers differently. Although I cannot say what truly made the difference, a series of specific experiences, small insights, revelations, new ideas, all addressing the same issue and coming over a period of thirty years, have caused me to change my views. I now have a new sense of what constitutes belief.

For a long time, twenty-five years or more, I kept trying to answer the questioner. I received little help from religious philosophers. The traditional proofs for God never made an impression on me. I did not find flaws in them; they simply seemed irrelevant. My empirical temperament and suspicion of grand systems worked against any enthusiasm for arguments about a prime mover. I never studied those arguments or made the slightest effort to make them my own. My chief line of reasoning was based on the Book of Mormon. It was concrete and real and seemed like a foundation for belief, not merely belief in Joseph Smith but in Christ and God. Joseph Smith and Mormonism, as I said before, were never the issues; it was primarily God. Although it was a lengthy chain from the historicity of the Book of Mormon, to Joseph's revelations, to the existence of God, it was a chain that held for me. I felt satisfied that if that book were true, my position was sound. Without it, I do not know where I would be. I have imagined I could be a religious agnostic were it not for the Book of Mormon. That is why Hugh Nibley's writings played a large part in my thinking. Although I recognized the eccentricities of his style and was never completely confident of his scholarship, there seemed to me to be enough there to make a case. First Nephi could not be dismissed as fraudulent; and, so far as I know, no one has refuted the argument he made in *Lehi in the Desert.* Nibley offered just the kind of evidence I was looking for in my pursuit of answers: evidence that was specific, empirical, historical.

Nibley's style was important enough that I made one attempt myself to prove the Book of Mormon in the Nibley-esque manner, and this effort came about in such a way as to confirm my belief. When I was asked to give some talks in Utah during the Bicentennial of the American Revolution, I decided to examine the political principles embodied in the Book of Mormon and make some applications to our nation's Revolution and Constitution. I thought this would be simple enough because of the switch from a monarchy to a republic during the reign of Mosiah. I was sure that somewhere in Mosiah's statements I would find ideas relevant to the modern world. With that in mind, I accepted the invitation to talk, but I did not get down to work until a few months before I was to appear. To my dismay, I could not find what I was looking for. Everything seemed just off the point, confused and baffling. I could not find the directions for a sound republic that I had expected. Gradually it dawned on me that the very absence of republican statements might in itself be interesting. Long ago I learned that it is better to flow with the evidence rather than to compel compliance with one's preformed ideas. So instead, I asked: what does the Book of Mormon say about politics? To my surprise I discovered it was quite an unrepublican book. Not only was Nephi a king, and monarchy presented as the ideal government in an ideal world, but the supposedly republican government instituted under Mosiah did not function that way at all. There was no elected legislature, and the chief judges usually inherited their office rather than being chosen to it. Eventually I came to see that here was my chance to emulate Nibley. If Joseph Smith was suffused with republican ideas, as I was confident he was, then the absence of such sentiments in Nephite society was peculiar, another evidence that he did not write the Book of Mormon. Eventually all of this came together in an article, "The Book of

Mormon and the American Revolution," published in *BYU Studies* in 1976.

While circumstances and my predilection to justify belief influenced me up to that point and beyond, my commitment to this kind of endeavor gradually weakened. Perhaps most influential was a gradual merger of personality and belief. By 1976 I had been a branch president and bishop, and was then president of the Boston Stake. Those offices required me to give blessings in the name of God and to seek solutions to difficult problems nearly every day. I usually felt entirely inadequate to the demands placed upon me and could not function at all without some measure of inspiration. What I did, the way I acted, my inner thoughts, were all intermingled with this effort to speak and act righteously for God. I could no longer entertain the possibility that God did not exist because I felt His power working through me. Sometimes I toyed with the notion that there could be other ways of describing what happened when I felt inspired, but the only language that actually worked, the only ideas that brought inspiration and did justice to the experience when it came, were the words in the scripture. Only when I thought of God as a person interested in me and asked for help as a member of Christ's kingdom did idea and reality fit properly. Only that language properly honored the experiences I had day after day in my callings.

More than anything else, church work probably quieted my old questions; but there were certain moments when these cumulative experiences precipitated new ideas. Once in the early sixties while I held a post-doctoral fellowship at Brown University and was visiting Cambridge, I happened into a young adult discussion, led by Terry Warner I believe. He had the group read the Grand Inquisitor passage in *The Brothers Karamazov*. The sentences that stuck with me that time through were the ones having to do with looking for reasons to believe that would convince the whole world and compel everyone to believe. That was the wish of the Inquisitor, a wish implicitly repudiated by Christ. The obvious fact that there is no convincing everyone that a religious idea is true came home strongly at that moment. It is impossible and arrogant, and yet that was exactly what I was attempting. When I sought to justify my belief, I was looking for answers that would persuade all reasonable men. That was why I liked Nibley: because he put his readers over a barrel. I wanted something that no one could deny. In that moment in Cambridge, I realized the futility of the quest.

I was moved still further in this direction by a lecture which Neal Maxwell invited me to give at Brigham Young University in 1974 as part of the Commissioner's Lecture Series. I cannot for the life of me recall why I turned to the topic of "Joseph Smith and Skepticism," but that was the subject. In that lecture I sketched in the massive effort to demonstrate reasonably the authenticity of the Christian revelation. The effort began in the early eighteenth century, when Deism first took hold in earnest, and continued through the nineteenth century. The Christian rationalists assembled all the evidence they could muster to prove that Biblical miracles, such as the parting of the Red Sea, were authentic and therefore evidence of God's endorsement of Israel. In the course of the nineteenth century, as agnosticism waxed strong among intellectuals, the volumes on Christian evidences proliferated. I can still remember sitting on the floor in the basement of the Harvard Divinity School library, flipping through these books, each one almost exactly like the others. I realized then that the tradition of seeking proof was very strong in the nineteenth century, and that Mormons had been influenced by it. More than any other Latter-day Saint, B. H. Roberts, a man troubled by questions as I had been, borrowed these methods. His *New Witness for God* was a replica of the books in the Harvard Divinity School basement, except with Mormon examples and conclusions. Hugh Nibley dropped the nineteenth-century format for works of Christian evidences, but his mode of reasoning was basically the same.

Awareness of the affinity of Nibley with these Protestant works did not dilute my own interest in evidences. The study of Book of Mormon republicanism, my own contribution to the genre, came along two years later. But the contradictions were taking shape in my mind and readied me, I suppose, for a personal paradigm shift. It occurred in the early 1980s at the

University of Indiana. Stephen Stein of the religion department had some Lilly Endowment money to assemble scholars and religious leaders from various denominations to discuss their beliefs. With Jan Shipps's help he brought together a handful of Mormon historians, some historians of American religion, a local stake president and regional representative, and a seminary teacher. The topic was Joseph Smith. The historians among us made some opening comments about the Prophet, and then over a day and a half we discussed the issues that emerged. It was a revelatory assemblage from my point of view because it brought together in one room representatives of the various groups involved in my religious life—Church leaders, non-Mormon scholars, and Mormon scholars. Although all of these people had been represented in my mind symbolically before, they had never been together in person before my face, talking about Joseph Smith.

Their presence brought together notions that previously had been floating about separately in my head. Sometime in the middle of the conversations it came to me in a flash that I did not want to prove the authenticity of Joseph Smith's calling to anyone. I did not want to wrestle Stephen Stein to the mat and make him cry "uncle." It was a false position, at least for me, and one that I doubted would have any long-range good results. I recognized then that the pursuit of Christian evidences was not a Mormon tradition; it was a borrowing from Protestantism—and not at a moment when Protestantism was at one of its high points. At any rate, it was not my tradition, and I did not want to participate in it. There was no proving religion to anyone; belief came by other means, by hearing testimonies or by individual pursuit or by the grace of God, but not by hammering.

By the time of the conference I had completed the manuscript of *Joseph Smith and the Beginnings of Mormonism*. The Book of Mormon chapter in that book hammered at readers. My urge was to show that the common secular explanations of the Book of Mormon were in error and to imply, if not to insist, that only a divine explanation would do. In the revision, I tried to moderate the tone without complete success. I did not wish to dissipate the basic argument, which is that the counter-explanations did not adequately explain the complexity of the book, but I sincerely did not want to push readers into a corner and force them to come out fighting. The desire to compel belief, the wish of the Grand Inquisitor, was exactly what I had abandoned.

At the present moment, the question of why I believe no longer has meaning for me. I do not ask it of myself or attempt to give my reasons to others. The fact is that I do believe. That is a given of my nature, and whatever reasons I might give would be insufficient and inaccurate. More relevant to my current condition is a related question: how do others come to believe? I would like to know if there is anything I can do that will draw people to faith in Christ and in the priesthood. My answer to this question is, of course, related to my personal experiences. I no longer think that people can be compelled to believe by any form of reasoning, whether from the scripture or from historical evidence. They will believe if it is in their natures to believe. All I can do is to attempt to bring forward the believing nature, smothered as it is in most people by the other natures that culture forms in us. The first responsibility is to tell the story, to say very simply what happened, so that knowledge of those events can do its work. But that is the easy part, the part that could be done by books or television. The hard part is to create an atmosphere where the spiritual nature, the deep-down goodness in the person, can react to the story honestly and directly. Some people can create that atmosphere quite easily by the very strength of their own spiritual personalities. It is hard for me. There are too many other natures in me: the vain aspirer formed in childhood, the intellectual fostered at Harvard, the would-be dominant male created by who knows what. But I do believe that when I am none of these, and instead am a humble follower of Christ who without pretense tells the story to a friend whom I love and respect, then they will believe if they want to, and conversion is possible. Questions may be answered and reasons given, but these are peripheral and essentially irrelevant. What is essential is for a person to listen carefully and openly in an attitude of trust. If belief is to be formed in the human mind, it will, I think, be formed that way.

3

John T. Kesler

Facing Spiritual Reality

John Kesler is a convert to the Church. His honesty and sensitivity to an "inner beacon" led him to embrace the gospel—to "face spiritual reality"—after exploring a bewildering array of philosophical and religious claims. Educated at the University of Utah, Columbia Law School, and the University of Hamburg, Brother Kesler has been Executive Director of the Utah Bicentennial Commission and Regional Director of Development for the LDS Church. He has been the area legal counsel of the Church for Europe and Africa and is currently a partner in the Salt Lake City law firm of Woodbury, Bettilyon and Kesler. He has served as a bishop and a high councilman, and he and his wife Colleen are the parents of two children. His essay was originally published in Sunstone *magazine, and is reprinted here by permission.*

"Would I like to know more about the Mormon Church? I can't believe my friends are asking me this. I'm sure they realize that I grew up in Salt Lake City and already know about their religion." Such were my initial thoughts one evening in New York City when some Mormon friends sprang the "golden question." Yet I found myself saying that I would take the missionary lessons. I was almost surprised to feel an urging within myself to more thoroughly investigate something which I had rejected so long ago.

As I went home that night I mused about why, at 25 years of age in New York City, I would take another look at a religion which I considered to be a small and somewhat eccentric branch of Christian fundamentalism. The main answer I came up with was that I had investigated about everything else under the sun; so why not take one more hard look before I dismissed it for good.

My life to that point seemed like a never-ending search for some reality deeper than I found readily apparent in my day-to-day environment. At first I was fascinated by the frontiers of the mind. By the time I was eleven I had read most of the books in the Salt Lake City Library on extrasensory perception and mental telepathy. During junior high school years I became an expert in hypnotism and the power of suggestion and did research on optical illusions.

As a child I attended an Episcopal church, but developed an increasingly cautious attitude about religious conversion. My studies of the mind had revealed to me how prone individuals are to self-deluding leaps of faith. Consequently, I vowed that I would resist such leaps to the utmost of my ability until I had searched as honestly and thoroughly as I was able, and until what final leap might eventually be necessary would be based, to the extent possible, on knowledge and self-knowledge. This attitude resulted in most of my youth being spent as a skeptic and a critic of others' beliefs. If I was outwardly tolerant, it belied the processes of my mind which were constantly analyzing and picking apart what I felt were the inadequacies of the world views of those around me. By the time I graduated from college, however, I realized that somehow I must find some affirmative belief of my own.

Soon after I started doing graduate work in Germany, I decided to put myself through self-analysis. I wanted to see if there was some mechanism within me which could recognize personal truths.

After about a month of trying to purge myself of all elements which had been imposed by others or picked up by habit rather than emerging from some truth or essence within, I began to feel as if I were falling into nothingness. The sensation was like jumping into a well, falling further and further into darkness with the light at the mouth of the well, representing all that was recognizable and secure, becoming less and less distinct, and at the same time falling into a dimensionless void without parameters or signposts to orient oneself. Eventually I felt that I had hit bottom and then began to rebuild. I was surprised how few perspectives I had that seemed to be purely in tune with what I felt was an inner essence that I had discovered.

This internal mechanism was not like a book which I could open at will, reading what was right and what directions I should take in life. It was more like a tuning fork. When thoughts or experiences rang true to me or at the right pitch, to use the simile, the tuning fork within would begin to resonate, to signal that I was receiving ideas or directions or concepts which were in harmony with this internal signal.

I wasn't sure if this dimension within me was a synthesis of all my intellectual, emotional, and instinctive faculties or whether it found its source from something outside myself. In any event, I came to trust that this signal should be the source of the final discernment of a matter after all thoughts and emotions had been consulted. In the next several years I learned by trial and error that not paying attention to that beacon was a mistake.

I now had a firm sense that if there was a way of life that was true and right, I would recognize it if I found it. So I began a renewed effort to review different moral, philisophical, and religious outlooks as well as scientific views of man, particularly psychological and behavioral views. After a year in Germany, I spent a year working and then entered law school. In every moment I could spare from my legal studies I pursued my personal investigations. Sometimes I would stay up an entire night poring over the writings of an original thinker such as Nietzsche or of some other particularly penetrating moralist. I finally became rather discouraged about the prospect of finding any absolute answers. So I put my search in low gear for the time being and began to pursue more immediate concerns.

Still, I could not deny the force within me which somehow told me that I should persevere in my search for more universal perspectives. More than anything else in the last year my inner beacon had responded affirmatively to Christ's message of love. I had a difficult time conceiving of his actual divinity, but I felt that I probably needed to reconsider the implications of his life and ministry. I was in the process of doing so when my Mormon friends asked me if I wanted to investigate their church. When I recalled the past several years, I had to admit I had given about everything else a chance. Now was the time, I thought, to make a final appraisal of even this unlikely church.

During the first several missionary lessons, it was reconfirmed that I was already reasonably well informed on the basic doctrines of the Church. In later lessons I became more aggressive in trying to contradict the two young men who were teaching me, and pointed out many of the strongest arguments against the Church that I had learned so well growing up as a non-Mormon in Salt Lake City. Yet despite the ease with which I could sometimes bring their arguments to a dead end, I was impressed by their reaction to my analytical stories. They would always fall back on their personal testimony, that they had an inner knowledge that what they taught was true, as though they were in tune to their own inner beacons. I was well aware that a clever arguer can seemingly make a shambles of any message, whether it is true or not, and began to think that perhaps I was trying to be a little bit too clever.

I was skeptical, though, because when I analyzed the Church and its claims from a purely intellectual point of view, it was my honest assessment that the whole thing was simply not believable. From what I had read it appeared that there was not a prominent non-Mormon archeologist who felt that there was much of a possibility that the civilization described in the Book of Mormon existed. As far as I knew, similar conclusions seemed to hold true for non-Mormon anthropologists who had looked at the Mormon claims that Indians are direct descendants of Old Testament Semites. I also had a hard time understanding why the Mormon Church should be the only group or institution I had ever found that denied privileges to the Negro on other than man-inspired discriminatory grounds. In short, it seemed that if one was going to be rational by twentieth-century standards, there was not much likelihood that one would end up believing in the claims of the Church.

In spite of such questions I decided to try to live their religion. I thought that if there was a chance in the world that it was true in spite of my best rational assessments to the contrary, I was going to let that inner beacon, or what the missionaries called the Spirit of Christ, give me feedback on the matter.

To my surprise, over a few months my commitment to living their way of life increased. Each step I took in living the tenets of this Church led me to take another. I was by no means desperate to leap into something just to find security; as a matter of fact, it was with reluctance at some points that I decided to make additional commitments. For instance, going to church had been a distasteful thing for me ever since I was quite young and had noticed the piety that some people exude only this one day a week. Yet before long I began to go to church regularly. In each case when I took another step in living the gospel as taught by the Church of Jesus Christ of Latter-day Saints, I could feel the seed that was planted there grow and yield satisfaction and fulfillment.

Learning to pray was the most difficult initial step for me. Getting humbly on my knees to pray about material, some of which I assumed down deep was nothing but fantasy, to a God I couldn't conceive of, seemed almost absurd at times. Yet I kept faith with that urging within me which kept telling me that there was truth to be discovered which was better and truer than what I had yet found, and I bowed my head and prayed. It was a futile exercise at first. Eventually, though, I felt a longing to return again and again, to come in tune with the currents in the depths of my self in search of the eternal within, and a sense of the infinite beyond.

Soon I began to feel a polarity within myself. My mind would go over it again and again, but I could not escape the conclusion that the claims of this church were simply not believable; they just seemed too unlikely. On the other hand, I had never before experienced such a constant and growing satisfaction from anything in which I had previously been involved. I began to feel that whether or not final truths were ever discoverable in a pure form, I should grasp that which best brings me most in harmony with what I feel in my inner essence, with what the missionaries called the Spirit of Christ. In other words, whether or not the claims of the Mormon Church were literally true, I was beginning to feel that there was no reason not to embrace their way of life since it was superior to all other philosophies, religions, or outlooks I had yet found or manufactured.

After I reached this conclusion I began to pray more fervently concerning the truthfulness of this church. One evening after reading one of the last sections of the Book of Mormon, I decided that now more than ever before I must completely absorb myself in prayer, somehow communicate with God, if He was there. I knelt in deep supplication for a few minutes, then found that thoughts and temptations began to enter my mind. I felt as if some force was trying to keep me from praying. I tried in vain to break out of a darkness which engulfed me. After some time I lay on the floor of my apartment, exhausted, but free from this influence. The next two evenings much the same type of occurrence ensued when I attempted to pray for an answer to my questions about the Book of Mormon and the Mormon Church.

On the fourth evening I completed the Book of Mormon for the first time since I had finished the missionary lessons. With all the earnestness I possessed I prayed once again. Almost immediately a power came over me that was so strong it pulled me out of the concentration of my prayer. I got up to see if someone was in the darkness of my room, for I felt something there. Finding nothing, I dropped to my knees again, but immediately I felt completely engulfed in a suffocating darkness. I had the sensation of being thrown by someone or something, and fell against the wall by which I had been kneeling. As I struggled to get up off the floor, I had never been in such despair in my life. With every ounce of strength that I still possessed I returned to my knees and called for my Father in Heaven.

At that moment a warm, burning sensation came flowing into my body. In concurrence with this feeling a light surrounded me and filled my entire being. Then a voice spoke to me which filled me as completely as the light and the burning. It said, "John, the Book of Mormon is true. Let your Uncle Joseph know that I have answered your prayers. You will see him before he leaves this earth." Then the light and the burning subsided. Exhausted, I went to bed.

In the morning I got up and wrote to my great uncle, Joseph Fielding Smith, President of The Church of Jesus Christ of Latter-day Saints, whom I had never met. I explained who I was, that I had received an answer to my prayers and was joining the Church. Instead of mailing the letter I pushed it to the back of my desk and went on to my responsibilities. As the letter lay on my desk for several days, I went over and over what had happened. I explored the possibility that I had become so worked up in my desire to receive an answer that my unconscious had fabricated the sensations that came over me and the voice which spoke to me. On the other hand, that force within me that had pushed me my entire life and had never let me rest or be satisfied with what I had found said, "Yes, you have found the truth." Finally I gave in to my inner promptings. I mailed the letter to President Smith and communicated to the local bishop that I had decided to join The Church of Jesus Christ of Latter-day Saints.

I was in an interesting predicament. It seemed as though I had progressed from faith or hope to real personal knowledge that the gospel as taught by this Church was true, but at the same time my critical intellect still questioned various claims of the Church. I had never expected that faith and knowledge would precede belief, but in some respects, it had happened.

A short time after my baptism I experienced a confirmation of the truthfulness of the communication I had received in response to my prayers. I recalled that the voice had told me that I would see President Smith "before he left this earth." President Smith had not responded to my letter, but I thought that perhaps someday I might be able to meet him. Shortly after I was baptized, however, I was in Salt Lake City and an aunt of mine said out of the blue, "I'll bet you would like to meet and talk with President Smith, wouldn't you?" I was very surprised, but within a few days I had the singular opportunity to meet him and to sit down and converse with him for about an hour and receive very personal counsel. A few days later he suddenly died. I thought back to the promise of the voice and felt humbled and gratified. Doubts were gradually dispelled from my mind after that event; not, I believe, because I had given up maintaining a critical intellect, but because I would better allow communications from God to reach me and the blessings and realities of the gospel to take their proper perspective in my mind as well as in my heart.

It may appear to a non-Mormon reader that I have fallen victim to self-delusions of a type which I had wanted so much to avoid, a spiritual conversion through emotional catharsis based on an overwhelming desire to confirm what I wanted to believe. All I can say to the skeptic is that living the gospel of Jesus Christ as taught by the Mormon Church works. It changes one's life for the better, and one receives spiritual confirmation of the correctness of this commitment.

My entire life, I searched as much as was humanly possible to discover truth. Armed with the best theories of man and a skepticism that had kept me from accepting any other religion, philosophy, or definitive outlook during periods when I needed security much more than when I investigated the Mormon Church, I had to face spiritual reality when I found it. I feel I have continued to maintain a critical intellect. The result has been that my commitment and conversion to this Church and to Christ have kept growing, for I have received confirmation many times since, in many ways, of the truthfulness of this Church.

It is difficult for many people today to bow their heads and humbly pray about a "new" church with claims that are so dramatic. Yet it is my firm belief that whoever plants the seed of this Church in his heart and humbles himself just enough to let it grow will travel down the same road that I have. As so many people in all walks of life all over the world are experiencing, he will come to know that Christ's true church exists on the earth today: The Church of Jesus Christ of Latter-day Saints.

4

Kenneth W. Godfrey

From Farm Boy To Believer

The most frequent justification for the rejection of God is the staggering fact of unexplained suffering and evil in the world: "If God is good, He is not God; if God is God, He is not good." Very early in his life, Kenneth Godfrey felt the impact of that challenge to belief, and here explains the course his faith has taken despite his deep sensitivity to the world's unfairness. Brother Godfrey received his Ph.D. in the History of Religion from Brigham Young University. He is the author of three books (most recently Women's Voices, An Untold History of the Latter-day Saints, 1830-1900, *which was co-authored with his wife, Audrey Montgomery Godfrey, and Jill Mulvay Derr). He has also written nearly one hundred articles. He is a past president of the Mormon History Association and has served in the Church as a high councilman, bishop, mission president, and on the Chruch's instructional development committee. He is presently the Director of the Utah North Area of the Church Educational System. He and Audrey are the parents of five children.*

I first became aware that the world was unfair when I was in the sixth grade. Our teacher read to us Victor Hugo's *Les Misérables*, and Jean Valjean became both a hero and a tragic figure in my mind. While milking cows and doing other chores, I thought deeply about his life and the suffering, anguish, and physical pain he endured just because he stole a loaf of bread to feed his hungry family. I began to question laws that allowed public officials to punish in excess, and even wondered why God would permit such things to happen if, indeed, He did have all power. Today I think I was extraordinarily fortunate, living in the very small agricultural community of Cornish, Utah, and going to a four-room school, to have had a teacher, a farmer's wife, who both knew and loved great literature.

A year later, a boy a year older than I climbed to the top of a grain elevator, lost his balance, and plunged to his death on the concrete floor a hundred feet below. We had played together when our houses were scarcely half a block apart, and though I did not particularly like him I did not sleep the night I learned of his death. When I was asked to be a pallbearer, I saw his casketed body still and powdered. For the second time in my life, I really pondered death. The first time I had realized that death was as real as life was when I saw our brown mare, Molly, savagely thrash her head on the ground and finally die of brain fever. But a human's death seemed still more tragic, and left behind a deeper sadness and more loneliness than the demise of a horse I had loved. I thought how unfair life was, when a boy just thirteen years of age could have his life cut short in a wild five-second plunge. That night, I imagined what it would be like to fall and then die. What did one think about in those five seconds? Was there terror, contact, pain, and then nothingness? I even dreamed that I was the one who had fallen and spontaneously jumped when, in my imagination, I struck the floor.

Another year passed, and a young father of two very young children slipped in the snow and fell under a moving truck loaded with sugar beet pulp. His head was crushed. Because he was my Sunday School teacher, I went to his funeral, saw his weeping wife and wiggling babies, and wondered anew why life was so unfair.

As I grew up, I went on to Primary and Sunday School. There I was taught the "plan of salvation": that men lived before they were born, that earth life has purpose and meaning at its core, and that men will live again after death. I applied those conceptions when I kissed my ninety-four-year-old great-grandfather on his deathbed, where he lay white-bearded, skinny, and blood-red beneath his thin pale skin. I imagined that soon he would embrace my great-grandmother (who somehow looked, in my mind, a lot like my mother) and all would be well once more.

A few years later I was jolted when I saw my father weep until his whole body shook as they closed the casket lid on his father. More than ever before, I was struck with just how agonizing parting can be for those left behind. Having just lived through the Second World War and having listened to the music of that period, which was dominated by songs about love, parting, and hopeful reunions (many of which never occurred), I continued to contemplate the meaning of a life that carried with it so much pain.

For some reason I found it extremely difficult to believe all that I was taught in church meetings, and I was often driven to the edge of despair. I sometimes felt that the most depressing teaching in Latter-day Saint theology was that man would always exist as an individual. Intelligence, I was told, was co-eternal with God; it was not created by Him, but had self-existent properties.

My teachers, basing their lessons on the writings of B. H. Roberts, told me that even when I was an intelligence I knew that I was me, and that I was different and unique from everyone else in the universe. Sometimes when I was discouraged, or immediately after doing something stupid, I wished I had been born a Hindu, and that rather than always existing I would one day dissolve into a state of never-ending, collective, impersonal peace and happiness. I longed for the annihilation of desire, freedom from attachments, and the nirvana of extinction. Some days, "being" felt like the most unfair aspect of life itself. That condition of "being," of contemplating that no matter how badly I felt I could never, in all the eons of time, escape from myself, sometimes brought with it an almost overwhelming despair. I was trapped within my own identity.

But one day my despair was displaced by a new awareness. Following the birth of our youngest son, the doctor telephoned and told me that my wife had only three or four hours to live. Returning to the hospital, I found her unconscious. I hurried home to try to prepare our four children for their mother's death. Suddenly I was aware not so much of how unfair life was, but, rather, how badly I needed her. I did not merely need her service to the family, or her work around the house; I needed her being, her personality, her totality. And then I thought, "If I were to cease to exist, to go into nothingness, are there people who would need me just as much as I now desperately need her?" In that moment I learned that parting is less difficult if reunion is also a principle of one's faith. Life seemed less unfair with the possibility of meeting again. My wife miraculously recovered, and I have never looked at her in the same way since the day that we almost parted more than a decade ago.

Now, when I leave home for a lecture or to teach a class in some far-off city, I begin to think about parting, and how much my children mean to me. I find I have hope (which the scriptures say is the forerunner of faith) that existence is eternal because of the need I have for them, and the need we all have for each other. If only one soul is destroyed and becomes nothing, all mankind ought to feel a great loss. God, part of whose work is to immortalize souls, may feel the need for us as deeply as we feel the need for Him.

Brigham Young expresses this belief in what is, for me, one of the most moving accounts in all of religious literature:

> God is the father of our spirits; and if we could know, understand, and do His will, every soul would be prepared to return back into His presence. And when they get there, they would see that they had formerly lived there for ages, and that they had

> previously been acquainted with every nook and corner, with the palaces, walks, and gardens; and they would embrace their father, and he would embrace them and say, my son, my daughter, I have you again; and the child would say, "O My Father, My Father, I am home again."

Enos, that great Book of Mormon prophet, did not fear the resurrection nor the judgment, but declared that he contemplated meeting Christ with pleasure. His was a great faith in reunion and love.

Thus, rather than being a threat to my faith, the need we have for each other and the loss we feel at times of parting is, instead, a consolation. When I am near the precipice and wishing, like Alma the younger, that I could cease to exist, I am jolted back into hope and faith by the thought that there are those on earth who, I believe, need me.

The second principle of my faith is that the gospel is so true that a person need not be afraid to study and explore any topic. Like the first principle it, too, was planted at home and nurtured and cultivated while I was in college, and it became firmly rooted in the challenging world of academia where I have spent my adult years.

Like many other Mormon families, my family's consciousness was largely shaped by its religion. Early in my youth I became fascinated by the theology I learned on Sunday, in M.I.A. on Tuesday nights, and every morning in seminary. Classes never bored me because I always had questions to ask. Because of my interest, we often discussed theology at home. Although my father had little secular education, he knew the gospel and had a faith so firm that he was not afraid to explore any issue that I wanted to raise. We talked about how God came to be God, who His Father was, the Adam-God theory, plural marriage (which my father had observed first-hand because his grandfathers each had more than one wife), and countless other Church-related topics. From his example, I learned that the Church's theology was so firmly rooted in truth that no question need go unexplored, nor any topic be barred from research. I came to believe that my father could answer any gospel question and, moreover, that his character was above reproach. (Later I learned that he could not answer every question, but that his character really was above reproach.) We could ponder any issue with integrity. I also learned from him to trust the Church, and the shepherds who protected it.

In addition, I had a Sunday School teacher who affected my faith. This teacher, a farmer in the community in which I lived, had been expelled from Mexico with other Latter-day Saints in 1912. He loved the scriptures, devoured James E. Talmage's writings, and taught me for six years. He, too, gently and lovingly answered my questions from the scriptures; even now, three-and-a-half decades later, I can still remember his teachings. He once gave a sacrament meeting talk concerning God's origin and announced to the ward that his subject was motivated by a question I had asked in class, thus wisely reinforcing the inquisitiveness of a young boy. Like my father, he had a character that matched his knowledge and commitment to the Church. The example of my father and my Sunday School teacher taught me that one need never fear if his character is pure. This gave me great solace.

Nevertheless, I still wondered, doubted, and questioned. Whether sitting in Church, or in school, or hoeing corn, I searched for meaning in my life, looked for purpose in existence and significance in daily routine. While some modern scholars argue that Mormons characteristically find religion primarily in such practical, mundane tasks as digging canals and building villages, that was never the case with me. I looked at the heavens on those dark summer nights, and wondered what life was really all about. I wondered whether or not I really mattered, and whether thinning sugar beets mattered, whether milking cows mattered, whether irrigating mattered. And if it all did, then to whom? And why?

One thing that helped me address these issues resulted from a death that occurred when I was in high school. My five-year-old cousin drowned in the irrigation ditch next to his home. I had disobeyed my father that day and gone swimming. When I returned home I found no one there. However, I saw a large number of automobiles surrounding my uncle's home, south and east of our house. Only thirty acres of farmland separated the two homes. I ran through the fields to see why all of the people had gathered there, and saw my cousin's motionless body with four medics busily kneeling around him as they tried to start him breathing again. Just the day before he had been singing "Bell Bottom Trousers," a popular song of the day; now he was dead. His mother, my aunt, began to sob when they told her that they could do nothing more for him. Then I watched them take his body away.

As I lay in bed that night, I listened to the water running in the irrigation ditch next to our house. I did not sleep. I wondered why something as helpful, as beautiful, and as necessary as water would snuff out the life of a little boy who had done nothing wrong. My prayers for understanding and comfort went unanswered, and only time made it possible for me to sleep again. More and more, I was coming to realize that most questions are rarely answered fully. Thus another essential of my faith was born. I came to believe that we all must develop the ability to live with questions and doubt. Furthermore, I decided to put those things I could not explain at the time "on the shelf" until I had an answer. I continued to read, study, and live the teachings I found in the scriptures and in other good books. My father, my Sunday School teacher, and my experiences were beginning to teach me that one can both know and doubt at the same time. A paradox, but in my case true. I became convinced that while I could not find the answers to all my questions, not even to all the important ones, I could discover in the gospel the solution to enough of my queries that faith was more than possible; it was an actuality and an exciting force in my life.

Still another aspect of my faith developed in my early twenties. It came about as a result of my being selected as the young man to represent our ward in the mission field for the year 1953. (The Selective Service had just approved the policy that one boy a year from each ward could serve a mission instead of going into the army.) My first two years of college had not had much impact upon my faith, but the mission call that followed the Selective Service announcement did. My parents were not secure financially and had little hope that they could support me. Yet when the call came they told the bishop they would be glad to sustain me. Then my father went to the barn and pleaded with Heavenly Father for the means to keep his promise. I saw in him and in my mother the sort of faith that allows one to step into the darkness, the unknown, without the light of solutions, and commit to the Lord, financially, more than their all. That act had a profound impact on my life, and made me a far better missionary than I otherwise would have been.

While attending a week's seminar in Salt Lake City to prepare for missionary service, I suddenly realized, while listening to a talk about the Book of Mormon, that I believed it was true but did not know for certain that it was. I also became aware that I would have to bear witness to the divinity of that book on my mission. Therefore I began to pray, even as the man talked, that I might receive such a witness. In that moment there came over me an indescribable feeling that removed all doubt, and I knew that the Book of Mormon was true. As Elder Boyd K. Packer has described, the knowledge came more as a feeling than as a sound. Yet it was a feeling so powerful, so convincing, that all doubt fled, though I had read the entire book only once. A side effect of this very special experience was a feeling of happiness and peace that I had not experienced up to that point. Little did I realize then why such an experience was so suddenly granted me.

Upon arriving in the mission field, I was assigned a companion who had fought with the U. S. Marines in the Korean War. He had gone through a sudden conversion to the Church in the middle of the battle of Seoul while fighting the Chinese Communist forces. While he was now willing to serve the Church and his God, he knew far less about them than I did, even though he had been on his mission for more than a year. The second day we were together, we knocked on the door of a small house and were immediately invited in by a tall, gregarious, confident man who we later discovered was a

Church of Christ minister. He read things to us from old Mormon documents that I had never before heard. From David Whitmer's *An Address To All Believers In Christ*, we heard that Joseph Smith translated the Book of Mormon by putting a rock in a hat and then placing the hat over his face; that Joseph did not even have the golden plates in the same room with him for most of the translating time, and that he both smoked and drank. He told us Martin Harris had written that the Prophet was drunk some of the time he was working on the Book of Mormon translation. I saw my companion go white, and he was, to borrow a phrase from Peter, unable in that moment to give a reason for the hope within him. Suddenly I found myself saying, "I don't know very much about the things you have been telling us but I do know that the Book of Mormon is true, because God Himself has told me so."

That night I thanked my Heavenly Father for giving me that assurance which has remained with me to this day. At the same time, however, I vowed that I would do everything I could to make certain that I would never again be surprised by the content of obscure historical documents. I have not always been successful in keeping this vow, but this concern inspired in me a deep affection for Church history.

When I returned from my mission I continued to be fascinated with our theology and history, and read every chance I got. This desire persisted after I enrolled at Utah State University. Then a new challenge to my faith appeared. I took a series of courses in political theory from a professor who had been excommunicated from the Church, and began to learn that several things I had been taught in Sunday School were questionable. The professor taught that there had been no prayer in the Constitutional Convention; that the fathers of the Constitution framed it, in part, to curb democracy; that they were acting, furthermore, partly from selfish monetary motives and that there were flaws in the finished product. Earlier I had been taught, or had decided on my own, that the Constitution was an inspired document, close to scripture, and these new ideas now caused me to question my religious faith. I was learning that religious historical facts can not only jolt the perceptions of a believer, but that they can have an impact on accepted secular knowledge as well.

I also began to learn that Joseph Smith had been less unique in his theology than I had been led to believe, and that the New York environment of the Prophet could account for many of his teachings and beliefs. During this period in my life I discovered Hugh Nibley. I heard him speak, read his books, and through him learned that the Book of Mormon was a far more sophisticated work than its critics had allowed. For this and other reasons I continued to read the Book of Mormon and our other scriptures and remained active in the Church. Moreover, I felt good when I did so, and I believed that their teachings were making me a better person and bringing me closer to Christ.

A great institute teacher, Jack Kidd, had me read Lowell Bennion's book *Religion and the Pursuit of Truth*, which helped me both as a person and as a scholar in embryo. But it was while "pitching manure" (that's what we called it) with my father on Saturdays that I began to understand that although many could appear to tear Joseph Smith's teachings apart, the structures they built in their place were infinitely inferior to the one the Prophet, by whatever means, had constructed. I also began to feel more deeply than before the importance of family, sociality, and the bonding together of peoples that the gospel accomplished. My crisis of conscience was over. Though I emerged not quite so trusting and gullible as before, the structure of my faith was much more durable. I had learned, both emotionally and empirically, that while truth is ultimately truth, still secular knowledge and religious truth are nevertheless not discovered and secured in the same ways. Moreover, I was convinced that both were important and necessary for me to be happy. Like Herman Hesse's *Siddhartha*, I found peace and comfort, as well as stimulation, in seeking truth both through reason and through faith.

While living in southern California I became a serious student of LDS Church history, and I began to read every book on the subject I could find. I devoured the *Journal of Discourses* as a research assistant for the Dean of the College of Public Administration, and had discussions on theology with members of the University of Southern California LDS Institute staff. My faith changed somewhat as I discovered that prophets were human, expressed their own opinions, and sometimes erred. Yet I found far more to emulate in them than to discard, and my personal contacts with them were sweet and uplifting. I felt their spirit and sensed that it was wholesome, caring, and holy. Associating with Spencer W. Kimball, Hugh B. Brown, Marion G. Romney, Boyd K. Packer, Ezra Taft Benson, Paul H. Dunn, and Marion D. Hanks, to mention only a few, brought me closer to Christ, not further from Him.

While doing research for my Ph.D. dissertation in the Church archives, I found my faith growing even more. "Skeletons" that I had heard so much about were simply not there. The more documents I read, the more convinced I became that Joseph Smith believed that he had seen God, Jesus Christ, and angels, and that he was convinced that he spoke for God. Joseph had to be understood in those terms, and if one were to be true to the records and documents, then the Prophet could not be dismissed as a deceiver, a rake, or a charlatan. He was best explained as a man called by God.

The more I learned about Joseph, the more I loved him. In Missouri, after having seen Joseph's comb, brush, Hebrew book, and other memorabilia, I sang with some other historians the W. W. Phelps hymn, "The Spirit Of God Like A Fire Is Burning," and then knelt with the others in prayer. While so engaged, I felt the Spirit remind me with great power that Joseph was indeed the Lord's prophet. That impression was strong, clear, and undeniable.

After being warned in a dream, I was called by President Spencer W. Kimball to be a mission president. In this capacity, I came to personally know that God loves missionaries and missionary work and inspires and directs not only elders and sisters, but also their presidents. I walked those three years with my hand in His, and while it was the most difficult assignment I have ever had, it was also the most spiritually rewarding. I came to know Heavenly Father and His Son in powerful new ways. I felt their presence, knew their will, and participated in their love.

Books, too, have helped increase my commitment, and have become important pillars of my faith. Upon graduation from college, I resolved that I would read one book a week for the rest of my life, and I am well ahead of schedule. I realize that many Latter-day Saints mouth a great desire for knowledge while displaying, at the same time, a deep-seated fear of intellectuals and the intellect. Nevertheless, I have found the Latter-day Saint devotion to the acquisition of all truth to be a great source of satisfaction.

My study of Aleksandr I. Solzhenitsyn has sharpened my integrity and my desire to be willing to sacrifice everything on the altar of honesty. Furthermore, his awesome devotion to telling the story of his gulag comrades and his ability to memorize their experiences until it took him weeks to recite the details (and his having done this just in case the account of their experiences he wrote on scraps of paper was confiscated and destroyed) inspired me to persevere in my quest to write the story of the Mormon people with as much integrity as I possessed. I have come to believe that their history, too, deserves to be written with as much exactness and love as is humanly possible. Their faith has helped sustain my own, and I have found additional strength and conviction in their heroic past.

As I read the theology of Tillich, Buber, Barth, and other great theologians, I found that by comparison Mormon thought is far more exciting and has more depth. My questions as a young man—"Where did God come from? What is Man? How did we get this way? Where can we go to from here?"—are uniquely well addressed in Mormon doctrine, especially in the writings of Joseph Smith. I have concluded that it stretches credulity more to believe that an obscure Palmyra farm boy, even an extremely bright youth, could, from his own mind, have invented Mormonism than it does to believe his own story: that God, angels, and the Holy Ghost instructed him all along the way.

My commitment has also been deepened by some of the more original thinkers in the Latter-day Saint tradition. I grew up on James E. Talmage, B. H. Roberts, and John A.

Widtsoe; was held close to the faith in my college years by Lowell L. Bennion, Hugh Nibley, and Hugh B. Brown. My adult life has been theologically enriched by Neal A. Maxwell, Eugene England, Clifton Jolley, Richard Bushman, Louis C. Midgley, and Gerald Bradford. My theological construct has also been strengthened by Joseph Fielding Smith, Bruce R. McConkie, Boyd K. Packer, and Spencer W. Kimball. Further, I have enjoyed and profited by long discussions with my institute and seminary colleagues, the professors I have worked with, and my friends in the Mormon History Association. Their honesty in confronting tough theological and intellectual issues has given me comfort and hope.

While I have loved books all my life, the scriptures continue to hold a special place in the development of my faith. Over the years, I have loved my walks with the Master through the rocky hills and valleys of Palestine and the less rocky lands of the Nephites. Adam and Eve, Jeremiah, Amos, Hosea, Abraham, Enoch, Alma, Nephi, Mormon and Moroni, have also accompanied me on many stimulating strolls.

One special nocturnal experience occurred while I was the mission president. One gloomy, rainy night, I had seen my wife and oldest son board a bus with other Latter-day Saints, bound for the Washington, D.C. temple. My son had received his mission call and was going to the temple for the first time. Because I was mission president, and the temple was located outside mission boundaries, I was not allowed to accompany him. As I returned home, I was feeling sorry for myself, and my depression was deepened by some severe and challenging problems in the mission. Upon falling asleep, I found myself in the presence of the Savior, and my joy was so great as He embraced me that I began to cry. I awoke and I found my pillow wet with tears. This dream happened to me twice again, and the last time Jesus seemed to be saying, "Whatever sacrifices you have to make to regain my presence are worth it, because the joy you feel now is just a sample of the happiness we will share for eternity." After awakening that third time, I wept again and then thanked my Heavenly Father for giving me such a taste of what lies ahead. I came away from that experience convinced that Christ was not only real but that he loved me, and all people as well. That knowledge has been especially sweet. In a significant way, my study of the scriptures made such an experience possible, because I believe that I had to come to know the Master first through the documents He had inspired before I could be embraced by Him.

Finally, when my questions have sometimes seemed of greater weight than the answers, I have been held to the faith by President Kimball's example of honesty. His forthrightness, and his allowing us all to see the challenges of his marriage, his family life, his personal life, and his Church callings, have not only inspired me to greater effort but have given me new courage to face my own challenges. He has convinced me that life is a journey worth taking, and that suffering, sorrow, and feelings of inadequacy may be important in the fashioning of true character.

Though I am not fully at peace in this alien world, I am convinced that I am on the right, though rocky and twisting, trail that will one day allow me to spend eternity with those I need the most, and who perhaps, in some measure, need me.

5

Thomas B. Alexander

The Faith Of An Urban Mormon

In clear contrast to Kenneth Godfrey's rural Mormon background, Thomas Alexander grew up in what he calls the working class section of Ogden, where he was socially and politically conscious at an early age. How does a passionate political liberal remain faithful when a politically conservative Church leadership seems occasionally to press its cause with vigor? This and the problem of writing responsible history as both a professional historian and a faithful Latter-day Saint are among the issues with which Professor Alexander deals. Among the conclusions he draws from the several questions he asks, however, one stands out as perhaps the simplest, yet most telling: Latter-day Saints who are "active, committed, and faithful [tend] to live the happiest lives." Brother Alexander is Professor of History and Director of the Charles Redd Center for Western Studies at Brigham Young University. He is the author of numerous works, including, most recently, Mormonism in Transition: A History of the Latter-Day Saints, 1890-1930. *He has served as a bishop and in many teaching positions in the Church. He and his wife Marilyn are the parents of five children.*

In his autobiography, Mark Twain wrote: "In the small town of Hannibal, Missouri, when I was a boy everybody was poor but didn't know it; and everybody was comfortable and did know it."[1] In the world I knew as a boy, such a statement would have been incomprehensible. Anyone with open eyes living in Ogden during and after the Second World War could easily see the contrast between our working class section in the north part of town, the poverty of the Grant Avenue district in the central city west of Washington Boulevard, and the splendor of the homes on the bench east of Harrison Avenue. Then, it seemed, you had arrived when you lived on Marilyn Drive or belonged to the Country Club. Both seemed quite beyond our reach.

While on the surface it might seem that my father's occupation as a drafting instructor at Weber Junior College would have placed us in the upper middle class, that was not the case. Our family was on about the same socioeconomic plane as the others in the neighborhood. My friends' fathers included a lumberyard worker, a postal clerk, a workman in a bakery, a milkman, and even a fireman. Some in the neighborhood worked at the new Defense Department installations like Hill Field and Utah General Depot.

A teacher by profession, my father was also a carpenter by trade. During the summer vacations, he generally plied his trade, and throughout the year he worked actively for the local carpenters' union, serving for a long time on the northern Utah building trades council. Born on a farm in Panguitch, he had left home after the depression of the early 1920s to learn carpentry and to work his way through Utah State Agricultural College in Logan. In Logan he met my mother, a farm girl from Mendon who had moved across the valley to work as a clerk in the county courthouse.

While both my father and mother had come from farms, their backgrounds differed markedly. Many in Dad's family had been inactive in the Church, and he was inactive most of his life. Except for a short stint as teachers quorum advisor, I can remember him holding no job in the Church during the time I was growing up. His politics, as befitted a union leader, were strongly New Deal Democratic.

My father's inactivity did not result solely from his childhood. Circumstances and the intolerance of many Church leaders for his political, social, and economic attitudes reinforced my father's reluctance to identify fully with the Church. As a union leader he was firmly committed to the cause of laboring people. He had seen the New Deal provide jobs and opportunities for people and firmly believed in the strong role of the worker's rights. His recognition that a number of Church leaders disliked the New Deal and that many preached against the policies of the Democratic administrations of the 1930s and '40s reinforced his inactivity. He saw little room within the Church for those with lower-middle-class social, economic, and political views, and local leaders did little to try to fellowship him.

Mother, on the other hand, came from a strictly orthodox Latter-day Saint family. Her father had served as a bishop for fifteen years and as a stake high councilman before his ordination as stake patriarch. A staunch Republican, he had garnered an appointment as postmaster in Mendon—probably a legacy of one of the Republican administrations of the 1920s. Somehow, he managed to survive the Democratic purges of the 1930s, and he kept the position until he retired. Mother was a fine pianist, and I remember her playing the organ or piano in Church meetings while I was growing up. She took us kids to Church; Dad seldom went with us.

Socially, I was always much closer to my mother's family than to my father's. As a child I went on regular summer vacations to my grandfather's farm in Mendon. Those were idyllic days. For me, rural life was a place of escape. Reality was the bustling Second World War atmosphere that transformed Ogden from a junction city to a colony of the Defense Department (then the War and Navy departments).

My father's political, economic, and social beliefs together with my perceptions of the social inequality I found in Ogden undoubtedly shaped my own attitudes. These feelings were personal as well as general. Always one of the smallest boys in my class, I had endured a series of childhood diseases including whooping cough, bronchitis, and chronic ear infections that left me with inner ear damage and poor physical coordination. I was generally the last chosen when the boys picked the baseball teams—usually ending up in right field.

Horatio Alger did not live in our neighborhood. Neither did Charles Atlas. The stories of little boys with pluck standing up to bullies and getting the best of them rang hollow to me. Like the rural life on my grandfather's farm, these were fantasies. In real life, the little guy got beaten up by the bullies, and those with the least native strength suffered the most discomfort.

My own activity in the Church stemmed from two sources. Mother and her family always encouraged activity, and I grew up in a neighborhood with friends who came from active families. I will always remember Ken Hull, a boy my age who lived across the street. Shortly after we moved to Ogden, he came by to invite me to go to Sunday School with him. I went, and he and my other close friends like Vance Pace developed a lifelong habit of going to church together. In my life, there followed the usual succession of church positions including Sunday School class offices, positions in the Aaronic priesthood quorum presidencies, and ordination as an elder.

In the meantime I had found a way to cope with my less than generous physical endowment. I learned quite early in school that I had an above-average mind. School work came relatively easy for me, and I enjoyed reading and learning new things. In junior high school and high school I expended considerable effort in debate and drama, achieving some success in both. I enjoyed singing and participated in some choral work. I even took up the cello for a time—though that was largely a disaster.

As time went on, my intellectual and religious life tended to separate into two compartments. Study of debate topics and American history reinforced the political, social, and economic attitudes I had learned from my father. The New Deal had been good to Utah in general and Ogden in particular. Contrary to the image portrayed by conservatives, the main emphasis in the New Deal was not the dole. Rather, New Dealers like Harry Hopkins stressed the need to invest workers' lives with dignity by providing public works to employ those who could not find jobs in the private sector. In Ogden the WPA had constructed a number of buildings, including Ogden High School, the City and County Building, and the Forest Service building. My grandparents spoke derisively of the privy in their back yard—calling it the WPA—but it seemed to me that any effort to help people by providing jobs for them deserved praise, not ridicule.

I was convinced then, and I still am, that social, economic, and political conservatism is morally indefensible. Conservative ideals placed the greatest burdens upon the socially and economically disadvantaged—exactly the people who are least able to bear them. The New Deal had inculcated a new definition of morality, since immorality could be collective as well as personal. Providing the dignity of work for people in need seemed exceedingly more Christian than forcing them to starve or to go on the dole. To take the position that the only people Church members had to concern themselves with were the worthy poor seemed un-Christian in the extreme.

On the other hand, the principles of the gospel were important to me. I had learned the rudiments from my mother and her family, and personal activity and study in Primary and Sunday School reinforced them as did my association with committed friends. My testimony of the divinity of Christ and of the restoration of the gospel through the prophet Joseph Smith grew.

Moreover, I recognized that something was missing in my family life. My friends' fathers baptized and confirmed them, ordained them to priesthood offices, and went to church with them. We went without Dad, and men in the ward whom I respected, but who were not really close to me, performed those ordinances instead.

Still, I was a bit resentful because I believed that Church leaders had had a great deal to do with my father's inactivity. The gospel taught me that each of us bore personal responsibility for our activity, but that we also bore responsibility for the offense we gave to others. If the gospel meant anything, it meant that Christ offered salvation to all mankind, not just to conservative Republicans. On balance, my father simply did not feel welcome to carry his economic, political, and social beliefs into the Church when so many leaders preached against those views.

Clearly I faced a dilemma. On the one hand, I had a strong testimony of the Church, and I wanted the gospel in my life. On the other, I found the political views of many in the Church repulsive. On the one hand was the Church which offered teachings revealed by God to the prophets. On the other was the everyday life of a lower-middle-class urban American boy which many Church leaders seemed not to understand. I resolved the conflict at the time by compartmentalizing my life into a Church domain and civil domain. In the first area, I followed the Church leaders implicitly. In the other, I remained independent of the Church, developing my own views in school and in personal study.

Moreover, I found considerable justification in the scriptures and in Church history for my political views. Both Jesus Christ and Joseph Smith had preached economic and social equality. The equality reported in Acts, in Third Nephi, in the Law of Consecration and Stewardship, and in the United Order seemed closer to New Deal principles than the individualistic and exploitive ideas I found so often in contemporary conservatism.

Occasionally, a Church leader had seemed to agree. I learned that B. H. Roberts and Anthony W. Ivins had both supported the New Deal, that Senator Elbert D. Thomas and Governor Herbert B. Maw were both active Churchmen. I concluded that I could indeed separate religious advice and political advice and that, while I accepted and followed the former, I could respectfully disregard the latter.

As a young man with a strong testimony, I had always wanted to serve a mission. My father, however, was not particularly keen on the idea. I completed two years at Weber College in engineering and then transferred for one quarter to the University of Utah. In the meantime, my close friends had left on missions. Ken Hull went to Illinois, Vance Pace left for Brazil, and Bob Standing, whom I had met in high school and to whom the rest of us had grown much closer in college, went to Finland. I knew that I should be in the mission field as well.

One weekend while I was home from the "U," I went to see Bishop Harmon Cutler of the Ogden 29th Ward. I told him that I really wanted to serve on a mission but that my father did not particularly want me to go. He agreed to meet with the two of us, and after some discussion, my dad agreed to let me go and to support me in the mission field.

I received a call to the West German Mission, and my experiences there changed my life. While preaching the gospel with some success, I found some of my attitudes changing. I reflected on the culture and history of the German people, and decided that I wanted to change my major and to study European history.

After returning home, I went to see Dello Dayton, a history professor at Weber College who had served as advisor for the social club to which I belonged. Dello had a Ph.D. from Berkeley, but he had retained a firm commitment to the gospel. I told him of my desire to major in history, and I explained also that my father would undoubtedly be upset at my decision. Dad wanted me to become an engineer, but even though I had spent two years studying in that field, I didn't want to spend the rest of my life working in it. I wanted to teach history and do research, not to design machines.

I told Dad of my decision, and it nearly broke his heart. I don't think he ever completely reconciled himself to my choice. I persisted, however, completing a bachelor's and master's degree at Utah State University, and a Ph.D. at Berkeley.

At Utah State I changed the emphasis within my major. The department there was not particularly strong in European history then, but it had some fine professors in the American field. Those who influenced me most were undoubtedly George Ellsworth and Leonard Arrington, and with both men I have maintained a life-long friendship. From George I learned a commitment to integrity and a concern for students, while Leonard taught me the joys of the scholarly life. Both were strongly devoted to the Church and active in responsible ward and stake positions.

In the meantime, I had married Marilyn Johns of Ogden, and our marriage reinforced the commitment to the gospel I had before. Mother attended our wedding in the Logan Temple, but Father's inactivity excluded him from the ceremony. I did not want that sort of life for my family. Ours would be a marriage in which both of us shared a commitment to the Church, though ironically, our political views are different, since Marilyn is an active Republican. During my university years after our marriage we both served in various Church positions, particularly in the Sunday School and MIA. I also served as an early morning seminary teacher in the Lafayette-Orinda Ward where we lived in California.

After I completed my Ph.D. at Berkeley, I began searching for a professorial appointment. By now, I had begun to collaborate with Leonard on articles dealing with the Defense Department in Utah, and I had also completed a dissertation on the Interior Department in the Intermountain West. Under the circumstances, when I received offers from both Fresno State University and Brigham Young University, I accepted the latter position. At Fresno I would have become their expert in California history. At Brigham Young I could work in Utah and western history—exactly what I wanted to do.

In my research, I followed two main paths. My master's thesis at Utah State had dealt with the nineteenth-century Mormon-Gentile conflict in Utah as it related to the federal courts, and I had written a seminar paper at Berkeley on territorial judge Charles S. Zane. At the same time, I continued to study federal activities in the Mountain West generally.

My research and study led me to believe that some Latter-day Saints had not always been honest about their past. Some of the official histories tended to gloss over problems, and some writers even denied that they existed. I learned that the numbers we had been taught to use in the mission field on the extent of people who practiced polygamy were quite erroneous, that plural marriage had not ended with the Manifesto in 1890, that John D. Lee and the Indians were not solely responsible for the Mountain Meadows Massacre, and that contrary to much that was written, Joseph Smith had undoubtedly engaged in digging for buried treasure. I resolved that whatever else I did I would try to be honest about the Church's past.

At the same time, I remained actively involved in the Church. After our move to Provo, I was called to serve in rather rapid succession as an assistant ward clerk, elders quorum president, and second counselor in a bishopric. After teaching on BYU's Semester Abroad program in Salzburg, I served as high priests group leader, then successively as assistant and acting stake executive secretary and as a member of a stake high council. There I developed a close friendship with men whose political and social views were quite at variance with my own, but whom I admired and respected and still do. This was particularly the case with the late President Richard A. Call, a conservative Republican, whose commitment to the gospel and whose compassionate service in the Church impressed all who knew him, and with President Keith H. Hoopes, with whom I had served in the bishopric and under whom I served on the high council.

These experiences left me with more to compartmentalize. The Church ministered to the spiritual and social welfare of those within the fold. Governmental activities helped those who were outside, and those who agreed with my political views sought social and economic justice for all. Still, my spiritual life and my professional life did not have to interface.

I found other things to compartmentalize as well. My historical education had led me to believe that historians could not deal properly with religious experience, since such experience could not be encompassed by ordinary historical methodology. This caused me no concern during the early years at BYU since none of my research dealt with religious experience.

Nevertheless, I had come from graduate school with a personal historical philosophy of relativistic historicism, largely because of my training under George Ellsworth at Utah State and Raymond Sontag at Berkeley. I rejected the possibility of objectivity, since I knew that the cultural baggage any historian carried inevitably affected his interpretation of the past. Reading in the works of historicists, and particularly the theoretical writings of R. J. Collingwood, Carl Becker, Charles Beard, Marc Bloch, Pieter Geyl, George M. Trevelyan, and Isaiah Berlin, led me to that conclusion. I rejected both positivism and determinism, the one because of my belief that objectivity was impossible and that the historian spoke—history did not speak through him as Fustel de Coulanges insisted—and the other because I recognized that anyone who knew enough about a historical period or subject could poke holes in a deterministic model.

The turning point that allowed me to join my religious faith with my historical study came between 1969 and 1971. During that time, I read Thomas Kuhn's *The Structure of Scientific Revolutions*, Robert Berkhofer's *A Behavioral Approach to Historical Analysis*, and Richard Bushman's essay "Faithful History." Each of these corresponded with ideas already formulating in my mind. Kuhn reinforced my belief that positivism and its accompanying objectivism were impossible to attain. I knew that each historian carried his cultural heritage, but Bushman helped me to see that the historian could use his biases as an aid in interpreting the past. Someone who understood Mormonism could interpret the Latter-day Saint past with much greater facility than one who did not. Berkhofer particularly impressed me with his argument that the historian must try to understand the past as the actors in past times understood it.

Since then, reading in the work of the founders of modern historicism has reinforced the attitudes that began to develop at that time. Most important have been the works of Wilhelm Dilthey, Benedetto Croce, and Max Weber.

By the early 1970s I was prepared to apply my interpretation of historicist principles to the study of the Mormon past. At about that time, a group of historians were planning a series of biographical essays on Mormon leaders. They asked me whether I would like to participate, and I told them that I would. I said that I wanted to write on Wilford Woodruff. George Ellsworth had introduced me to Woodruff's diary as an undergraduate, and I knew that it contained large blocks of information on both his spiritual experiences and his everyday life.

The attitudes that had coalesced in my mind by this time led me to believe that I could combine secular and religious knowledge. These did not have to occupy separate realms. Thus, I began to read extensively in the literature of religious experience. At the same time my research assistant, Jessie Embry, and I began to take notes on the religious experiences Woodruff reported in his diary. After conducting the research, I began to search for a way to interpret those experiences. Concluding, with Berkhofer, that I must try to understand them as Woodruff did, I believed also that I needed to reinterpret them for a late twentieth-century audience. The result was "Wilford Woodruff and the Changing Nature of Mormon Religious Experience," which I gave as my presidential address to the Mormon History Association in 1975 and which was published in 1976 in *Church History*.

In essence, my work on this essay had helped me to integrate my religious and professional life. No longer was it necessary for me to compartmentalize the two. If, I believed, an actor in past times reported particular religious experiences, and if his or her personal life and activities were consistent with those experiences, the historian could accept the report in the same way he would the report of any event to which there was only one witness. That the event was supernatural was irrelevant. In my view, the only question the historian had a right to ask was whether the reported experience was consistent with the other aspects of the actor's personal life. The historian had no right to reject it or to bracket it by referring to an experience as alleged simply because he or she had never had a similar experience. Thus, I could write that Woodruff's experiences in Kirtland included visitations by heavenly beings, speaking in tongues, receiving washings and anointings, formal blessings in which the power to heal the sick and other gifts were given him, manifestations of clouds of blood and fire in the heavens, and the overcoming of the power of Satan.[2]

Moreover, I found that non-Mormon scholars could accept this methodology as easily as those in the Church. By reporting Woodruff's experiences as he reported them and interpreting them in the context of the scholarly literature, I could deal with his religious life without raising questions about the reality of those experiences. Nowhere in that essay did I imply, as some critics have been wont to insist, that the experiences were unauthentic or pathological.

Nevertheless, while I had resolved the compartmentalization of my professional and religious life, the division between my political views and those of many others in the Church remained. Church leaders continued to take positions on political, social, and economic questions with which I disagreed. I knew, however, that I had the right to ask the Lord whether those views were revelations of His will, and thus binding on me, or whether they were expressions of opinion to be accepted or rejected like any other opinions. I have the same right to the confirmation of the Spirit on such matters as any other Church member.

I find absolutely no need to be disrespectful on those matters where there may be disagreements. A statement B. H. Roberts made in his address to the October 1912 general conference strikes me as relevant in this regard: "In essentials let there be unity; in non-essentials, liberty; and in all things, charity."[3]

My recent position as a bishop in the Church has led me to believe that my initial recognition of the importance of the Church in the lives of people was not misplaced. Those people in my ward who have been active, committed, and faithful have tended to live the happiest lives. Those with problems have tended to remain farthest from the Church. Each of us needs to recognize the strong sense of community that must exist within the Church and do all in our power to make others feel welcome and comfortable within the fellowship of the Saints.

Notes

1. Samuel L. Clemens, *The Autobiography of Mark Twain Including Chapters Now Published for the First Time,* ed. Charles Neider (New York: Harper, 1959), p. 28.

2. Thomas G. Alexander, "Wilford Woodruff and the Changing Nature of Mormon Religious Experience," *Church History* 45 (March 1976): 62.

3. Church of Jesus Christ of Latter-day Saints, *Report of the Eighty-third Semi-Annual Conference* (Salt Lake City: Deseret News, ca. 1912), p. 30.

6

Eugene England

On Finding Truth And God: From Hope To Knowledge To Skepticism To Faith

Few minds have ranged so broadly and so deeply as Eugene England's in probing the profundities of the gospel and in successfully relating those profundities both to philosophical inquiry and to everyday Christian living. The title of his essay well conveys the heart of England's message: arguing that skeptics are not often skeptical enough, *he suggests that the path to truth for some may lie on a road of "Hope to Knowledge to Skepticism to Faith." Brother England and his wife Charlotte are the parents of six children. He is Associate Professor of English at Brigham Young University and the author of, among other things,* Brother Brigham. *He was the founding editor of* Dialogue: A Journal of Mormon Thought. *He writes poetry and criticism of American (especially Mormon) literature. He is a master of the personal essay, and some of his best are gathered in the book* Dialogues with Myself. *He is currently working on a new book:* Shakespeare and Melville: Man's Final Lore.

Nearly twenty years ago, a student came to me for counsel. I had taught him at the Institute of Religion and had served as a member of his bishopric while I was doing graduate work at Stanford. He told me that he had tried on his mission—and with particular intensity during the year since he had returned—to get a spiritual witness of the Book of Mormon. He had read and reread the promise of Moroni and had tried to fulfill the conditions, reading the book, pondering, praying, yearning. But, he told me in tears, he simply had not experienced any response—any knowledge or even spiritual comfort. How, he begged, could I explain this "failure"—or better, how could I help him find success?

I don't think I was very helpful. I didn't know then—and don't now—how to "explain" and thus control the *gift* of grace or the meanderings of the breeze of the Spirit, which "bloweth where it listeth." The operative word in Moroni 10:5 is "may": "And by the power of the Holy Ghost ye *may* know the truth of all things." And that is the word used by Alma in his great chapter (Alma 32) on epistemology, on the process of finding (creating) truth in this lone and dreary world: "Now, if ye give place, that a seed *may* be planted in your heart, behold, if it be a true seed..., if ye do not cast it out by your unbelief, that ye will resist the Spirit of the Lord, behold it will begin to swell within your breasts" (verse 28). The processes of knowing and the role of our individual agency are so subtle and intertwined yet so important that neither pride nor despair behooves any of us engaged in this pilgrimage. And I can only be thankful that I did not further burden my young friend with allegations that he had not *really* fulfilled Moroni's conditions—or that he must be sinful or at least delinquent in obedience to the gospel if the promise wasn't being fulfilled. I think I did the best I could do then: I mourned with one that mourned and comforted one who stood in need of comfort.

But the years since then have brought much experience and perhaps a little wisdom that I could share with those who may be feeling some of my young friend's anguish; perhaps I can provide some help for all of us who have difficulty making the process of finding truth work as quickly and easily as we would like.

The title of my essay contains both my subject and my conclusions: I am convinced, both in theory and from experience, that it is possible to find truth and to find God—truth that matters and a God who is personal, ravishing, and a trustworthy and accessible model. I believe the quest must start in *hope*, which I define as an active desire that this universe we live in is a meaningful and potent one. Such hope includes an energetic yearning for immortality—for meaningful, individual life after death—and also some willingness to accept the responsibilities that such potential life implies, such as eternal marriage and continual repentance and preparation to meet God. I know from experience that knowledge comes in abundance from such questing—but if the quest is honest much skepticism also comes. All the faith that is possible in this vale of tears lies on the other side of the skepticism and is made possible in part by our being energetic and persistent in that skepticism. (A famous couplet from Alexander Pope's *Essay on Man* reminds us that "A little learning is a dangerous thing"—but so is a little skepticism.) And finally, I believe that there is precious little faith possible for many "intellectuals," that is, for those who are blessed (and cursed) with the "gift of knowledge" (which includes everyone reading this essay). But it *is* precious—above all that is sweet and precious—and it is sufficient for our needs.

It may seem strange that this essay, which is essentially upbeat and affirmative, should depend so much on such seemingly weak reeds as skepticism and later on what I call "the null hypothesis" and "the insufficiency of human satisfactions." But I hope you will come to agree with me that such weak things of human experience shall be found more reliable and important than objectivity, reason, etc.—the mighty and strong in the world's eyes.

Indeed, the increase in skepticism since the Enlightenment, even since the Renaissance, has become most dramatic since the Restoration and seems to have undermined religious faith irreversibly, which some see as evidence of Satan's battle against the Restoration. But, on balance, I believe that this skepticism has been positive. It has certainly undermined false religion and bad faith—all to the good, and in fact it can easily be seen as a necessary part of the Restoration and preparation for the Eschaton, the final great drama. Though skepticism has sometimes destroyed true religion and good faith, when properly understood and used it reinforces the need for both religion and faith. It has, in the hands of faithful thinkers like Pascal, Coleridge, Kierkegaard, Popper, and Hayek, undermined the excessive faith of many modern thinkers in such previously intimidating giants as Plato, Aquinas, Hegel, and Marx; and it has successfully countered the modern tendency toward naive faith in science as our savior. Skepticism has successfully refuted reductionism—the pervasive modern idea that all reality is matter and all theory of matter is reducible to physics. Skepticism has helped us rediscover the law of unanticipated consequences—that social experiments often fail, even when we possess moral truth and good intentions, because human nature is more complex than we have assumed, and that it is therefore dangerous to give great power to anyone on the basis of their claim to special truth or ways of knowing truth. In the perspective I am seeking here, skepticism leads directly back toward the balance of humility and fearlessness of true faith—that very thing Mormons understand is among our chief purposes in life to develop.

But let me first establish that perspective from two basic Mormon texts, both from the Book of Mormon. The first gives the most challenging and yet satisfying basis I have been able to find for *ontology*, that is, a concept of what the universe basically is. The second gives what I have found to be the most convincing and workable *epistemology*, that is, a concept of how we know anything. In 2 Nephi, chapter 2, Lehi teaches his son that "it must needs be that there is an opposition in all things" and goes on to explain that this is not merely a descriptive statement about the divisions and conflicts of human personality and social interaction in history but a proscriptive assertion about what the universe *must* be like, not only in order for righteousness and good to be brought to pass but in order for life, sense and sensibility, the earth, God, and even the universe itself to exist. The crucial thing this opposition at the heart of things makes possible is the creative activity and freedom of intelligences, initiated (at least in our sphere of present understanding) by God: "For if [opposition is] not there is no God. And if there is no God, we are not, neither the earth; for there could have been no creation of things, neither to act nor to be acted upon; wherefore, all things must have vanished away."

This crucial ontological point is reinforced in a revelation that was given to Joseph Smith three years after the Book of Mormon was published: "All truth is independent in that sphere in which God has placed it, to act for itself, as all intelligence also; otherwise there is no existence" (D&C 93:30). This scripture bridges ontology and epistemology because it not only suggests that the very existence of the universe depends on the dynamism of opposition and the perplexing, joy-bringing but also pain- and sin-bringing, creative play of intelligences, including God. The passage also states that "truth," which we have been tempted to regard as static and permanently fixed, however elusive, is also inseparably connected to the creative activity of intelligences and relative to the sphere of existence where it is pursued. As the Lord told Joseph Smith in that same revelation, "Truth is knowledge of things as they are, as they were, and as they are to come," and knowledge, as we have learned so well since the Romantic revolution, changes as the knower changes. Thus, truth may well be called, as it is in an LDS hymn, "the sum of existence," but by that very token it is *not* "eternal, unchanged evermore," because that sum is always changing.

I believe that the second text I will use, Alma 32, gives us the best help both in understanding how the knower knows and what the process of change is. It also helps move us to engage in the process. Alma puts his finger on the essential dilemma of any epistemology. He points out that in his time, just as in ours, many start with a self-defeating condition before they will risk the search for truth and God: They say, "If thou wilt show unto us a sign from heaven, then we shall know of a surety; then we shall believe" (verse 17). Human beings *claim* they are perfectly willing to believe, if only someone will provide perfect knowledge—clear, rational argument and evidence—in advance. But Alma knows from experience that such a condition, such prior "knowledge," is a snare and a delusion, because "if a man knoweth a thing he hath no cause to believe"—that is, he will be satisfied with those static, unprogressive, essentially trivial aspects of existence which are available for perfect knowledge, and he will not be moved to change his life to conform to the active knowledge of self and God that comes only through faith. As Alma warns, "How much more cursed is he that knoweth the will of God and doeth it not" (verse 19).

Alma is interested in something much more important than the knowledge available empirically and rationally. He is interested in *faith*, which he says is "not to have a perfect knowledge of things; therefore if ye have faith ye hope for things which are not seen which are true." In other words, we live in a universe (not of our making, nor ultimately of God's, but just irrevocably there) in which the most important spiritual realities and meanings are not empirically available to mortals. Some of those realities in fact seem to be merely potentials, yet to be built by beings willing to hope and to proceed without perfect knowledge. Truth is to be found in the process of *creating* the true realities possible in our universe. God is to be discovered as the being who guides and nurtures that process, but only as we create the beings we may become in that process.

How then are we to proceed in such a strange universe, so unresponsive to our desire for a sign, for perfect clarity and assurance? Alma is extremely fair: He asks the bare minimum required for the process to begin: "Awake and arouse your faculties, even to an experiment upon my words, and exercise a particle of faith" (verse 27). This is *hope* being described, a motivating wish that certain things *could* be true, because he goes on to ask of us, "Even if ye can no more than desire to believe, let this desire work in you, even until ye believe in a manner that ye can give place for a portion of my words."

At this point alarm bells go off for all skeptics, especially those aware of "cognitive dissonance" and the numerous ways mortals can delude themselves that Leon Festinger and others—notably in the book *When Prophecy Fails*—have documented so well. Such are convinced that *any* tilt in the experiment, any emotional hangup, any desire for social approval, any congenital or learned need, even any desire to believe, destroys complete, disinterested neutrality—and thus the reliability of the experiment. And they are right about the destruction of neutrality—but not about the value of the experiment: because all experiments *unavoidably* have *at least* those limitations, even the ones upon which the evidence of Festinger is based. No human endeavor at all, including science, would be possible without some desire, some chance-taking, some hope and vision, some assumptions—if no more than faith in the reliability of our senses as they perceive and measure things. And there are some good safeguards against these minimal tilts, ones well-proven in science and ones that Alma not only accepts but firmly insists upon. He is perfectly aware that the process he is describing, central to the life of the universe, is a fragile one, much like the growth of a plant—which is the very metaphor he chooses. The process can be aborted by tilts in either direction: On the one hand the seed, even a "true seed," a "good seed," can be cast out by unbelief, by resisting the Spirit of the Lord; on the other hand the seed can be bad, and "if it groweth not, behold it is not good, therefore it is cast away" (verse 32)—that is, it *should* be cast away. But clearly Alma understands that some of us, because of cognitive dissonance, or pride, or fear, or some other weakness, may go on harboring bad seeds (whether false doctrine, Mormon mythology, or simply incomplete notions that need to be improved before they are planted and nurtured). And, not being skeptical *enough* at this point, we delude ourselves that these bad seeds are growing. Thus we invalidate the experiment and do real damage to ourselves and others.

But Alma realistically views even a successful experiment as only a beginning, though a crucial and rewarding step:

> Ye know that the word hath swelled your souls, and ye also know that it hath sprouted up, that your understanding doth begin to be enlightened, and your mind doth begin to expand. O then, is not this real? I

> say unto you, Yea, because it is light; and whatsoever is light, is good, because it is discernible, therefore ye must know that it is good; and now behold, after ye have tasted this light is your knowledge perfect? Behold I say unto you, Nay; neither must ye lay aside your faith, for ye have only exercised your faith to plant the seed that ye might try the experiment to know if the seed was good.... And now behold, if you nourish it with much care it will get root, and grow up, and bring forth fruit. (Alma 32:34-37)

This all strikes me as eminently reasonable and fair and modest, yet it does not shrink from suggesting how difficult and risky the business of learning to know through faith really is.

Though we may be blind and gullible pilgrims in a strange and deadly universe, assaulted on all sides by claims and counter-claims, there is an orderly way to begin to sort things out. We need only have the courage to hope, to desire a living and responsive universe no matter how responsible that makes us—and whatever increasing demands that places on us. If we refuse to begin or to continue the process, the judgment lies not on the universe—despite Albert Camus's pained and painful arguments—but upon ourselves:

> If ye neglect the tree, and take no thought for its nourishment, behold it will not get any root; and when the heat of the sun cometh and scorcheth it, because it hath no root it withers away, and ye pluck it up and cast it out. Now, this is not because the seed was not good, neither is it because the fruit thereof would not be desirable; but it is because your ground is barren,...and thus, if ye will not nourish the word, looking forward with an eye of faith to the fruit thereof, ye can never pluck of the fruit of the tree of life. (Alma 32:39-40)

On the other hand, Alma's promise, which I have tested

many times and found as true as anything I know about, is that...

> because of your diligence and your faith and your patience with the word in nourishing it, that it may take root in you, behold, by and by ye shall pluck the fruit thereof, which is most precious, which is sweet above all that is sweet, and which is white above all that is white, yea and pure above all that is pure; and ye shall feast upon this fruit even until ye are filled, that ye hunger not, neither shall ye thirst. (Alma 32:42)

No wonder that fruit was so desirable to Adam and Eve. I mean that very seriously, because I believe that was precisely the fruit they learned to partake of in the Garden, through great effort and moral anguish and courage. Their brave choice to partake of the fruit of the Tree of the Knowledge of Good and Evil began for us all the opportunity to engage in a similar process of growth through faith. It is a process not available in any other way and one that therefore our heavenly Father and Mother, in great sorrow but in great hope, had to send us forth to do—on our own, though with Christ's necessary and sufficient help.

I know I have not pinned down precisely the only true way for finding God and truth. But it is one way—one that I, as your fellow pilgrim in this lone and dreary world, can bear fervent witness about. I really know of no better way to describe it than Alma's, because he not only persuasively argues for its viability, but his words convey with the power of great literature compelling evidence of his conviction and of the desirability of the way. What I can do at this point is relate some contemporary ideas and experiences that might increase our understanding and willingness to try that way to the fruit of knowledge. For instance, many modern scientists and philosophers have carefully removed any basis for undue pride in—or even much confidence about—the once touted powers of critical intelligence and the certainties of science. For one example that is available to rather general audiences, see

Lewis Thomas's essay, "On the Uncertainity of Science," in the Sept.-Oct. 1980 *Harvard Magazine.* He argues powerfully for humble attention to our still very mysterious but essential human gifts for ambiguity and for language: "The culmination of a liberal-arts education ought to include, among other matters, the news that we do not understand a flea, much less the making of a thought." Another example is Alston Chase, who in a forum address at BYU (published in *BYU Today*, August 1985) recently presented a striking description of what we have lost since the Renaissance by exalting knowledge over virtue and faith, not only in public and private evil committed by perfectly intelligent beings like the Nazis (who increased through science their power to do evil but not their will to avoid it), but also in educational disarray and general anxiety:

> The academic community, by putting scholarly ideals above spiritual and moral ones, has forgotten how to make value judgments, and therefore does not know how to say what ought to be taught.... Nuclear bombs, genetic experimentation, industrial pollution, carcinogens in processed foods are all products of our own ingenuity and unlimited desire. In the end our fears remain because we have chosen neither to limit knowledge nor to rein in the human will. Instead we have decided to follow our curiosity wherever it will lead, even though this random wandering of the intellect leaves our fate to chance. In all of history, this unleashing of reason and ego is unprecedented.... Only in my lifetime have educators abandoned all pretense to limit reason by faith.

But, you may be saying, didn't you earlier praise desire and knowledge as parts of the process of finding truth? Yes, certainly, but only in the context of Alma's thorough and balanced treatment of the process of gaining faith. The process begins in a "hope for things which are not seen, which are true." But where do we get any idea about what Paul called "the substance of things hoped for" so that we can go on to develop (through Alma's process) some evidence for "things not seen"? Joseph Smith, in his *Lectures on Faith*, taught that three things are necessary for viable faith—that is, faith unto salvation: the idea that God exists, a correct knowledge of His attributes, and confidence that we are living in harmony with those attributes of integrity, charity, etc. The first two conditions are provided in history and revelation: God has assured us that He will not "leave us comfortless," and throughout the scriptures He both gives us the evidence and reminds us how important that evidence is to assure us of what Moroni calls, in the preface to the Book of Mormon, "what great things God has done for our fathers." But though God, through His loving watchfulness over human history, makes available to us all the essential knowledge on which hope and proper desire can be based, we must finally reach out to Christ for the power to repent and put our lives sufficiently in harmony with the divine nature that our hope can be properly directed and our knowledge sufficiently humble. Then, if our skepticism is adequately persistent, we can begin to develop a growing and saving faith.

I remember with continuing pain a conversation I had nearly thirty years ago with a friend, a fine young poet and thoughtful, sensitive husband and father. He and his wife had decided to no longer be involved with Mormonism, not because it wasn't true but because they were afraid it *was*. He had considered carefully the prevailing Mormon rhetoric about the celestial kingdom, apparently a place of organizational charts, high-powered administration, constant progress measured by graphs, assignments, and evaluations—and constant cheer of the kind best imagined as a perennial missionary zone conference or an Amway sales force meeting. He had accepted the image as accurate and decided that he wanted no part of such a heaven, because there would obviously be no place for poets. Like Huckleberry Finn, he said, "All right, I'll go to hell," because his sound heart would not accept the racist values—though he uncritically accepted them as true—of the imperfect society that had conditioned him. But my friend, right as he was to resist a false image of heaven, was wrong; his desire was not Christ-centered enough and his skepticism not persistent enough to help him beyond a community-taught "knowledge" that was flawed and limited, to help him move on to a growing and life-giving faith in the living God of the scriptures and of his own best imaginings—a God who, I believe, is a poet.

Besides the skepticism my friend needed in order to find faith, the other "weak reeds" I mentioned earlier were "the null hypothesis" and "the insufficiency of human satisfactions." The first refers to a process, familiar from algebra and best used in Mormon thought by Hugh Nibley, by which the apparently negative, even corrosive power of skeptical logic can be turned to the service of *affirming* propositions rather than constantly attacking them. For example, rather than merely pointing to logical and evidential weaknesses or problems in the claim that the Book of Mormon is of divine origin (a very easy thing to do) or trying to prove the claim directly (an impossible thing to do), we can make the "null" or negative hypothesis that the book is not divine, was written by Joseph Smith or some other early nineteenth-century person, and then apply all our skeptical, logical tools scrupulously to that proposition; the result, I believe, is a powerful argument that the null hypothesis is *not* true and by logical implication the opposite *is* true—the Book of Mormon is divine. In general, if we would be as rigorously honest and thorough in questioning our negative conclusions as we are our positive ones, we would find God and truth more easily. Skepticism should keep us from accepting inadequate answers and merely wishful hope—but also from accepting inadequate refutations and self-indulgent or cowardly despair. And if anything, as Pascal taught, the possibility that God exists, the mere chance that he guarantees human immortality and joyful eternal purposes, is so stupendous a possibility that we ought to risk all for it, gamble everything, certainly time and intellectual persistence and "working out our salvation in fear and trembling" rather than getting lost in some absurdly fair or "objective" game of letting all the negative evidence overbalance the little, but sufficient, positive evidence. If I am marooned on a desert island, absolutely dependent on finding another human being to comfort and perhaps save me, the one little swale where I find a single footprint is more important, more true, than the other hundreds of square miles where I find nothing.

My last weak reed is "the insufficiency of human satisfactions," which is Samuel Johnson's phrase for a reality he analyzed brilliantly throughout much of his great work on moral philosophy. Johnson was concerned to understand and combat the universal phenomenon that "few of the hours of life are filled up with objects adequate to the mind of man, since the mind of man can conceive so much more than the present can ever supply." He saw this as the reason we are continually caught up in "the vanity of human wishes," dwelling on past and future, letting our fears and hopes, our regrets and voracious desires, consume us and others around us. But I also see there, as I think Johnson did, an unusual but helpful argument for the existence of God and the divinity of human potential. Humans are unique, at least on earth, in having that potential—that appetite—and the language to express it and to imaginatively, and thus constructively, deal with it. I leave it to you to apply a null hypothesis argument to the situation: Assume that we are merely the products of evolution—not of divine origin and destiny—and then falsify that assumption by showing how difficult, even absurd, it is to explain the development and persistence of that continually thwarted human aspiration and imaginative restlessness and creative though often destructive yearning *except* as divine.

I believe that the struggle to find truth is only really successful when united with the struggle to find God and that the struggle is worth the pain and setbacks, worth enduring to the end. I believe the evidences God has provided in history and in the scriptures are adequate to show what great things he has done for our ancestors and can do for us if we will persist in the hope that such evidence provides. I believe his grace is sufficient, that he will visit us with assurance and spiritual confirmation from time to time—not as we demand it but as he knows we need it. And I believe the Church of Jesus Christ is the best context on earth in which to carry on the struggle—because it provides ways to know and serve Christ that can direct and discipline our desires and thus help us to hope genuinely in things that are real but not seen. And through the sacrificial service it requires and unconditional love it thus helps us learn, the Church can teach us to persist in humility, not to be consumers of truth but rather servants of truth and to affirm the struggle, becoming as little children, willing, as Joseph Smith the boy was, to ask and let it be given, to knock and let the door open.

In a recent interview (published in *Dialogue*, Spring 1984), Sterling McMurrin, one of the brightest people I know and truly a post-Enlightenment rationalist, bore his testimony as follows: "I came to the conclusion at a very early age, earlier than I can remember, that you don't get books from angels and translate them by miracles." I find that a remarkably unskeptical assertion, one that manifests much greater faith than I am capable of—a faith, that is, in a dogmatic and quite limited view of the world. I am inclined to believe what Shakespeare's Hamlet reminds us—that there are stranger things than are dreamed of in any of our philosophies. Joseph Smith was more skeptical than Sterling McMurrin, more willing to question the most basic assumptions and thus to make contact with the most basic, divine realities and learn basic truths about the universe. As we learn more about young Joseph as a practitioner of folk magic, one still in tune with forces and perceptions that had not yet been destroyed by Enlightenment rationalism and thus able later to look back to what he called "the ancient pattern of things," I hope we will not let our own rationalist limitations shock and disappoint us too much. We may even open up a bit ourselves. After all, it seems to me that the living God of the scriptures (the one whom I desire to love and serve and know) could make himself known to a boy still capable of seeking treasures in the earth more easily than to someone who is certain you "just don't get books from angels."

Finally, let me say something about the role of the Church in our quest for truth. Not too long after that conversation with my young friend at Stanford who was struggling to get some divine confirmation, I heard President David O. McKay give one of his last addresses, one that was a little disturbing to those who thought the process of getting divine manifestations an easy one, especially for potential prophets. He told how he struggled in vain all through his teen-age years to get God "to declare to me the truth of his revelation to Joseph Smith." He prayed, "fervently and sincerely," in the hills and at home but had to admit constantly, "No spiritual manifestation has come to me." But he continued to seek truth and to serve others in the context of Mormonism, including going on a mission to Britain, mainly because of trust in his parents and the goodness of his own experience in the Church. And finally, *during* that mission in England, while witnessing some remarkable spiritual outpourings at a conference, including the presence of angels, he realized that "the spiritual manifestation for which I had prayed as a boy in my teens came as a natural sequence to the performance of duty." I have had many personal confirmations of that prophetic witness. Most of my profound spiritual manifestations that have confirmed and strengthened me in the struggle to create truth and find God—as well as my most soul-stretching moral challenges and my most precious though painful opportunities to learn how to love—have come "as a natural sequence to the performance of duty" in the Church.

I believe that, together with the scriptures which it plays a major role in preserving and teaching, the Church is one of the major gifts of grace God provides in His promise not to leave us comfortless in a difficult world. It is the most tangible, day-to-day reminder of "what great things the Lord hath done for [our] fathers," the chief way we "may know the covenants of the Lord, that [we] are not cast off forever." And according to Moroni, this is precisely the evidence of "how merciful the Lord hath been unto the children of men" and what we must "ponder" in our hearts in order to be *prepared* to know the truth of all things through the power of the Holy Ghost (see Moroni 10:3-5).

I know from experience that there are many ways to improve our receptivity to divine confirmation of truth. Pride and despair, seemingly opposite, are very similar in their preoccupation with self, their inclination to put immediate success *or* failure in the quest for truth ahead of sacrificial love or even patience: "He that would save his life shall lose it." And a persistent inclination to extreme skepticism—or cynicism, whether intrinsic or adopted as a modern fad—can be a problem: "If ye do not cast [the seed] out by your unbelief, that ye will resist the Spirit of the Lord" is one of Alma's conditions for tasting the fruit of faith. But the essence of my wisdom is simply that one must keep trying, patiently and humbly, and that by far the best place to do that is within the bonds of brotherhood and sisterhood created by a covenant community; for all of us who have it available to them, the Church of Jesus Christ is that community. I just don't buy the objection that church participation is too stressful, too boring or painful or degrading or whatever. I have encountered most of those stresses quite directly and I'm not persuaded the price is too high, especially as I have found that the very problems and stresses that a demanding, authoritarian, but lay church places on us are a good part of its blessing to us in teaching us to love so that we can more ably create truth and find God.

Finally, I just can't accept the claim of some people (though I certainly feel the pain they reveal) that we must get on with our lives—that if there is no sure answer, fairly soon, to the question of Joseph's divine calling or the truth of the Book of Mormon claims, then we can't wait around but must try something quite different. This takes us back to Alma's condition of *desire*: What do we *want* to be true? The claims of the restored gospel, beginning with Joseph Smith and the Book of Mormon, are simply on the face of it the most intellectually and morally and spiritually exciting available on the earth. If it is true that we are eternal intelligences, gods in embryo who can fulfill our infinite potential only in an ever-ongoing process of perfecting the very best of what we know and find joy in—love, marriage, friendship, service, integrity, learning, pursuing beauty, creating—then it is worth every effort, every sacrifice, to engage in the process sufficiently to find out. Certainly, short of convincing evidence that such a possibility does not exist, we would be foolish to turn our energies to lesser options, especially those, however brave-sounding, that are content to limit our vision and responsibilities to this mortal, that is to say, material and doomed, life. So I encourage us to keep trying, however long and difficult the way.

It seems that all of us must go through some kind of Gethsemane, some version of Abraham's test when he was asked to give up his beloved son and his most cherished moral beliefs in order to know God. This may be the only way in the universe to be prepared to understand and accept for ourselves what Christ learned in the Atonement—and thus learn to forgive ourselves and others and develop faith unto repentance so we can be redeemed. For some of us that test may come in our challenge to keep trying, to keep planting seeds and nurturing them, without feeling any clearly recognizable swelling motions or spiritual confirmation, but simply enduring in desire and hope until, after long and patient service in love, the joyful taste of the fruit comes "as a natural sequence to the performance of duty." If my young friend from Stanford were here, this is what I would bear my own witness to—and hope for him.

7

Carlfred B. Broderick

The Core Of My Belief

Carlfred Broderick's autobiographical essay on belief is a powerful caution to those who draw unfair conclusions in their criticisms of Church leaders. Broderick is frank about the spiritual realities he has experienced and, despite a brilliant scholarly career, is well aware that "when the Savior greets me at the veil, it will not be my scholarship that will be examined." For thirty years Brother Broderick has taught and researched family relationships. He is an internationally recognized marital and family therapist and has been cited in Time, Newsweek, The Wall Street Journal, The New York Times, *and many other major magazines and newspapers. Among his books are* Couples: How to Confront Problems and Maintain Loving Relationships *and* One Flesh, One Heart. *He has appeared frequently on national television, including ten appearances on the Johnny Carson Show and recent interviews on ABC News. Educated at Harvard and Cornell, he is currently Professor of Sociology and director of the Ph.D. Training Program in Marriage and Family Therapy at the University of Southern California. He and his wife Kathleen have been married for more than thirty years. He has served in the Church as a stake president and in many other capacities.*

Many a night as I grew up I lay awake listening to my mother and step-father argue in their bedroom, which was separated from mine only by a thin wall. As I remember, two topics were the major themes of their sometimes heated discussions. One was me. It was my step-father's passionate belief that I was stupid, lazy, ill-disciplined and would never amount to a damn. My mother's more serenely held view was that I was like cream and would rise to the top in any situation by virtue of my natural superiority. I suppose it is not overstating the case to say that I have spent most of my life attempting to prove him wrong and her right.

The other topic of contention was religion. It would be hard to imagine two less evenly matched debaters on the subject. He was a gospel scholar of the first rank who could, literally, tell you the content of any chapter in the standard works without looking it up. My mother, as he used to say, was not certain whether Second Nephi was in the Old Testament or the New. But though he was remarkably knowledgeable about the gospel, he believed none of it. Mother said he lost his testimony on his mission where he was appointed the personal secretary to the president the day he arrived and for three years spent his full time dealing with troubled and rebellious elders or Church politics (his president was an outspoken general authority in temporary exile from Salt Lake City). In all that time he never knocked on a door or bore his testimony, but he did study.

In their standard argument he would point out to my mother (*forte*) the contradictions in some series of scriptures (such as the various accounts of the resurrection or the conflicting revelations on the foundation of Zion in Missouri or Zion's Camp or the United Order or polygamy). Her response (*piano*) was always that she didn't know much about this particular issue but she did know this..., and then she would bear her testimony to him and he would, likely as not, put his fist through a wall or door out of sheer frustration.

Early in my life I decided which side of that argument I was on. But I think I also must have decided that I wanted to match his scholarship with her faith.

He died when I was 12 and I inherited his extensive Church library. By the time I was 14 I had devoured all of it, including his well-marked standard works. Not that I waited for him to die to begin reading scriptures or Church books. I remember once at age 11 being reprimanded by my mother for missing the afternoon session of stake conference because I was engrossed in a new book on Book of Mormon geography that was in the seventies book display in the foyer.

It goes without saying that all of that religious precocity made me an obnoxious child, the bane of every Sunday School teacher. Once when I was ten I was sent home for explaining to the class what "Thou shalt not commit adultery" really meant. It had seemed clear to me from her explanation that our teacher did not quite understand the concept. Indeed, Sunday School would have been totally insufferable to me if it had not been for one other smart kid in the class, Kathleen. My habit was to attack the teacher's point (whatever it might be) and Kathleen's was to defend it. Since we were evenly matched this added some life to the otherwise tedious and repetitious material. I eventually married her, having become addicted to the intellectual stimulation which her independent intelligence added to my life.

From the beginning, I suppose, my life experience predisposed me to segregate matters of *faith*, which were based on personal experience with the Spirit (my mother being the model), and matters of *doctrine*, which were subject to derivation, documentation, and debate. I read every word Joseph Fielding Smith (and later Bruce R. McConkie) ever published and honored them as among the greatest scriptorians and doctrinal expositors of the Church. Yet I was always aware of some of the alternative views of Elders Talmage and Widtsoe and President McKay. I remember as a teenager that Kathleen and I approached President McKay (who had come to dedicate the new stake center) and asked him to resolve an issue concerning evolution which we had been discussing. He looked at us and said, "The thing you need to remember about evolution is that the Lord has never revealed anything about the matter. People have their opinions but the Lord has not revealed the details of how He created the earth."

At a less sublime level I remember the time our bishop came to talk to the priest's quorum on "self-abuse." This was a man whom I looked up to as a spiritual giant, who could bring tears to my eyes with his testimony. Yet I heard him explain on this occasion (with the same fervency of conviction that he evinced when bearing witness of more sacred things) that we ought not to abuse ourselves because the practice would weaken our minds—literally (he seemed to tie seminal emission to the loss of spinal fluid in some mystical way)—and that if we spent all of our life fluids as young men we would have nothing left when we needed it later in life. I don't suppose that there was a priest in the room who believed a word of this. The disturbing thing, to me at least, was that he did not differentiate between what he knew by the Spirit and what he believed from folklore. I was grateful that my testimony was independently derived and not dependent upon his credibility as a witness. And I think I vowed to myself never to repeat his error, that is, always to differentiate the core of my faith from the extended corpus of my beliefs.

One last experience in my late teens might perhaps be cited as contributing to my differentiation between spiritual leadership and doctrinal sophistication. As a 17-year-old freshman at Harvard I had the great privilege of getting to know my first general authority on other than a conference-visitor basis. S. Dilworth Young was the mission president and would invite students over to his home for firesides once a month. I was delighted at the opportunity to get an informed opinion on many of the doctrinal imponderables which I and the little clutch of faithful LDS Harvard students debated in our weekly Sunday afternoon discussion sessions. For starters, one evening I cornered him and asked how he had resolved the paradoxical issues around the nature of our spiritual birth as described in the early chapters of the Book of Moses. It took several minutes of confusing non-communication before it dawned on me that this great man not only did not have an informed opinion on the matter but he scarcely understood the issue and frankly concerned himself very little with such obscure doctrinal points. Once more I had confirmed the lesson of my childhood—that spiritual maturity and inspirational power (which this man unquestionably had in abundance) need not be packaged together with advanced intellectual questing.

Meanwhile, my own experiences led me to pursue each half of the equation. Harvard (and later Cornell, where I got my Ph.D.) were wonderfully challenging environments. I scarcely read a textbook in my whole educational career—always I was sent to the original sources, even if it was in a different language (I remember having to learn enough Portuguese to get through the reading assignment for a course on world exploration in the sixteenth century). At the same time I was constantly being given levels of ecclesiastical responsibility beyond my age or experience because I was living in the mission field. The Church's policy of lay leadership has always struck me as one of the most ingenious mechanisms of socialization ever invented. I am puzzled that social analysts and commentators take so little note of it. It is sheer genius to take the very groups that in the ordinary nature of things are most likely to challenge authority and orthodoxy and put them *in* authority and *in charge* of orthodoxy. So they call 19-year-old males (surely the most ungovernable and intellectually rebellious group imaginable) to convert the world to believe our doctrine and follow our authorities. Similarly they choose the educated, active, competent, and critical man or woman to head up Church units and become the very agents of orthodoxy. I was not called on a mission, mostly because the nation was involved in the Korean War at the time and Truman had slapped a quota on the Church of one missionary per ward (being of the opinion that missionaries were merely draft-dodgers in dark suits). The other part of the reason was that at the tender age of 20 I married Kathleen and took her back to share my senior year at Harvard with me.

But if I missed the experience of a full-time mission, I was fully engaged in various leadership opportunities. In Cambridge Branch I served as Aaronic Priesthood general secretary (roughly equivalent to the Young Men's president today) and in the elders quorum presidency. At Cornell I once held six jobs; I served as Young Men's president at the mission, district, and branch level, as high councilman in the district, and as elders quorum instructor. When I took my first job at the University of Georgia, Kathleen and I founded the branch and I became its first branch president. Later when we moved to Penn State I served in the district high council, on the mission board in various capacities, and finally as district president. When we moved to California I eventually became a stake president. From all of these opportunities has come a rooted certainty that the work is true. The evidence is experiential and overwhelming in its depth and breadth. I have never been permitted the luxury of being a dabbler in the gospel or in the Kingdom. At every point I have been up to my elbows in prayerful application of gospel principles to the real challenges of individual lives and of humanly textured Chruch organization.

As district president in State College, Pennsylvania, I was frequently confronted with Ph.D. candidates who informed me that they felt their call was to complete their degree and that they intended to abstain from all other Church callings until they had finished. I invariably reminded them that the keys for making calls resided not in them but in their branch and district and mission presidents. Not one (of several dozen) ever escaped being given substantial opportunities to serve, and not one went sour from over-extension of their intellectual development while their spiritual selves atrophied. I believe this is the key to the resolution of intellectual and spiritual tensions: full-throttle involvement with both.

That is not to say that I have never experienced serious conflict between these two components in my life. My research efforts in the early 1960s were centered on tracing the development of normal heterosexual development among children and adolescents. In fact my first book was entitled *The Individual, Sex and Society* and my second (which was translated into German, Dutch, French, and Italian) was titled *Sexual Development in Childhood and Youth.* The publication of these materials, plus research articles in professional journals, placed me in the forefront of research in this area for a time, and in addition to receiving a great deal of media attention I was frequently invited as a consultant to school systems which were beginning to awaken to their responsibility to provide information and guidance to their students in this area. I traveled all over the world in this capacity during the late '60s and inevitably was invited to be a member of the Sex Information and Education Council of the United States (SIECUS), which was the informal resource center for the whole burgeoning sex education movement of that decade. I was honored to take my place among such distinguished colleagues as John Money, David Mace, Ira Reiss, Harold Christiansen, William Masters, Wardel Pomeroy, and Mary Calderone, to mention only a few of the great scholars who constituted that blue ribbon board. Moreover, I felt that the movement could use an LDS perspective to balance some of the more radical views held by some of its members. The board came under a great deal of attack from the far right, but I knew from my own intimate involvement that their charges of communist allegiance and corrupted morals were baseless and irresponsible. Even when a little film strip put out by the John Birch Society entitled "The Rape of Innocence" singled out me and two other board members as "Comrades" with red hammers and sickles superimposed on our photos and referred to us as the corrupters of youth, I was more flattered than perturbed. I knew I was no such thing, and that the entire purpose of the sex education movement was to inform children about their own bodies and about the realities of the socio-sexual world, which information could not corrupt them. Ignorance can corrupt, not information. Besides, I was at that time anxiously engaged in good works and bringing to pass much righteousness as president of the Central Pennsylvania District of the Pennsylvania Mission, which stretched across the entire rural diagonal of the state, at various times including branches as remote as Scranton-Wilkes-Barre in the northeast and Uniontown in the southwest corner of the state. Every Sunday I was on the road in all types of weather, shoring up the Saints and helping to sustain the struggling branches throughout the area. The work was gratifying, the people were responsive, even the statistics looked good (compared to other districts of similar makeup). We had the highest hometeaching, most organized auxiliary programs, most building funds begun, etc., etc. I knew I was guided by the Lord in my ministry and I felt comfortable with the virtue of my work in the sex education movement too.

As a result I was totally unprepared for what happened...well, no, that is not true. The Lord had actually prepared me in a fashion that I did not appreciate until later. I had received a letter from a professional colleague whom I had known for years and who, like myself, was involved in Church leadership positions and in what he used to refer to as the "forefront of the explosion of information and understanding of man's sexual nature." His interests were different from mine, and in my view, more fringy. Among other things he had become involved in research into nudist groups and had eventually come to feel that the innocent frankness of the sunshine set was wholesome and ought to be emulated. Apparently he had discussed his activities and enthusiasms with his own stake president, who had taken a sophisticated, permissive posture on the matter. But eventually he wrote a paper on his work which attracted general media attention and got a letter from a general authority suggesting that the roles of priesthood leader and nudist advocate were incompatible and he would have to choose which he wanted to be.

He was mortally offended and intellectually outraged. He was confident that the brethren were reflecting their "Wasatch Front" culture and not the will of the Lord who, he pointed out, had created us naked. But he was also shaken to be put in jeopardy of losing his capacity to serve in the Church. He wrote me an agonizing letter asking for my counsel, feeling that I might be someone who could understand his plight.

I took the responsibility of replying very seriously. I began by acknowledging that it was cheap to give advice from the outside of a situation but that I had tried to put myself in his place, supposing that, for example, the brethren had come out against sex education, which I was passionately committed to. Then I told him that I had searched my soul as deeply as I could as to how I would respond in that situation and that I could only come up with two possibilities: either 1) I would conclude that the brethren were exercising their appointed duty to keep watch over the Church and were legitimately calling me back from a path I had wandered into that could lead me away from the goal that we all share, or 2) I would conclude that the brethren were reacting to my work from a position of differing cultural and generational background rather than revelation; but in that case I would consider it my duty to make the Abrahamic Sacrifice and sustain them anyway as I have, after all, covenanted to do. I could not, for myself, entertain any third alternative.

Three weeks later my family and I were watching General Conference on television and heard Elder Alvin R. Dyer of the First Presidency describe SIECUS (by then, I was a member of the five-person executive committee) as an organization led by evil and conspiring men who were seeking to lead the youth of our nation astray. I felt I had been cleaved asunder by an ax. There were only three men on the executive committee and two of us were Mormons. My oldest daughter got up and stalked out of the room, declaring that she didn't listen to Conference to hear her father slandered. Once I recovered enough to begin to think clearly I decided that what had surely happened was that some of the scurrilous anti-sex education material put out by the far right had been given to the brethren. Taken at face value it would alarm anyone. What I needed to do was write for an appointment with Elder Dyer to put the record straight. But before I wrote to Church headquarters I went to my office at the university, pulled out my correspondence file to reread the letter I had written to my friend. As events transpired, he chose not to follow my counsel, but I did. I fully believe the Lord provided that opportunity for me to formulate my response in a non-defensive mood so that when I needed it I was certain what I must do.

President Dyer did agree to meet with me and the other Mormon on the SIECUS executive committee. To my surprise he brought with him a staff (for some reason it had escaped my awareness that general authorities had staffs) who in turn brought a traveling file drawer with every article I and the other brother and the rest of the SIECUS Board had ever written—all content analyzed. Actually they did not criticize my own writing, but they did find in general the SIECUS position was value-free and that that was exactly the opposite of the gospel position. My colleague tried to defend this as the position required of all scientists and scholars but President Dyer kept coming back to the point that it was contrary to the gospel position to treat these matters in a value-neutral way.

The bottom line was that it would please the brethren if we let our association with SIECUS lapse lest we lend our reputations to a movement which ran counter to the Plan. In all honesty, my non-renewable term was about up so it was little sacrifice to agree to follow their counsel (it was not coercive; there were no threats). I did ask what I should do about the address urging parents to take a more active role in the sex education of their children which I had contracted to give in New York at the American Medical Association meetings and also in San Francisco at the National School Board Association meeting that June. President Dyer suggested I submit the talk to President McKay, who was ill but still lucid at that time. I did and received back a letter approving the talk "provided it was delivered with the proper spirit."

That may be the only talk on behalf of sex education ever approved by a prophet. It is also the only time in my life I gave a speech with no jokes or adlibs, exactly as it was written.

But a hard thing happened just a week or two after my meeting with President Dyer and his staff. One of the elders who chauffeured the mission president confided to me that he had overheard a visiting general authority tell the mission president that in his place, he wouldn't leave a man like me in a position of authority for five minutes. The following Sunday the mission president made an unscheduled visit to our district and released me. He had a hard time explaining why he was doing it, so I helped him out: "Nothing personal, just to give various brethren a chance to serve, right?" "Oh yes! That's it!" he replied gratefully.

I was wounded. I felt I had taken counsel and done everything I had been asked to do; in fact, no one had even accused me of doing anything wrong, yet I felt I was being punished. I loved the people of my district and I loved the particular claim on the Spirit of the Lord that is incident to such a calling. I had plans and projects and commitments that would now fall to another to implement or ignore. For a year my only calling was as a home teacher.

I will say on my own behalf that I did not withdraw from Church or from my personal prayers. I never spoke a word of complaint to anyone, including my wife and children. I do not remember taxing the Lord with the unfairness of it all, but in my heart I felt that I had been tried out of court and blackballed. At thirty-eight, I felt that my years of service to the Church had been unfairly, prematurely, and permanently ended.

Soon afterwards I got a job offer from the University of Southern California. It was an exciting opportunity and all of our relatives were in California, but I would never have left the Central Penn District if I had not been previously released from my responsibilities to it.

Our new stake president was a contractor and had never heard of me or of SIECUS. He came to like me and within a few months of our arrival I was the stake Sunday School president and then stake Young Men's president. After about a year they split our ward. As always happens when the news of such a plan is announced there is speculation about who the new leadership will be. I had myself participated in the process of dividing Church units and felt I knew how it worked. As it happened, on our side of the line there were a couple of older brethren who had been bishops twenty years before, and a whole rash of young couples in their late twenties with small children—but in the middle, in the thirties and forties from which bracket bishops are usually chosen, there was an echoing emptiness—except for me. Frankly, if I had been the stake president, I would have chosen me as bishop. Nor did this possibility escape the notice of others. People started calling me "Bishop" and watched my response to get a clue if they were right. At least one such was a high councilman's wife. I figured she might know. I got a haircut and waited for the call. It never came. The 27-year-old elders quorum president was sustained.

The scenario was plain to me. The stake president had nominated me, the high council had approved the nomination (leaked it to their wives) and sent it on to Salt Lake City—where it had been disapproved. I smiled grimly at the scramble there must have been to come up with the final candidate in time for the advertised date.

However, I continued to serve as the Young Men's president, and when the stake president's second counselor left the stake, he started to use me informally as a counselor. When stake conference came I overheard a somewhat heated discussion between the president and the visiting general authority in which my name occurred. The conference came and went and the second counselor's chair remained empty. Once again I had no trouble imagining exactly what had happened. However, three months later the stake was divided, and I was sustained as second counselor. I was amazed and could only conclude that the brethren had yielded to the stake president's importunity, doubtless charging him to keep a close supervisory eye on me.

A year and a half later when the stake presidency was reorganized I was confident that the first counselor, an excellent, well-organized man would succeed to the post. Elder Packer was the visiting authority, and although I had always admired him I knew he had the reputation of being one of the more conservative brethren.

I believe many were surprised when I was chosen as the stake president, but none more that I.

In order to check my perspective I, as president, went back in the minutes of the stake presidency to see whether I had been right about what had happened. I wasn't. I had never been nominated for bishop. When I later asked the former president why not he answered, "Why would I do that? I was grooming you for my replacement." The heated exchange over my appointment to the counselor's spot had nothing to do with me. The president had not submitted the nomination to Salt Lake City in advance, feeling that with a general authority scheduled for the conference it would not be necessary. He was told that that was not the way to proceed and could jolly well send in the paper work and wait three months until the stake division for his new counselor.

The "blackball" had been a figment of my imagination. I had suffered needlessly. Yet I suppose it does not matter very much if the trial of one's faith is based on a real or only a fancied issue. There is value in the experience.

The seven years I served as president of the Cerritos California Stake were among the most satisfying of my life. I am not certain how others would characterize my presidency but my own goals were: 1) to focus the teaching and preaching and testifying in the stake on the Savior and His mission, 2) to establish scriptural scholarship at the expense of creative theology, and 3) to govern by the handbook and to do all within my power to encourage the other leaders in the stake to do likewise.

When the letter came announcing my imminent release (it came a year sooner than I had hoped but this time I resisted the temptation to interpret the move) I recommended myself to the L.A. temple presidency as an ordinance worker and called the brother teaching the Gospel Doctrine class to the high council. These two responsibilities, I knew, would provide the structured opportunities for spiritual feeding that I would need to deal with the withdrawal symptoms.

These have been the main currents in my life as I have striven to integrate and coordinate my intellectual and my spiritual life, but of course there have been many points at which the struggle has been joined over the years. Among them are these:

The Policy of Blacks Not Holding the Priesthood

During the years that this policy prevailed in the Church I had many very difficult confrontations with friends and acquaintances, both black and white, who could not understand how I could support a church that promulgated such doctrine. My only answer then and now is that the priesthood belongs to God, not to me or mankind. He is not accountable to me as to how He uses it and distributes it. His ways are just but He has never explained, so far as I know, the basis of His former policy or of its change. I am grateful, personally, to live in the time of universal access to priesthood blessings.

Succession in the Presidency

It has sometimes been painful for me to see the struggle that some of the general authorities have had in performing their duties in the face of overwhelming illness, weariness and age. Often I have wondered whether a policy that permitted members of the Twelve and First Presidency to retire when they can no longer function would not be kinder and more effective. I confess that I am one who, at the time when President McKay was lingering beyond his ability to function, wondered aloud whether this was the Lord's means of protecting Joseph Fielding Smith from the burdens of that onerous office and more recently wondered also about a similar function in President Kimball's extended illness. However, when President Smith survived to take the mantle of the prophet I was given a surging testimony that the Lord was the architect of that transition (as did everyone who was attuned to the Spirit at that time). More recently I have had a witness that President Benson was elected by the Lord, not by chance. On another occasion I remember deciding that it was not kind of the Saints to keep President Kimball alive with their prayers and decided to be courageous enough to take a more enlightened approach and pray for the Lord to take him Home. I experienced such a darkness of spirit on that occasion that I will never make that mistake again.

I still do not pretend to understand why the Lord uses this system rather than others I could recommend, but I have a perfect faith that at this point it is His will.

Evolution

From my youth forward it has been clear to me that a Latter-day Saint is required to believe that Adam and Eve were real people from whom we are all descended. Beyond that I have felt that we know next to nothing about the creation of the earth or its calendar. I think it presumptuous for someone who could not repair his own TV set to think that he understands how the universe was put into operation. As I understand it, the Lord has promised to reveal more about this at some future time (D&C 121:28-31). In the meantime I am content to have geologists and biologists put together the information available to them according to the best models they can devise. When the full truth is revealed it will encompass all that is real, not merely all that is in the understanding of a particular person or group of persons. If dinosaurs were some cruel hoax, would God have buried so many in Utah?

Homosexuality

I think that I am as knowledgeable about the condition we call homosexuality as any heterosexual in the Church. My life has brought me into close association with many fine people whom, fortunately, I had the privilege of knowing well before I knew of their sexual orientation. My professional activities have led me to be a student of the research on this condition. As a priesthood leader and therapist I have worked with many people over the years as they have struggled with difficulties they face in resolving the tensions between the homosexual lifestyle and the gospel path. No one knows what determines that one individual will be drawn toward members of his own sex and another to the opposite sex. There is beginning to be some evidence that there may be a biochemical factor. Perhaps certain life experiences make the opposite sex seem more dangerous and less attractive to some than to others. Whatever the origins, I have never met a homosexual who remembered *choosing* to be so oriented. Each experiences it as an unbidden affliction.

Given that premise, it has nevertheless been my observation that those who act on those unbidden feelings lose the Spirit and before they know it are pulled step by step into a world at complete odds with the Kingdom. Those who earnestly seek to conform to the Plan are provided small miracle after small miracle until they are able to experience every blessing of the gospel. I have yet to find an exception to this rule. This puts me at odds with both those who treat men and women with homosexual feelings as though they were voluntary pervert's and also with those who insist that there can be no genuine reconciliation between such persons and the highest standards of the Kingdom.

Church History With and Without Warts

I am impressed with the enormous amount of scholarship which has, in recent years, provided us with a far more textured picture of our history. I am not always equally impressed with the intellectual honesty of those writing some of that history. I have always believed that whatever is true should not be flinched from. But I am often appalled at the criterion for truth that some embrace. It is fashionable these days to portray Joseph Smith as a charismatic leader who, however, did have a certain tendency for creative thinking and sexual adventurism. When I read these historical accounts I always check the footnotes. It is not too surprising to find that the evidence for these"historical" conclusions is the testimony of those who hated him and did all in their power to destroy him. It does not seem to me to be good historical practice to present such material as though it were true rather than merely alleged. Indeed, many of these allegations were made in Joseph's lifetime. Concerning those who made them, the Lord made a number of uncomplimentary and cautionary remarks (D&C 121:11-20). Out of my own experience with the Spirit of the Lord I *know* that Joseph could not have done the things they said he did with the motivations they ascribed to him because if he had he would have been deserted by the Spirit and replaced by one who would keep a pure heart.

In a similar vein I find the analyses of post-Manifesto polygamy, which put the First Presidency in such an untenable light, do so by accepting the self-serving claims of those facing Church courts at face value while placing no value at all on the testimony of the men in the Presidency themselves. I would not mind if they cited both and let the reader make up his own mind as to whom to believe, but I object to their taking one set as the truth and the other as the lie in their presentation.

At the beginning of this article I suggested that I have attempted to achieve my mother's faith and my step-father's scholarship. I have been richly blessed by both pursuits but of the two, faith is at my core, rooted in my most unchallengeable experiences. Scholarship is my most valued auxiliary. Through it my mind is enriched, my relationships enlivened, my living procured, and such worldly reputation as I have sustained. But I never forget that when the Savior greets me at the veil, it will not be my scholarship that will be examined.

8

Francine Bennion

A Large And Reasonable Context

Authentic faith, like life itself, is not easily reducible to tidy theological structures. For Francine Bennion, faith and thought are an organic part of her being. In this carefully worded paper, she gives them a "large and reasonable context." Sister Bennion is a woman of highly diverse talents and interests. She has taught at Ohio State University and Brigham Young University in such fields as English, piano, and scripture. She has served the Church on the Young Women's General Board, the Relief Society General Board, and the Church Writing Committee, and has taught in several Church auxiliaries. She is married to Robert G. Bennion and is the mother of three children.

At one point in my life, I thought I had become indifferent to matters of the intellect, academic or religious. I had seen too much collecting, collating, cataloguing, and cross-referencing by persons eager to reveal and defend a "new" insight, which as often as not had already been expressed in one form or another hundreds or thousands of years ago. I had seen long years, lives even, spent in "proving" the internal consistency and logic of systems based ultimately on unexamined assumptions. I had seen too much effort spent creating human ideas and cultures, including our own, which became the only reality experienced. I decided it would be better to start baking good chocolate cakes. Knowing the reality and goodness of God would be enough, and for some purposes it was.

But I found that though I can turn off academic game-playing, I cannot turn off lively seeing, analyzing, and questioning, or constructing sense, and making new (for me) metaphors. I cannot divorce thinking from religion, or from human relationships or, for that matter, from taking a shower or doing the dishes. It is all very well to say that what matters is love, kindness, humility, and knowing God, but the fact is that none of these can be separated from what I think.

Those of us who have profound spiritual experiences continue to live, make decisions, and structure our worlds in part because of what we *think* about such experiences, not just because of our feelings or faith about them. Moses, Jacob, Isaiah, Nephi, Laman and Lemuel, Peter, Joan of Arc, Gerrard Winstanley, William Blake, Joseph Smith—all these and others who said they talked with God or angels make clear that a divine experience does not transform prophets or other persons into puppets with strings controlled by God: a human being thinks.

When a person with me shows tears, anguish, or confusion, or when I experience these things myself, or when I go out for the morning paper and see Mount Timpanogos all aglow, or for the evening paper and see richness of light on the dry mountain, how can I pretend indifference to matters of the intellect, as though thinking is irrelevant?

Faith in God's ways, and commitment to them and to the

people of my Church, are in my bones, at the core of who I am. So is knowledge that God is real, and good, and powerful. To abandon this faith, commitment, and knowledge would be to become a different person. To abandon them would be as difficult for me as to abandon thinking. However, the faith, commitment, and knowledge have not been matters of unconscious habit, or absence of seeing, hearing, and change.

As a child in Western Canada in the 'thirties and 'forties, I was among friends, neighbors, and schoolmates of diverse origins and religions. I heard from one friend that the Pope was infallible, and from others that God created us and the world out of nothing, that God was three in one and one in three, and when you prayed, He heard without ears and listened to everyone at once but wasn't a person. None of it seemed reasonable to me (a man who couldn't make a mistake? three and one at the same time? somebody who was nobody?), but they seemed satisfied. They prayed for help when they needed it, and tried to be good. Some of my schoolmates went to church when it wasn't Sunday, and some didn't go at all that I ever heard of, and others sang in Mrs. Cull's United Church choir all year and went to Bible school in summer but not to church in July because there wasn't any: it was vacation for everybody. There was more than one way to do things, and it seemed to me that while some choices mattered greatly, others mattered not at all.

Though vulnerable to many other personal hurts, I found no need to be defensive about my religion among friends in the United (Methodist-Presbyterian) Church, the Anglican Church, the Catholic Church, the Baptist Church, and the synagogue. Many of the people I knew were first generation immigrants, and few had grandparents born in Canada. A flood of displaced persons came from all over Europe after World War II, along with Australians and even an occasional American. I thought hardly anyone was particularly peculiar—or rather, everyone was, including me. I was aware of persons, not groups. Once when I cut through the back alley coming home from a piano lesson, a boy pointed his finger at me and stroked it with a finger of his other hand calling, "Stinky little Mormon, stinky little Mormon," his voice rising and falling in singsong melody. I was hardly surprised—after all, it was Denny Burton.

Joseph Smith and Church history were not as important or as real for me then as Heavenly Father, Jesus, and the Holy Ghost. Till I was grown up, I had little awareness of my own pioneer ancestors: pioneers and early Church leaders were another kind of creature, not like me. Stories I heard about their unqualified virtue didn't seem as real as stories about the Council in Heaven, or walking on water, or a little bread and fish fed to five thousand, or Christ's letting the children come to Him, or the decision of Eve and the struggles of Moses, Abraham, David and Jonathan, and Esther. My faith was in Heavenly Father; Church was where I learned and sang about Him and Jesus, and later the Holy Ghost, and where as I grew, I saw my parents and other men and women building and worshipping together in His own church because they loved Him, and would give skin, muscle, life savings, and faith to Him. Because of Him they also gave much to each other, teaching rowdy classes, mashing big pots of potatoes, and standing in long lines at receptions.

General authorities who drove the long road from Salt Lake to Lethbridge Stake Conference several times a year, even in -40 degree blizzards, often ate in our home, and when they stayed with us we'd double up on bedrooms so they could have one. I stood silently watching a presiding bishop play with my blond, dimpled little sister on his knee, and noticed that he seemed as delighted with her as my parents and everyone else did. When one apostle eating supper with us spilled crumbs on his tie, my sister observed, "You're as sloppy as I am," and when he took some berry jam from a crystal dish, my brother politely said, "When I take that much, I have to go without for a week." My mother blushed; Christ's apostle smiled. These authorities were fallible men, not infallible popes, not God Himself, but His dedicated servants. With no patina of perfection, they sacrificed, taught, and testified, at times lifting young and old alike in packed meetings, giving us awareness and courage. Whatever the topic, for me the cumulative song of their sermons was a state of being: eternity, intelligence (the glory of God), joy, love, and height of soul.

Perhaps my physical landscape was important to my context for stake conference sermons. The sky was clear, and the stars countless at night. Even now when I visit that country and the wind blows so I must stand against it to keep my balance, the expanse in all directions invites to ends of the earth beyond the prairie rim except to the West, where mountains loom a hundred miles away, not a barrier but a more visible invitation to explore and know.

Though our family at times had "home evening," or whatever it was called in the 'forties or 'fifties, I remember little about explicit instruction there or at regular Church classes, and there was no seminary. Far more important than lectures was the implicit framework my parents and teachers had for what they did. My parents didn't need to *tell* me about prayer or God, or *tell* me to give to the Church, or to set goals. These were self-evident parts of a whole. They didn't need to explain sacrifice and consecration. I saw theirs, and was involved in them. There were of course occasional lectures at home, but I don't remember systematic "religious" ones. I do remember my father sitting at the opposite end of the table in our small breakfast nook telling me week after week, year after year, to sit up straight, put my shoulders back, and quit slouching. The fact that he had to keep telling me suggests something about the relative effectiveness of that kind of instruction.

Most important by far to my religious convictions was the quality of a few experiences that were not matters of teaching, authority, social habit, or abstract belief. They were not matters of so-called "faith" or "reason." They were matters of immediate absolute reality. I knew about the fabrication of fairy tales and night or day dreams—I could create them all, and make them go as I wanted them to go. I knew that when my cousin Tom and I acted out stories, or the novel we were going to write, we were making up what we wanted to think and feel. But I knew my own imagination could not fabricate the astonishing transcendence I experienced when I was alone in the temple for a few minutes before baptism, or sitting on a folding chair far back in the recreation hall at a stake conference in my early teens, or receiving a blessing from David O. McKay, or in my middle teens knowing a few hours of absolute faith and almost immediate healing after long weeks of uncontrollable infection when I discovered the first part of D&C 88 one night while alone in a hospital far from home. I told no one of these experiences, because it seemed to do so would profane them, and because they are beyond the thousands of words I knew then and have learned since, and because there was no need: anyone who had experienced such things didn't need to hear about them, and anyone who hadn't probably *couldn't* hear. Besides, I was a private person. I didn't talk about things most important to me.

Running through all my world, earlier than I can remember, were questions, and the lively searching they provoked—the most exciting kind of learning. The first "religious" (I made no such distinction then) question which I can remember came with a great shock a few weeks after I turned six. For the Dominion Day celebration in July, my parents and some friends arranged to meet in the afternoon for a picnic at Park Lake. My family and two others arrived first. Camp kitchens were filling fast, and we needed a stove for hamburgers and hotdogs. The men stayed at the entrance of the park to meet our other friends, and under a darkening sky the mothers and children walked some distance round the lake to a three-walled rectangular shelter complete with roof, two wooden tables, and a metal-covered cement stove for wood fires. A violent thunderstorm came up, splits and rumbles shaking the universe and us with light, sound, and finally a deluge. Under the sheltering roof we huddled in wonder, till an astonishing clap of brilliance, tingle, shaking, and smell came all together: lightning down the chimney exploded our stove. Pieces of cement flew into bare arms, children were thrown against walls, purple-brown lines streaked down necks to ankles, and I ran out into rain and tall wet weeds screaming my question: "I thought Heavenly Father would take care of us?" No one was dead or permanently damaged, and my mother came into the rain answering me, "What do you think He did?"

What did I think indeed? Amidst crying children and

frightened adults, I thought to myself about the meaning of "take care of us" and I later thought about it again. My fifth-year-thinking about God, myself, and the world hadn't taken into account complexities I met at six.

I've not had a chance since to assume I knew everything or could, though I kept trying. Years later, riding the train 140 miles home from a visit to the only orthodontist in the province, I saw a line of telephone poles getting smaller till they disappeared across the distant prairie, and that night in bed I thought about following such a line beyond the horizon, then around the earth till I came back to the beginning, or better still, taking such a line out past the stars to the end of space. But in space could there *be* an end? If there were, how could it be an end unless there were something "outside" it? And if there were nothing outside, *nothing* would then be *something*, wouldn't it? There couldn't be an end of space as I'd assumed, or, by the same reasoning, of time either. I glimpsed infinity then, without bounds, and in sudden terror looked to my own windowsill for familiar definition of glittering stars and black space beyond me.

Hearing in Church another day that the purpose of earth life is to get a body so we can be parents forever, I thought as I undressed that night that if I had come to get a body so I could have children, so they could get bodies so they could have children, so theirs could and theirs could, on and on in a chain through boundless eternity like paper dolls, then the whole business had no meaning. What was it *for*? Something was being left out. Then I heard in Church that we are here so God could test us, which suggested contradictions and more questions than it answered no matter how I interpreted it. Something was still being left out. How could my Catholic friend be satisfied with a catechism which supposedly gave her all the questions as well as all the answers?

From the time I started giving two-and-a-half-minute talks in Sunday School, scriptures were like a dictionary—a good reference book when there was a particular word I wanted to use. I'd look up *baptism* or *faith* in the index, find a verse, and make a talk around it without ever knowing or wondering who said it to whom, or when, or why. Verses of scripture, or even parts of verses, stood on their own.

The importance of context for a given scripture finally dawned on me one cold winter day when I was home alone practicing the piano and was interrupted by a knock on the door from a Jehovah's Witness whom I invited in. It was hardly a visit, but rather a matter of two persons thinking in mutually exclusive closed circles. The Witness did most of the talking, among other things proving to me from the Bible that we had no existence before birth. After two non-stop hours, as I finally ushered the earnest Witness out into arctic air, I thought, "One can probably prove almost anything with scripture if one is narrow, closed, and sure enough of being right." Then I thought, "A verse of scripture is in frameworks—several frameworks, the writer's and the reader's," and with new awareness I went back to the piano and my versions of Bach, Beethoven, Chopin, Prokofiev, and Pinto—each uniquely himself, writing music both like and unlike the others'.

That probably contributed to my decision to read the Book of Mormon right through instead of just picking verses from it. I'd begun several times, and knew "I, Nephi, having been born of goodly parents" by heart, but I'd never got past the first few chapters except to get a verse when I needed it. When my older sister came home for a few months and I saw her steadfastly studying the whole book, I decided to do it too. This time I was captured by the reading, which went quickly till I got to the chapters from Isaiah. They seemed to me the ravings of a madman. Why would scripture be so crazy? I put the book down. Later I hurried on to more straightforward chapters, got lost in the wars for a while, and finally finished the book quite unchanged. The good parts confirmed what I already thought, and I ignored Isaiah. You could say I consciously put it on the shelf, but the truth is I simply forgot about it for a while.

I can't ignore the Book of Isaiah now. None of it seems madness. Much of it exhilarates me, and after many readings, I still discover sudden illumination in an image here and there. But Isaiah also disturbs me. In more than one chapter, the writer(s) of Isaiah affirm human agency and divine justice and love, but in the same chapter give assurance that God manipulates human beings and then punishes or rewards them for the results of His own manipulation. Isaiah makes God a respecter of persons, who will not let His sun shine on both the good and the evil, i.e., Israelites and non-Israelites. Such a God is consistent neither with the Father of whom Christ tells, nor with what some other scriptures seem to say. Like some other Old Testament scriptures, the Book of Isaiah seems to affirm some teachings of Christ and contradict others, and the mix causes confusion in some persons' relationships with God. I have not put the mix on the shelf, because the confusion has mattered much to persons I care about, and also because in context the mix and confusion make sense.

I am fifty now, and know both more and less than I did as a child. Tonight, coming up the stairs, I saw one of my scientific sons getting Snelgrove Canadian Vanilla ice cream out of the freezer. "I saw that," I teased. "How did you see it?" he answered, calmly putting cinnamon and applesauce on the ice cream. "With my eyes." "How did they do it?" Thinking of something else, I lost the connection for an instant, wondered who "they" were, and absently replied, "Why don't you ask them?" "They can't talk. You tell me." Remembering what our lighthearted exchange was about, and aware of research studies, quantum mechanics, and some ideas which have been around for hundreds and thousands of years, I said, "Well, that depends. Either some particles or some waves struck either some so-called matter or some so-called energy and...." "Don't get technical. Just tell me what happened." "I can't," I said.

Sometimes increased information and alternative theoretical approaches make simple accuracy hard to achieve, at least temporarily. But information, experience, and theories that are used as such can also make simplicity and accuracy easier to achieve. It is ignorance and inexperience, not a little knowledge, that make confusion.

A couple of years ago, I answered the phone. After some conversation, the voice at the other end shook and finally broke: "Does God love me? *Can* God love me?" "Why don't you try asking Him for yourself?" "I've tried. I try and I try, but I don't get any answer: I wonder if He's even there, or if He pays attention to me. *Can* He love me?"

It was not the time to talk about what prayer is, or why there might be no apparent answer. It was not the time to talk about important differences between feeling guilty and being evil. It was not time to say, "Well, let's just put this on the shelf a while. You don't have to get all heated up about it." It was certainly no time to refer to scripture.

Once, it had been profoundly comforting to this person to read,

> But Zion said, The Lord hath forsaken me, and my Lord hath forgotten me.
>
> Can a woman forget her sucking child, that she should not have compassion on the son of her womb? yea, they may forget, yet will I not forget thee.
>
> Behold, I have graven thee upon the palms of my hands; thy walls are continually before me. (Isaiah 49:14-16)

But now, after reading in the Doctrine and Covenants about the wrath of God, and then going to Isaiah for comfort but instead chancing on verses about unforgiving divine vengeance, this person found scripture to be the problem, not the solution. Discussion of context would not erase deep despair at that moment, and any ignorant call to repentance for uncommitted sins would make it worse. What was needed was knowledge that God's love for a struggling human being is real—not just likely, logical, promised, or assumed, but real.

The voice on the phone came again: "Do you *know* He is real? Do you *know* He can love me?"

It is one of the few things I absolutely do know. Several years ago, while on a Church writing committee, I was asked to do a lesson on love for all persons. I wasn't qualified for the task. I myself didn't love everybody, didn't know what it felt like, not the all-encompassing continous state of being we wanted to teach. For several weeks I focused on learning. I cut out newspaper articles about loving persons and nasty persons and indifferent persons; I skimmed and reread assorted essays, discourses, biographies, autobiographies, short stories, poems, and sections of novels; I watched and listened; I consulted concordances for everything I could find in scripture (in context) on *love*, *charity*, other relevant words, and characters I remembered as loving or unloving. The scripture I found most powerful, Moroni 7:48, impelled me to pray with all energy of heart for the love I wanted to teach, and I did so at night and at assorted odd moments during the days. I was full of the search, and knew quite a bit.

One morning I took some clean clothes into my son's room. It smelled terrible. A search finally revealed the odiferous source: several of Brett's dirty socks were in a heap with his cross-country running shoes. That night I reminded him to use the dirty socks basket outside his door by the washer. A few days later, the room stunk again, I found a pile again, I reminded him again, and a few days later again, and then again. Finally frustrated one evening, again, by the powerful air emanating to the hall from his room, I exploded (not my usual style).

In the middle of hot angry generalizations about his intractable laziness, I suddenly saw the great crack between how I'd been studying about love all afternoon and how I was feeling about my son now. What kind of person was I?

In the middle of a word, in shame and despair of doing anything right that mattered, I went to my room, shut the door, and went to bed though it was hardly 9 p.m.—no toothbrushing, no prayer, no looking or analyzing. I slept deeply and blankly until just before morning, when I learned, to my astonishment, things I had thought I already knew about God, love, and human relationships.

When I was young, I dreaded becoming middle-aged and believing *all* to be just as I thought it was. When I was older, I had a period of wishing I might believe that *anything* was just as I thought it to be. One of many tensions in mortality is that between knowing and not knowing. We are likely to forget some things and remember others, to notice some things and ignore others, to assume some things and search for others. In all this mix, it is easy for most of us to trust ourselves too much or too little.

I know a little. I believe much and assume much—as most persons must do about anything. I know God now in ways enhanced by my questions and my experience. Though such knowledge does not solve all questions, or smooth all hills and valleys, at the core of my context for current experience is the certainty I have about God and His relationship with us.

From the earliest years I remember, I have wanted a large and reasonable context, logical and internally consistent. I do not want it based only on human assumptions or secondhand reports, important though they be. I do not want my only realities to be those which I and others have created, important though they be. Though it is useful to know that someone says a thing is true, I want to learn whether it *is* true. I want to know reality beyond my own window sill. I want at least some acquaintance with ultimate, eternal truth, though I see it through a glass darkly till I die.

I need a reasonable context for diversity, suffering, confusion, sacrifice, and love, a context for delight and discovery, questions, and the lively exchanges repeated over and over for thousands of years without universally complete conclusions on everything, except those supposed by persons unwilling or unable to go beyond their own thinking. I need not only a good context of time, place, and circumstance for a given event or idea, but a large and reasonable context for looking at what scripture is, what humans are, who God is, what life is for, and how we do and don't make sense of things. Such a context is important for understanding not only answers, but also the questions.

From LDS scriptures I draw the basis for such a context. It certainly is not the only view which can be drawn from them, but is a framework which for me is logical, useful, and consistent with my experience with God and my fellow human beings, a framework different in important ways from traditional Christianity and many other religions and philosophies. My understanding is that God and His Son have given and continue to give help we need to preserve our individual diverse wills, and our capacity for both confusion and understanding, costly though that preservation be for us all. Otherwise, how could we continue to exist as individuals, capable of choice and change, capable of learning to deal with realities of personal relationships and natural "law" as He does, capable of rightness and truth without cracks or shadows if that is what we want, capable of knowing Him and ourselves, capable of joy and love, of choosing from all other possibilities to *be* as He is?

Last month, our Sunday School class discussed D&C 132. One man was disturbed by language suggesting that women are property to be given to men, to be owned by them. Another man said that, personally, he puts his wife on a pedestal; in fact, he puts most women on a pedestal. A woman objected to that. A wonderful assortment of heads and faces responded to each comment, and a forest of lively but not hostile hands arose. Men and women talked about God, scripture, and men and women.

After the closing prayer, one man who didn't get to speak before the teacher closed the discussion in time for sacrament meeting, said to another: "I don't know why anyone gets upset about men's higher position, their power over women. It's the way things were in the pre-existence, and it's the way God wants it. Women had just better obey and be happy about it." He was serious, and so was his neighbor, whose assumptions were different.

The two are friends. Both are committed to the Church and God, and both read scripture. Both have seen how men treat women, and each thinks differently about that and about other things. Each thinks his choices matter.

Who can say that faith and reason are separate categories? Those who have faith think about it. Those who reason, even (or especially) scientists, must begin with ultimate assumptions they cannot incontrovertibly prove, assumptions which they must rely upon with a degree of faith. It is not easy to define such complexities, or to be simple and accurate in expressing all the things important to us. Alive, we move in darkness and light, expressive and inarticulate, inventing and discovering. That makes sense to me, in context.

9

E. Gary Smith

Faith And Knowledge: Products Of An Open Mind

The Savior admonished us to "be believing." Unfortunately, some people extend this counsel beyond its probable intent. They try to deal with religious doubts by repressing them, or by partially deliberate ignorance. However, doubt can, when coupled with patience and honesty, actually aid the quest for a deeper faith. As Gary Smith suggests, "a degree of uncertainty is not the same as disbelief." Brother Smith received a J.D. degree from the University of Utah in 1965. He is a senior partner in the California law firm of Booth, Mitchel, Strange & Smith. He is a specialist on the history of the office of the Church Patriarch, has published and presented papers on the subject to professional groups, and is currently extending his treatment to book-length in a work he is co-authoring with Irene Bates. He has a broad background of Church service, including work as a bishop's counselor, as a high counselor, and in numerous teaching positions.

> ...the things of God are of deep import; and time, and experience, and careful and ponderous and solemn thoughts can only find them out. Thy mind, O man! if thou wilt lead a soul unto salvation, must stretch as high as the utmost heavens, and search into and contemplate the darkest abyss, and the broad expanse of eternity—thou must commune with God. (Joseph Smith, letter from Liberty Jail, 25 March 1839)

As a full-time missionary over twenty-five years ago, I regarded an investigator's attendance at a testimony meeting as a watershed in his or her progress toward baptism. It seemed to me that if an investigator could weather that experience, then tithing, the Word of Wisdom, or even the issue of the blacks and the priesthood could be no great hurdle. After all, few people outside the Mormon Church are exposed to anything like the testimony meeting experience. There are no controls. No one has a prepared text. Time limits do not exist. Anyone in the congregation can stand up and say just about anything, no matter how trivial, melodramatic, irrational, or emotional. Indeed, tears seem to be the one constant in the meeting.

Yet I was consistently amazed at our investigators' tolerance for such an unusual practice. I have now come to believe it is the very lack of structure that allows the meeting to rise above its inherent opportunities for excess. The lack of structure makes it easier to communicate sincerity and commitment, no matter what the words. The testimony meeting has become a time when I attune myself more to the feelings than the words expressed by my friends and fellow strugglers.

This approach provides me a comfortable personal

harbor, but I have never been able to entirely suppress my missionary discomfort on others' behalf. I am concerned that for many the testimony meeting vocabulary is actually counterproductive to the development of a mature and stable faith. Although the format allows some refreshing flexibility, it seems to me that the language used does not always demonstrate the same flexibility. For example, there is an unspoken expectation that at some point certain statements must be made. These statements all begin with "I know" and end with one or more items from a predictable list: "that Jesus is the Christ," "that Joseph Smith was a prophet of God," "that [current president] is also a prophet of God," "that the Church is true," etc.

Sociologically, these affirmations bring group acceptance and show that the speaker participates with the audience in "active" church status. This is not an undesirable result. We all need to feel accepted, and a central purpose of the Kingdom of God (the Church) is to provide individuals with group support for the Second Estate journey.

Ultimately, however, faith is a personal thing. It is not borrowed from or bestowed by another. It is not found in litany or group expectations. Nor is it an absolute commodity—something we "get" and then automatically "have" for a lifetime. I probably do it an injustice when I attempt to analyze and write about it. Rarely does the communication of my faith to another accurately reflect the status of that faith so carefully kept within the protective cocoon of my heart and mind.

But to avoid all attempts at logical analysis of the process of my faith would also be wrong. The purpose of this essay is to discuss two concepts I have found to be inescapable: 1) developing and understanding faith is for me a complex, non-static, and difficult process, and 2) I must honestly and vigorously become engaged in that process without "copping out." I must not succumb to the various temptations to avoid, through rationalization, the honesty and effort required.

One of the most quoted passages in the Book of Mormon for members of the Church is the exhortation in Moroni 10:4-5 which promises that we can *know* the truth of all things by the power of the Holy Ghost, if we: 1) ask God in the name of Christ, 2) have a sincere heart, 3) have real intent, and 4) have faith in Christ. This scripture has been used so much in the context of missionary work that it has taken on secondary implications not inherent in the passage itself. For example, the knowledge (as opposed to faith, belief, etc.) mentioned is considered by many to be a prerequisite to baptism and acceptance of the gospel. Once baptized, or once a testimony is obtained, this knowledge is seen as a permanent possession to be protected, expressed, and only lost upon individual apostasy. Yet according to this passage, one of the conditions precedent to the obtaining of knowledge is an *existing* faith in Christ, and there is no time-table mentioned for the development of the promised knowledge.

Paul spoke of the tenuous and necessarily imperfect capacity of the human condition to know all religious matters with certainty in this life. "For we know in part, and we prophesy in part," he told us in I Corinthians, chapter 13. "For now we see through a glass, darkly; but then face to face: now I know in part; but then I shall know even as I am known." I have found it hard to "put away childish things," as Paul put it. Understanding as a child often means seeing with a deceptive clarity that which becomes complex with greater insight and understanding.

Growing into uncertainty seems the antithesis of what we normally associate with progress. Learning, by definition, connotes the idea that we come to know more than we knew before we learned. How can the two concepts—learning and uncertainty—be reconciled? We are all familiar with the adage: "The more I learn, the more I discover I don't know." Growth and progress, even in the spiritual sphere, incorporate this seeming dilemma.

As an undergraduate university student, I took a class in business law. We were required to learn the rules which govern the conduct of business enterprises so, as future business persons, we could engage in our professions with the confidence of knowing the applicable laws. We memorized a great number of rules. At the conclusion of the class I felt I had a pretty good knowledge of business law.

A couple of years later, while in law school, I attended a forum where we students were allowed to pose questions to a visiting U.S. Supreme Court Justice. One of the students asked why the members of the Supreme Court so often failed to follow existing law in their decisions, either by giving deference to legislative enactments or by honoring previous decisions reported by the court itself. The impatience and anger of the responding Justice impressed me as much as the answer itself. "Just what do you think 'the law' is?" he bellowed. "Is it something you bottle up or put in neat little packages?"

This wise jurist expressed eloquently the provisional state to which his great learning had brought him. The unlearned student had spoken from the certainty of intellectual immaturity. The jurist was open to refinements and adjustments in his perceptions of the law. The student had viewed the process for himself as complete. The uncertainty which we must engage, rather than avoid, is not the uncertainty of confusion or stasis. I see it, in fact, as exactly the opposite. It is a humility which, properly applied, leaves us open to further refinements or adjustments as our capacity and opportunity to know increases. The law is a good example of this process. Rules are promulgated upon circumstances and perceptions known at the time. While these rules (laws) are generally orderly and predictable, they also allow for adjustment through modifications either by way of legislative amendment or judicial interpretation to adapt to new circumstances and heightened social perception of what is right. To predict these changes in advance involves uncertainty.

Whether the subject is law, physics, art, or religion, there is a learning process which can bring us ultimately to an expanded understanding of truth. If we skip over the steps in the learning process, we may think we have knowledge, but we fool ourselves.

Two elements illustrate the elusiveness of "knowledge" which is gained without recognizing the provisional aspect of the process. First, exactly what is it to "know"? It is simple to conclude that we "know" the Church is true. But what does "know" mean in that sentence? Can we distinguish between the feelings inherent in good fellowship and moral teachings (found in most religions) and the promptings of the Holy Ghost? What part does the intellect vis-a-vis the Spirit play? Do we know or are we avoiding the effort it takes to really know? If we are unwilling to even ask these questions of ourselves, how secure can we be in our professed knowledge?

Second, what is the subject of the knowledge? When we say we know the Church is true, what do we mean by "Church"? Do we separate the body of teachings from the organizational institution? Or do we see the teachings and institution as one inseparable monolith to be known or not known together? Do we speak of the Church of Joseph Smith's time? Of Brigham Young's? Are some teachings less or more knowable or true than others?

I suggest the need for critical examination, not for the purpose of destroying faith, but with the firm conviction that no real faith or expanded understanding of truth can be gained otherwise. Certainly some will enter the struggle only to fail and retrogress rather than progress. It can be argued, as some in the Church have to me, that to introduce issues which have the potential for loss of faith is improper.

In *The Brothers Karamazov*, there is a "play within a play" wherein Christ returns to earth during the time of the Inquisition and is recognized by the Grand Inquisitor, who defends before the Savior his practice of requiring mindless obedience without questions from his religious followers:

> Thou didst promise them the bread of heaven, but, I repeat again, can it compare with earthly bread in the eyes of the weak, ever sinful and ignoble race of man? And if for the sake of the bread of heaven thousands and tens of thousands shall follow Thee, what is to become of the millions of creatures who will not have the strength to forego the earthly bread for the sake of the heavenly? Or dost thou care only for the tens of thousands of the great and strong, while the millions, numerous as the sands of the sea, who are weak but love Thee, must exist only for the sake of the great and strong? No, we are for the weak too.

The Grand Inquisitor then refers to Christ's desire that men have free love (or agency) and says: "But thou didst think too highly of men therein for they are slaves, of course, though rebellious by nature."

This line of reasoning is not new nor without insidious appeal. Satan, who is known for his subtlety, promised he would "redeem all mankind, that not one soul shall be lost" (Moses 4:1). The rejection by the Father of Lucifer's offer makes it clear that while God mourns over the many who will inevitably choose incorrectly, He accepts this price in order to give all the opportunity to choose. God will find happiness in those who achieve nobility through their successful struggle. Further, it suggests that without allowing failure through incorrect choices, all would fail by default.

I have been taught that those of us who are here on earth are those who chose to accept the struggle and to avoid Satan's offered protection from our own errors. Yet, if we here choose not to really choose, are we not insulating ourselves from the very process for which we opted? For many years I was not consciously aware that I was avoiding the struggle and sincerely believed that to question, doubt, or struggle would be an indication of weakness, inconsistent with finding knowledge or keeping the knowledge I felt I had. It has required sometimes painful honesty and effort to avoid such rationalizations, which in the past have kept me from reaching toward a greater faith and knowledge.

I am now comfortable with the provisional aspect inherent in the faith-process. In fact, as long as God continues in His perfection, to honor His children's free agency, perhaps even He experiences uncertainty. I do not feel myself less valiant because mine is not a perfect or all-encompassing knowledge of religious matters. If I encounter difficulty in understanding some theological or historical question, I do not conclude that I have lost my testimony. A degree of uncertainty is not the same as unbelief. Indeed, to question in an honest and constructive way should lead eventually to a stronger belief. And while I have doubts, questions, and less than perfect understanding, I hope to continue engaging positively in those areas where I feel more confident in my understanding. Commitment to the process can and should remain strong and constant while the good fight is being fought.

I look forward to the time when members can stand in testimony meetings and freely share their struggles with faith, doubts, or lack of full understanding, while committing publicly to the struggle before them. I am hopeful the time will come when more members understand not only the need to protect from failure, but the need to allow true success, through honestly facing the uncertainties of the unknown as they search for truth.

I suppose each of us as we were about to leave our First Estate knew somewhat of the uncertainties through which we must pass during our existence on earth. I can visualize the Father bidding us a temporary farewell and assuring us of that one anchor which never has been nor ever will be uncertain—His love. This is the truth of which I have no uncertainty and which maintains me in even the darkest hours of struggle. The apostle Paul, while confirming the partial and cloudy state of our earthly knowledge, left us with two very optimistic and positive truths: first, that we shall, if we persist faithfully, eventually see "face to face" and "know even as I also am known," and, second, that God's love is a constant on which we can rely though all else may fail for us. For "whether there be prophecies, they shall fail: whether there be knowledge, it shall vanish away..." But, Paul assures us, "charity never faileth."

In addition to God's love for us, our love for others is also a principle we can embrace without being tentative about its sustaining power as we experience the exciting adventure that the search for truth represents.

And it is exciting. The adrenalin that makes me feel critically alive when facing the unknown serves to make my journey into the faith-process one of joy. Sometimes I feel afraid: of peer disapproval, of learning things uncomfortable or unsettling to know, of the mental and spiritual energy it will take to absorb and incorporate new discoveries within the network of my previous assumptions, or simply of the unknown in general and a concern over whether I am capable of facing it. But I have found when I do face it (I don't always—yet) I find I can assimilate satisfactorily, and with it comes that third dimension of supreme exhilaration which can only be described as that joy for which men are created.

10

Robert C. Fletcher

One Scientist's Spiritual Autobiography

In general, this book does not purport to directly engage issues of "science and religion"; the backgrounds of its contributors are primarily in the liberal arts. Still, science and its methods are of course not irrelevant to the themes of this work, and Robert Fletcher's article serves as a representative link to a somewhat different world. How might an outstanding scientist, "whose training is to believe only in that which can be demonstrated by confirming evidence," function as, say, a patriarch—wholly dependent upon the brooding of the Spirit? Brother Fletcher's current Church position is that of patriarch (in the Caldwell, New Jersey, Stake). When he was first impressed that he might receive such an assignment, his soul "cried out that this was not the calling for me. I was a scientist." He accepted the call, however, and in it he has had confirmed what he already knew: "The methods of science, which deal primarily with the material world, do not necessarily exclude the existence of a world of spirit. In fact...the two worlds together represent the totality of reality." Brother Fletcher, a former bishop, is the executive director of computing technology and design engineering at AT&T Bell Laboratories. His essay is reprinted with permission of Sunstone *magazine.*

In reflecting on my own spiritual odyssey, I am impressed with the highly individualized nature of that path. The course I have taken is not one I would recommend for anyone else. Each person must find his own testimony in the light of his experience, education, and capabilities. I find that the vast majority of Church members have arrived at their faith without struggling with the troublesome questions I have had. Since their faith is enabling them to lead wholesome lives under the influence of the gospel, I feel it is a mistake to disturb that faith with my doubts unless I feel I have satisfying answers. I tell my story with the hope that it will help someone who is having similar concerns and perhaps reassure others that science need not be feared as a destroyer of faith.

I am a fourth generation Mormon, or more precisely a four-and-one-"quarterth" generation Mormon; that is, six of my eight great-grandparents were the first in their families to join the Church, and the other two were the children of first members. My heritage came from those valiant pioneers who settled the West and established a unique culture in the Rocky Mountains. Yet my parents were pioneers in a different sense. They were in the vanguard of those who emigrated from the West with the reversal of the "gathering of the Saints," arriving in New York City in 1916. I was born in an apartment bedroom in Manhattan in 1921.

Although I was raised in the mission field and thus had mostly nonmember schoolmates and friends, the branch (and later ward) in which I resided provided a good part of my social life. From an early age I felt committed to the Church.

This sense of commitment remained with me, at least at first, as my studies led me to an interest in science. My first real excitement with school came with a course in plane geometry. Although all my schoolmates regarded the teacher as a severe, ill-humored taskmaster, to me she opened the way to the marvels of deductive reasoning. I stood in awe as a whole book full of theorems on plane geometry was rigorously deduced from only a few axioms.

Significant involvement with science had to wait until I got to the Massachusetts Institute of Technology. In my freshman year there I was exposed to Newton's laws of motion. They seemed to explain so much of what I had always wondered about. At that time the courses in calculus and physics were synchronized so that we used the calculus to solve problems in physics and used the physics to illustrate the usefulness of calculus. I was impressed at how remarkable it was that mathematically expressed laws were actually obeyed in nature. This fascination with science led me to major in physics. After working at the MIT Radiation Laboratory during World War II, I went on to get a Ph.D. in physics and work in experimental research at the Bell Laboratories.

One aspect of science which I found to be particularly significant was the way "truth" can be extracted from experiment. For example, in the midst of investigating the effect of a magnetic field on the electrical properties of crushed silicon, a group of us discovered a magnetic resonance associated with the electrons in the silicon. Now what surprised us was that there were two resonances, not one. We speculated that these resonances might be due to a variety of causes having to do with the crushing of the silicon, e.g., dislocations, surface electrons, vacancies in the crystalline structure, etc. Then one of the group suggested that the two resonances might be caused by the magnetism of the phosphorus nucleus. Phosphorus is used in minute amounts to "dope" the silicon to give it its electrical properties. Its nucleus is known from other experiments to have only two possible orientations in a magnetic field. Maybe the electron whose resonance we were observing was associated with this phosphorus. At first thought, this hypothesis seemed unlikely since it didn't seem to have anything to do with the crushing. Nevertheless, it was a straightforward procedure to crush a silicon crystal which had been doped with arsenic instead of phosphorus and measure it. Arsenic has a nucleus with four possible orientations in a magnetic field. How exciting it was to find the four resonances when we did the experiment. We had moved the possibility of a hypothesis from about one chance in ten to a probability of maybe 99%.

Then we had the idea of trying antimony as a dopant. Antimony occurs naturally with two different nuclei (isotopes), one with six possible orientations in a magnetic field, and the other with eight. Sure enough we found all fourteen resonances, and in just the right magnitude to agree with their relative abundance and the right separation to agree with their magnetism. We now had a certainty of our hypothesis which must approach a 99.999999% probability of being right. We might be justified in saying we "knew" that the number of resonances was associated with the nucleus of the dopant. Later, we found the resonances in uncrushed silicon, confirming that the crushing was not the cause of the resonances but only served to enhance our ability to detect them.

The danger in believing this high probability that our hypothesis was "true" was in extending it beyond where it was "proven." The high certainty applied only to a very narrow part of a possible hypothesis, namely that the electron whose resonance we were observing was associated with the doping impurity's nucleus. This suggested other hypotheses about the localization of the orbit of the electron around each atom of the impurity, and the amount of time the electron spent close to the nucleus so its resonance could be affected, and on and on. But these additional aspects of the hypothesis had different probabilities of being correct, being dependent on theoretical calculations and other measurements.

Conviction as to the truthfulness of a hypothesis can thus grow from a 10% probability to a 90% probability to a 99.999999% probability as one performs successive experiments. This comes pretty close to "knowledge" that the hypothesis is correct. I was fortunate to be a personal witness to the excitement of discovering new knowledge by this process.

This process is characteristic of scientific "truths." Some things we "know" with high certainty when a wide variety of experimental observations hang together to confirm them. But as scientists, we are not always careful to limit what we think we know to that which has been confirmed, but instead tend to believe the whole body of scientific theory as proven, even beyond where it is confirmed. This point was to become very important to me.

While I was working at the MIT Radiation Lab during

the Second World War, I shared an apartment with three other bachelors, all of whom were members of the Church working at the lab. They were all called to be missionaries in the Cambridge Branch. Although I wasn't called at the same time, I attended all their study groups and was pretty well enmeshed in the missionary environment. When the teacher who was leading the study group discovered I was not called as a missionary, she went to the district leader and insisted that I be called. (Perhaps this by-passing of inspiration is what led to my subsequent problems.)

After I was belatedly called and set apart, I tried to apply myself conscientiously to the calling. I had a very demanding weekly schedule of working fifty hours a week (including Saturday mornings), trying to keep a bachelor household, and spending several nights a week on missionary work. In addition I had a keen sensitivity to rejection, and rejection at that time was the norm in our missionary work. I kept thinking that the fault was mine, that somehow if I could bear a more fervent testimony I would be more successful. Yet I found this very difficult. I didn't feel I "knew" the gospel was true in the same way I could "know" the truth of a scientific hypothesis. The more I tried to be a good missionary the more this inner tension built up. I'm sure I prayed very hard during that period for guidance.

One day, as I was walking back to our bachelor apartment from MIT and contemplating this problem, I had an experience which hit me with such force that I can only describe it as a revelation. The words came to me as though spoken: "God does not expect you to believe anything but what is true. Nor does he expect you to say anything but what you believe to be true." As I contemplated this, I was impressed that the whole gospel was built on this principle. By insisting that we discover for ourselves its truth, the gospel had within it the seeds of its own destruction if it were false.

This revelation persuaded me that I didn't have enough of a testimony to continue saying that I "knew the Church was true" and therefore to continue serving as a missionary. As a result I was left with the difficult task of reconstructing a philosophy of life based on a firmer foundation of conviction.

If God didn't make known to me his truth with the same kind of evidence as presented from scientific experiments, what was reasonable for him to expect of me? I decided he could expect me to order my life according to what I thought good even though I didn't have a perfect knowledge. Indeed, this seemed consistent with the teachings of the Church that all men were given a basic knowledge of right and wrong. By consistently following that which we deeply believe to be right, we will improve our discernment and be led to the kind of life that God desires of us.

I believed The Church of Jesus Christ of Latter-day Saints led to a good life and, at least for me, was the best life that I knew. I resolved to be committed to that church until or unless I could find something which promised a better life or was closer to the truth. Although outwardly my activity in the Church did not change greatly, inwardly my whole perspective changed. I came to appreciate the significance of the scripture, "and the truth shall make you free." Internal tensions were relieved since I no longer felt the compulsion to use the word *know* in a way that was different than the way it was used in science. After this experience, I was still able to accept calls as Gospel Doctrine teacher and Sunday School superintendent, honestly answer the questions put to me in a temple interview, and be married in the temple.

Marriage had a profound effect on my life. I married a fine companion, Rosemary Bennett. Sharing a life with her gave life more meaning. Before I was married, *truth* was lonely, abstract, and academic. After I was married, *truth* was living a good life with companionship and love. My faith was strengthened by the steadfastness of my wife's belief in the gospel. My daughter Peggy says that my wife is conservative in her beliefs and liberal in her actions, whereas I'm liberal in my beliefs but conservative in my actions. It makes an interesting life to couple opposites, not without its problems but also not without its rewards.

I would also like to acknowledge a debt to my children. The act of caring for them and watching them mature also added great meaning to my life. Each of them has been outstanding in his or her own special way. They have taught me more than I have taught them, and they are still teaching me as they have grown to maturity.

The next major turning point in my spiritual development occurred in the second year of our marriage. We were walking with another young couple, themselves struggling graduate students. I can't remember the conversation that led to this particular experience, but I do remember we were crossing a road together. By the time we reached the other side, I had had another of those flashes of deep insight: "The principal evidence for the existence of the spirit is within yourself." Miracles may have been witnessed by others. Prophets may have conversed with God face-to-face. Others could testify that they had had spiritual experiences. But none of those had as much evidential weight as the observation I had of my own awareness and consciousness. This must have been very similar to the insight which Descartes had when he said, "I think, therefore I am." The part of me that was aware and sensitive I had no difficulty identifying as my spirit.

By inference it then became easy to assume the reality of spirit within everyone. By further inference it was not difficult to believe in the independent existence of the spirit and hence immortality. With immortal spirits there must be a purpose for mortality and a Supreme Being (or Beings) who had such a purpose. This sequence of conclusions did not constitute a logical proof, but it was satisfying to me.

This greatly strengthened the basis for continued activity in the Church. In addition to a conviction of the goodness of the Church in the lives of its members, I had the basis for being convinced of its theology. I discovered Alma 32 as a logical way to get a testimony. Doctrine and Covenants 9 led me to believe that my way of approaching the gospel was consistent with Joseph Smith's; for personal guidance on a question in my life I should study out of the best books, listen to people I regard as well informed, then work out the answer in my mind, pray about it, and then examine whether I get a good feeling about the answer I had formulated.

Continued activity further strengthened my faith. The Church provided a great source of support to me. I became grateful for the many dedicated teachers who provided instruction to my children and the Church leaders who gave unstintingly of their time to lead us in the gospel. I came to tolerate the imperfections.

Prayer also became very meaningful to me. I came to appreciate that my prayers were being answered, not always in the way I had expected, but in the way that was good for me in the long run. I was able to accept calls as elders quorum president, as high counselor, and (a great surprise to me) as bishop. With time I learned in these calls to lean upon inner impressions ("burning of my bosom"?) which I do not feel too uncomfortable identifying with the promptings of the Holy Ghost. Indeed, I believe that the process described in Alma 32 worked for me in my life. I had practiced the gospel in my life, and I "knew" I had an inner peace and enlargement of my soul that said it was good.

After I had been a bishop for a number of years, I experienced a strong impression that I would be called as a patriarch. My soul cried out that this was not the calling for me. I was a scientist. Yes, it is true that I had come to terms with the concept of the Spirit. Yes, it is true that I had felt the influence of the Holy Spirit in my life. Yes, it is true that I had tried to use that influence as I pursued my responsibilities as bishop. But to have a calling whose whole activity demanded a constant influence of the Holy Spirit seemed inconsistent with the discipline of a scientist, whose training is to believe only in that which can be demonstrated by confirming evidence. I considered going to the stake president and saying that I did not want my name presented to the Council of the Twelve as a possible patriarch. I discussed it with my wife, who is wise and practical. She pointed out that it was presumptuous on my part to even consider going to an authority since no one had yet spoken to me. Even when I was interviewed by Elder L. Tom Perry, he didn't indicate what I was being interviewed for, so I said nothing.

By the time the call came, I had become accustomed to the notion for a period of time. I decided it was up to the Lord to say whether to call me or not. He knew me better than anyone else, even than my wife. If he thought I could fill the call, I would do it to the best of my ability. So I, the skeptical scientist, am operating as a stake patriarch. I have even come to a peace of mind with respect to the call. Although I feel inadequate, I still feel it's up to the Lord to decide whether he wants me to continue in this or some other calling.

A final pillar of my faith is the Book of Mormon. In my forty-ninth year as a member of the Church, I read this volume of scripture all the way through again. But in all my life up to that time, I had never put the challenge of Moroni 10:4 to the test. So I decided to pray to have the Holy Ghost manifest the truth of it to me. After several prayers, I was prompted to read on in that chapter to verse six. I received a flood of internal confirmation when I read: "and whatsoever thing is good is just and true." I recognized that I had had a lifetime of experience in seeing the good effects of the Book of Mormon in the lives of those who believed it and tried to live the gospel as preached in The Church of Jesus Christ of Latter-day Saints. Too, I had personally cherished the insights gleaned from the Book of Mormon. All of this was a testimony of the truth of the Book of Mormon.

Scientists can conclude many things with a high degree of confidence. They can indeed say they "know" those things. But there is a vast area of truth which they have not yet touched. In particular I find the methods of science, which deal primarily with the material world, do not necessarily exclude the existence of a world of spirit. In fact I believe the two worlds together represent the totality of reality. The world of spirit gives value, meaning, and purpose to our lives.

As I reflect back on my hesitance to use the word *know* in describing how I feel about the Church, I still feel that my use of the word is consistent with that described by Alma in Alma 32. We can know with some certainty of the burning within, or the enlargement of our souls, and yet have only faith in the truths of the Church. But at the same time I'm not inclined to be critical of the culture in the Church which requires good members of the Church to say they know the Church is true. To me it reflects an indication of a strong degree of conviction about the Church. It is not too hard for me to translate "I know the Church is true" to "I know I have had a burning in my bosom which confirms the goodness of the Church and the truth of the principles which it teaches." This feeling can be so consuming as to eliminate all doubt.

11

Emma Lou Thayne

The Landing

This essay, like much of Emma Lou Thayne's prose, is actually half-poetry. The author's Mormonism is so fully and so naturally integrated with the fabric of her life that she finds it impossible and unrewarding to separate them for analysis. She is less concerned with the outward formalities of her religion than she is with the process of being a full-blooded Mormon human being. Sister Thayne has published nine books of poetry and prose and one book club novel and is widely anthologized. She is listed in A Directory of American Poets, *and the* World's Who's Who for Women. *She serves on the Board of Directors of the Deseret News Publishing Company, on the Mountain Bell Board of Advisors, and is a recent member of the Utah Endowment for the Humanities and Utah Arts Council Advisory Board. A mother of five and grandmother of eight, Sister Thayne is on the steering committees of Women Concerned about Nuclear War and Utahns United Against the Nuclear Arms Race. Her essay is reprinted by permission from* Exponent II.

It was the 24th of July, hot and blue just as it should be in Utah. On the program for sacrament meeting in the Third Ward were a scout, a Merrie Miss, a fifteen-year-old teacher, a seventy-eight-year-old high priest, and an eighty-nine-year-old matriarch, all telling stories about their pioneer forebears. They were prepared, personal, touching. Each brought warmth, faith, information, even humor to the pulpit as the congregation radiated acceptance like hummingbirds at a feeder.

The bishop beamed; the song leader had us singing "Utah We Love Thee" and "Come, Come Ye Saints" at the top of our collectives; the sacrament had come and gone like a good dream in spite of one prayer's having to be repeated twice because the newly ordained nerves of the priest kept mixing *partake* and *sanctify*. Sitting in that red-carpeted chapel among the twenty-five-years-familiar dear faces and constantly changing backs of heads, I belonged as surely as my pioneers belonged to their wagon circles on the prairie or conferences on folding chairs in the half-finished Tabernacle on Temple Square. My head spun with being at home, and my spirit went shimmering off like the sun on Great Salt Lake to meet my mother and father, grandmas and grandpas who I knew were singing along with me on a blue sky 24th. It was my church, my culture, an intimate province that held and fed me among my people then and now. I absolutely loved it. And through it, the gospel.

But then the contradictions.

In the week since, a friend has been inconsiderately released from a responsible administrative position she occupied with candor and courage, not knowing of the change until her perhaps milder successor was announced. While a brother I know has escaped a coronary by-pass through prayer, a young friend who talked in profound confidence to her home teacher about an indiscretion has been excommunicated. In the past several weeks I've seen the Church mobilize generosity and stem a flood to win the amazement of the world, and at the same time be editorially petty about what an under-researched newspaper article in a neighboring state said about a "Zion curtain." I've listened to a lesson on compassionate service, but I've also heard of lessons on what *not* to read, seen the expulsion of a questing paper from the BYU campus and the investigation of writers for sister publications to the *Exponent*, and heard of machinations for positions that I in younger days might have expected to be filled by inspiration.

I've seen one missionary go out and come home under a mission president who built him, helped him master his diffidence, who gave him faith in himself and his relationship to Jesus Christ; I've seen another come home from another mission and another mission president, her self-worth bludgeoned by guilt and debasement for failing to find converts in a mission now closed for want of success.

Perhaps most unnerving of all, I see people afraid of the Church that I grew up regarding as refuge and sustenance, purveyor of truth and love. Who has not observed the historian afraid to write history, the young mother afraid to turn down a call, the parents panicked, expectations smashed for a son who doesn't want a mission. And all the time believers afraid to confront unbelief even as they search for believing.

Everywhere, every week, I see the good and the far from good influences and eventualities of life in the Church, my church. There have to be ways to come to grips with the contradictions, to have enough belief in the good to counteract distress at the bad. Maybe my willingness and ableness to handle the contradictions could be seen as a lot like the fear and faith I take to the big swing at our cabin.

The swing is up a gully and then up a steep dusty mountainside. You get on the single thick rope from a platform hammered to a rough pine, grab a knot straight out from your arms, see that the seat—a shiny skinned three-inch round of mountain mahogany—is pulled tight between your legs, shove up on your toes, and take off.

No matter if it's your first or two-hundredth time, your heart will tattoo your ribs and your mouth go dry as you drop and then swoop up over forty feet to look back—if you dare open your eyes—to the platform somewhere over there on the mountain you just left between two ancient spruces aching and swaying to hold your flight. It's a "beaut" of a swing, one we built as kids more than forty years ago.

The swing was always central to our parties from the time we were twelve until we had our own children daring their friends to try it. And still I get up there and take off with an assurance of terror that makes even my past half-a-hundred-year-old lungs need to "Wa-hoo" on that first plunge, as my legs kick me out and about for a heady landing three swings later on the bank grown steep and treacherous under the canyon boots of three generations of thrill seekers. I know I'll make it. I've never failed. Oh, sometimes I've missed my footing as I've tried to land and had to hang and dangle out and back for another try, sometimes even to have somebody grab and hold till I could get off. But I've always made it. It's something I can count on.

In like fashion in the Church, I've often gone off swinging onto new skies, examining, cheering, chafing, opposing, espousing, hoping for change, loving sometimes unequivocally a status quo. Most of all wanting urgently to continue—nay, grow—in my believing. I've found plenty to believe in—like the inspiration behind that program Sunday. But I go less often now up that gully and onto the swing. It seems OK simply to know it's there, that others are whooping on it, and that anytime I want to, I can go for it and be sure of both flying and finding a landing. I've learned that maturity can help positively only what I have control over, and more and more I gravitate to what little I can control—mostly in private spheres.

Maybe that's what's happened with other enterprises that used to compel and challenge me. Like getting up on one water ski. Or thinking it was possible to rewrite lesson manuals for the Beehives, Mia Maids, and Laurels with a General Board committee who thought with me that we could make them last even through Correlation for at least a decade. Or trying either to make sense of or changes in traditions that suppose credibility in the Church only for the playing of established roles, or the signing of class rolls, or the delivery of hot rolls around the block. I just quit needing to do all of it, maybe because I already knew I could and needed to move on. Or, more likely, because the ground for landing after even the most expectant foray can so often slide and break if not my spirit, very often my heart. Too often I sense a closing down of options of where to land, a suspicion of diversity and more often than not a landing in Leviticus rules and brimstone where John might offer spirit and hope.

Sometimes I find myself with a new gnawing fear of what power or insistence on conformity can unleash—and it's a far cry from the *Wahoo* of taking off on the swing, the challenge of a new idea or way of going. So I simply choose not to swing so much any more.

This is a good time of life. Mostly I am on solid but private ground, ground cut out and smoothed and made comfortable by my own landings or the landings of others willing to share their space with me. It is a place of believing, of letting in, and of being grounded in solid essentials. All intimately mine, all supplied by years of selecting and becoming comfortable with where I have come to flourish.

The arrival? When is there such a thing as arrival in believing? Nothing was ever more dynamic. But where I am now feels good. Full of believing—in the gospel of Jesus Christ and, if not in busyness in the Church, then in the support and camaraderie of those I love and in being about our Father's business as well as our own.

Of course I have often over the years pleaded, "I believe. Help thou mine unbelief!" But the unbelief has given way to—or been discarded in—the gradual and not always easy comings of belief. Time and inclination finally preclude my dealing with supposition or speculation—or even caring about what I don't know and have yet to encounter. There is little enough time for dealing with what is here and now, for trying to find out how to be human before I worry about how to be divine. But time is short. I'm about to turn the age my father was when he died—fifty-nine. It feels young, but now I'm the matriarch propounding by my life as he did for his following.

My mother and father talked little in a formal sense about what they believed. I never remember either bearing a traditional testimony. Their lives were their message: They were fair and kind and full of humor. And never condemning.

More, what they chose seemed to make them happy and replete with possibilities—as they expected their children to be. They never set us up for rebellion by removing our options. Swings were there to be conceived, built, and swung on. Each of the four of us remembers going with their sanction to our own ways in the Church, attending and not attending and staying together as we came back to the same landings—non-conformists in our conformity.

I'd like very much for it to work in such a fashion for our five daughters, each of them as different as her coloring, as "active" as her convictions and sense of well being.

Now in the Sabbath of my days, I claim more than ever the right to selective recall, endurance, ecstasy, expectation. "My" church is actually mine—a combination of "Abide With Me," "...that His Spirit may be with you...," and hugging in the foyer. I love teaching an institute class and learning more from my co-instructor and students than I ever teach. I watch "the word" in action up and down my block and among good people everywhere, LDS and not, all living what more and more makes ultimate sense in this passage from the Book of Mormon:

> And because of your diligence and your faith and your patience with the word in nourishing it, that it may take root in you, behold by and by ye shall pluck the fruit thereof, which is sweet above all that is sweet, and which is white above all that is white, yea, and pure above all that is pure; and ye shall feast upon this fruit even until ye are filled, that ye hunger not, neither shall ye thirst. (Alma 32:42)

What has been there for me to pluck seems most precious. But my feasting and not hungering or thirsting has taken different shapes over the years. It's been a long time since I've signed a roll or read a manual for the classes I attend or felt uneasy about missing Sunday school to visit my friend Margaret, 89, or to be home for house calls from my brothers, one at a time, between their comings and goings. Like one of my mentors of years ago, I'm reading less and thinking more.

I'm loving my children as adults, finding from them and their husbands new ways to see. My husband and I with our different approaches have broadened each other and learned together that to praise one thing is not to condemn another. In our now almost empty nest, we're realizing that constructive togetherness can mean sometimes prickly, often comfortable accommodation to difference.

In that accommodation I'm getting as addicted to solitude as I am to gatherings of kindred spirits, related or un-, the dozens gradually giving away to the one-to-ones.

If I like swinging over the kingdom of God in that gully and gasping at the thrill and the beauty of a green world, I also like inordinately having landed on the dark brown earth to watch the flights of others, knowing at least for now where I've come from, pretty much where I am, and not really a whole lot concerned about where I'm going. Only that it's bound to be full of wonder. And that the land under me and the people around me and the tetherings inside me all seem to make a lot of sense and connect me surely to what I know with the faith of my childhood—that someone way beyond me is there to make sure that the kingdom greens or sheds in the season thereof, with predictable unpredictability.

If I have come to live more easily with some of my own frailties—and they don't become fewer with age!—surely I can allow the same for the Church that I love and am so often dismayed at. It has given me far more than I it—and continues to. I have to play fair with it collectively as I would hope to individually. Its people, its practices, its truths have grounded and blessed me. I must grant it at least a modicum of the understanding I have come to expect from the Lord Himself for my struggles and failings. I must remind myself to be uncondemning as I pray for the patience and forbearance I hope just might be reciprocal.

With as many kinds of goodness to respond to as there are ways of looking at a sunset, I can be happy with my church only if I have neither the time nor the inclination to be unstrung by what might seem to me mismanagement, striving, discrimination, even witch hunts and paranoia. My landing and my being sure of my swinging, or of helping anyone else's, derive from that private kingdom that is within me telling me that only I can know when to go from the platform, how many times out before I lift myself from the seat and try for another landing, how long before there will be no swinging at all. And how to look for the serenity of having held onto the landings so I can love what the 24th of July is all about enough to counter depletions of what it isn't.

So far, what there is to love helps make manageable any perspective on the plunge. I trust it always will.

12

Victor B. Cline

The Faith Of A Psychologist: A Personal Document

Some studies indicate that psychologists and psychiatrists rank among the least religiously inclined of all professionals—to the extent that a belief in God and participation in an organized faith define "religiously inclined." "Several years ago," writes Victor Cline, "I found myself challenged by a friend to explain how I, as a clinical psychologist, could also be active religiously and believe in such a fundamentalist religion as Mormonism...." In the process of explaining how he holds together his faith and his professional knowledge, Dr. Cline addresses such issues as religion and psychopathology, guilt, and free will versus determinism. Brother Cline received his Ph.D. from the University of California, Berkeley, and is now Professor of Psychology at the University of Utah. He is a joint founder of Marriage and Family Enrichment, a non-profit foundation devoted to marriage renewal seminars and family life education. The author of some seventy publications, Brother Cline was formerly a research scientist with George Washington University's Human Resources Research Office. He and his wife Lois are the parents of nine children. His essay was originally published in Dialogue: A Journal of Mormon Thought.

In 1933 James Leuba[1] conducted a survey of the beliefs in deity held by scientific and professional men. He found that only ten per cent of the psychologists surveyed admitted to a belief in God. This compared with twenty-seven per cent for biologists and thirty-eight per cent for physical scientists; in effect, psychologists were the least "religious" of all professional groups studied. In a later study by Riggs[2] in 1956, the results generally showed an increase in the percentages of scientists believing in a deity (e.g., physical scientists fifty-two per cent), but again psychologists were at the bottom. This compares with ninety-eight per cent of the general American population who claim a belief in deity.

Some of the reasons for this are hinted at in the later work of Dr. Ann Rowe;[3] in her study of eminent scientists she suggests that many psychologists are a rebellious lot, fighting parents, authority, and religion. It would appear that many, when they reject the religion of their youth, find a new religion in psychology, psychoanalysis, secular humanism, or B. F. Skinner's operant conditioning. These seem to provide for them new, more up-to-date explanations and models of behavior for understanding man and his place in the universe.

Several years ago I found myself challenged by a friend to explain how I, as a clinical psychologist, could also be active religiously and believe in such a fundamentalist religion as Mormonism when many people in my field had rejected even a belief in a deity and conceived of the world from an extremely mechanistic, stimulus-response point of view. Was I being intellectually honest? Did I have a compartmentalized mind where I put religion in one corner and psychology in another, with never the twain to meet? What finally emerged was a brief chronicle of my own intellectual and experiential journey which had led to a religious commitment.

I must first confess that I am basically reluctant to put this in writing. My religious feelings are quite personal to me, and I feel somewhat uncomfortable wearing my religion on my sleeve, though I have found that at times I can be articulate about such matters if it is necessary and in the proper setting. Also, I am too aware of some of my own prejudices, biases, irrationalities, and at times intuitive (as opposed to logical) thinking to risk exposing these to strangers without some trepidation and misgivings.

To begin with, I had pleasant and happy experiences in my early family life and in my early associations with the Christian religion. My mother was an active and devout Mormon. My father was an inactive nondenominational Protestant who saw no harm in church attendance and activity for his children. My mother respected his free agency and never pressed him about religion (though he did in later years join the Mormon Church). Both were basically good people from agrarian backgrounds, of high personal integrity, and possessed of a keen sense of honor and justice. Education and intellectual achievement were highly valued and rewarded both openly and subtly. This climate was positive and comfortable rather than overbearing or oppressive.

The school years slipped by, and possibly by the end of the second year of college I made a definite decision to make psychology my career field. Though I was a member of a minority denomination, my religion fit fairly comfortably. No one ever made an issue of it or even of such peculiar habits as not smoking or drinking. In my eight years at Berkeley, where I received all my training, very few people even noticed my religion. To many of my peers there, religion was something they were indifferent about. This reminded me of an old saying that the opposite of love is not hate, but rather indifference.

The indifference to religion at Berkeley was obvious. To some, especially in psychology, religion hardly existed, and few paid much attention to it. In all of my years at Berkeley, I was aware of no psychology professor who ever discussed personality theory or people in our Western culture in terms of religion, worship, or the impact of belief in deity on people's lives. In my graduate seminars problems of religious guilt, values, and ethics or ways a therapist might help one deal with religious or moral conflicts were never even considered. Yet evidence from a variety of studies[4] indicates that at least ninety-six per cent of the citizens of this country believe in a deity. And later in clinical practice I found that one deals frequently with patients with religious problems, moral conflicts, and deep anxieties about death or about the meaning of their lives and places in the universe. Though I came to have a deep affection for the campus and the intellectual ferment which always abounded there, I was disappointed that religion was an issue which psychology as a field studiously avoided. The silence was deafening.

As I moved ahead in my discipline, repeated challenges and questions for my religious faith presented themselves. In a church that believes in "speaking in tongues," revelations, miraculous healings, and the like, one must face the very reasonable question of psychologists about the relationship between religious experience and psychopathology. For example, occasionally one sees people who are psychotic who may either believe they are divine or who claim to have visions or revelations, to hear supernatural voices, or to have extremely unusual religious experiences. How is this any different from a valid religious experience? How is it possible to distinguish between the two? This, for me, has never presented any great overriding problem of explanation or interpretation. If the individual is hallucinating and is sick or psychotic, his judgment will be impaired generally, and there will be an abundance of other evidence of sickness or confused thinking. Admittedly there are borderline cases where it may be hard to tell, but in cases of sickness or disease usually the truth will out. The same is true of the psychopath (e.g., the character disorder or criminal personality). Some psychopaths are very adept at deception and misrepresenting themselves; but these deceptions tend to catch up with them, and the fabric of their lies and claims crumbles under careful scrutiny and examination. In other words, "By their fruits ye shall know them."

If a person who is fairly religious becomes mentally ill, in most cases some religious symbols, ideas, and beliefs become mixed in with his psychopathology. This certainly is not unexpected nor unusual. It does not necessarily mean that his religion made him ill, but only that he makes use of whatever ideas and symbols he was familiar with before his illness (religious, scientific, vocational, sexual, etc.) to restructure the world during his illness. We have to be careful of the *post hoc ergo propter hoc* fallacy—that merely because B follows A, A is necessarily responsible for or causally connected with B. Because a person has been religious and has unusual religious beliefs while mentally ill, it does not follow that these beliefs or his religion made him ill.

A related question presented by some of my colleagues has to do with the possible role of religion in creating illness, such as through guilt. They point to such neurotic conditions as anxiety attacks and obsessive-compulsive neuroses. Their view is that religion makes people feel guilt about various real or even contemplated misdeeds (such as breaking sexual taboos), often greatly out of proportion to the severity of the offense. My experience, especially in the last five years, has often been to find amazingly little guilt among many patients for breaking society's so-called taboos. Ours appears to be an extremely permissive age. Adultery, for example, is committed by many church-going people, with easy rationalizations and remarkably little psychic pain, even though the results may ultimately be quite disastrous. The view that has made most sense to me is that guilt, remorse, and sometimes acute psychic pain are extremely important prerequisites to constructive change. When people exploit and injure others without remorse, empathy, or pangs of guilt, they are approaching the type of personality seen in the true criminal psychopath. I certainly have not seen many people clinically who have been "damaged" by the stern morality of their religious teachings. However, I have seen sick families inflict religion on their children in unhealthy ways. Neurotic, excessively hostile, or borderline psychotic parents can take certain facets of their religious beliefs and in almost diabolical ways torment and ravage their children with these. I do not, in these cases, blame the religion particularly, whatever the denomination, though I would recognize that certain religious groups do have more "healthy" techniques for instruction and control than others. If the sick parents happened to belong to no religion at all, they would seize upon other symbols or convenient values in their culture and in like manner inflict these on their children, with the possible production of neurotic or disturbing symptoms in their offspring.

One sometimes hears religion, belief in deity, and religious faith criticized rather disdainfully as a kind of crutch and a sign of weakness. This seems to be an entirely irrelevant point. Crutch or no crutch, the basic question seems to be, "Is there a Supreme Intelligence in the heavens, and if so, what is His nature and plan?" I am not afraid of being either dependent or independent, if my condition is in reasonable balance and appropriate to reality.

Another issue, with which many of my friends have struggled painfully, is the problem of free will versus determinism in the lives of men. The view of some has been that all of our behavior ultimately is determined by our genetic endowment plus the pattern of training, conditioning, and life experiences to which we have been exposed since our conception in the womb. They have further claimed that the subjective feeling one may have that he is an agent who can freely choose his destiny is really only illusory. This view posits that our every move, wish, choice, and thought could, if we had a large enough computer and sufficient data, be completely predicted and that in a true sense life is determined. This has been called by some the "new materialism." It implies that we are not really responsible for our behavior but rather are merely hapless pawns buffeted about by the winds of our environment on the sea of our self-duplicating nucleic acids (our genetic endowment).

My personal view is similar to that of Vannevar Bush,[5] wartime director of the Office of Scientific Research and Development, who states that of the two vital realities of man's being, his free will and his consciousness, science not only gives no proof but does not even produce evidence. Thus, rationally, empirically, or scientifically, there can be no absolute demonstration as to whether or not we are completely determined, as some would have us believe. I agree with Bush that, even so, one's sense of free will is still a vital reality (as are consciousness, love, and many other scientifically unmeasurable entities). However, people do vary in the amount of freedom available to them; some people are more free than others. The goal of successful psychotherapy is to free an individual from the tyranny of his impulses (frequently unconscious). Some individuals are slaves to obsessive-compulsive or other symptoms such as inability to stay on a diet or regulate food consumption, masochistic self-punishment, alcoholism (and other addictions), chronic depression, and the like. They have, in a sense, lost some measure of rational control over some or many aspects of their life or behavior. The apostle Paul put it well when he wrote, "I do not understand my own actions, for I do not what I want, but I do the very thing I hate."[6] One sees this in marriage counseling when an ordinarily sane and rational housewife with five children, active in her church, loses herself in an affair with a man she would never think of marrying; she risks disaster, loss of family, incapacitating guilt, and all the rest for a few words of flattery and moments of passion.

With regard to the contributions of the major philosophers to my religious growth, I'm afraid the cupboard is bare; most of the thinkers seemed merely analytic (though often brilliantly so), and rarely did they contribute anything to live by or any newer, higher morality. I also have found myself increasingly disappointed with the major Protestant theologians, many of whom, in my view, have pretty much written themselves out of Christianity. Christ and His role in history have been so emasculated as to be hardly recognizable and remain only as a caricature of what one reads in the Four Gospels. Or as O. Hobart Mowrer, professor of psychology at the University of Illinois, has succintly put it, "Theology has come near to spoiling religion—and life itself for modern man."[7]

Despite this blanket indictment, I must confess to admiration for such men as Robert Elliot Fitch,[8] Dean of Christian Ethics at the Pacific School of Religion, whose clear-eyed views on personal ethics and social responsibility, especially in the area of sexual conduct, much impress me. Even the maligned and often disparaged Reverend Norman Vincent Peale cannot be dismissed too cavalierly. I have seen patient after patient who obtains solace and significant help from such books as *The Power of Positive Thinking.* This may be an "out" book for the professional therapists, and the

Reverend Peale may be an embarrassment to the professors in schools of theology; yet, in fact, he does give people help, and his books do assist some people significantly in staying afloat. As a pragmatist and empiricist, I am more impressed by this than by his reviewers' disdainful comments.

Some people have mistaken notions about what psychology, psychiatry, or even psychoanalysis can tell us. These fields have made and do make major contributions scientifically, as well as relieving suffering and untangling deeply imbedded psychic conflicts. But they give us nothing in the way of values or morals. They say nothing, really, about what is right or wrong, good or bad; if anything they try to avoid making value judgements. And they tell us nothing about who man is, where he is going, or why he is here. Nevertheless, every psychotherapist seems to gradually assume the function of a "priest and prophet." He is almost forced into this by the very nature of his work; patients daily bring him their most intimate problems and challenge him to set their lives aright. This can be a very ego-inflating experience—especially if one has some measure of success. But it also poses the danger of creating unwarranted feelings of omniscience. It is not unusual to see some therapists become extreme cultists, no less fanatical than the extreme religionists one sometimes sees. Psychotherapy is not a science; it is an art. Ten therapists interpreting the same dream will come up with ten interpretations. We still are very much on the frontiers in our understanding of the behavior of man and of many aspects of mental illness, such as schizophrenia.

Frequently I have noticed that some people, when they move into a new town, choose their psychiatrist as others choose a minister. They pick someone with whom they feel some rapport. They may shop around awhile—visiting one therapist, then another—until they hit on someone who particularly suits their fancy. Thus the therapist frequently falls into the role of guide, father, financial advisor, second spouse, healer, priest, and so on. And my prediction would be that as our Western civilization becomes increasingly secular, the psychotherapist will tend to gradually replace the minister and priest as reliever of guilt and dispenser of comfort, wisdom, and personal counsel. Professional people in the arts, sciences, and particularly in the communications industry appear to be leading the way in this trend (substituting a therapist for a minister), with many middle-class people following suit. To counteract this there is increasingly a tendency of the ministry of the major denominations to move into clinical psychology, social work, and, to a lesser degree, psychiatry. This apparently represents an effort on their part to "legitimize" their function and become respectable. Thus, as I see it, the seeming convergence of psychology and religion is no convergence at all. Actually psychology (which includes the psychoanalytic view of man) has made no compromises at all toward religion. The religionists, primarily middle-class Protestant ministers, are doing most of the compromising; and if the trend continues, they will wind up as teachers of mental health to their congregations, with private psychotherapy being their primary responsibility and religion in the classical sense coming in a poor third.

Even though I consider myself a committed Christian, there are some loose ends, frustrating dilemmas, and completely baffling problems that at present defy all honest attempts at resolution. These focus in several areas. The first has to do with scriptural contradictions. While I accept the Bible and other sacred writings as, for the most part, inspired words from the mouths of men, at times I run into baffling contradictions. God seems to be saying one thing on one day and just the opposite on another. I might try to explain these as faulty translations arising over the centuries or the distortions of men somewhere in the receiving or editing process. But I am not always comfortable with these explanations. How does one distinguish which inspiration is the correct one? My way of dealing with such a problem is to admit that it is for the moment insoluble and to put it down in writing in a center section of my Bible where there are a number of blank pages for notes. I periodically come back and study the problem again, trying to look at it from another vantage point. Some of my conflicts have been resolved this way, meeting reasonable tests of evidence; others have not.

The second problem area has to do with people. Occasionally people in positions of religious authority say things that rouse my ire, that make no sense whatsoever, that seem calculated to offend and destroy, not heal and repair. Sometimes their biases and politics are very contrary to mine. The view I have finally come to regarding this is that a church can make all of its leaders strictly conform and follow a straight "party line" in expressing their thoughts and politics, or it can allow a certain amount of free agency and independence of thought and expression. Somehow, the latter course would seem to me in the long run to be the most healthy, even at the cost of occasional ruffled feathers. It permits some individual interpretations and personal biases to be expressed—and thus allows for some honest disagreement and the possibility of individual error.

The third kind of problem I run into has to do with my church's position or lack of position on certain social and moral issues which seem to demand some response. But I am painfully aware that some other active church members, men of good will, do not see eye to eye with me in defining which are the most pressing social and moral issues that should be immediately dealt with; and even if they did, they would not agree as to what would be the most appropriate action. I am not quite egoistic enough to believe that if the Church doesn't happen to agree with me on every social and moral issue it is wrong and I must walk out in a huff. But I am of the conviction that even though the Church has revelation and inspiration guiding its leaders, God is concerned that we exercise our intelligence, pursue truth diligently, and use our free agency. I don't think He wants to solve all of our problems for us, thereby creating an extreme dependence; I think we must sweat it out sometimes. If this is true, it means that occasional tension and disagreement are healthy for the Church. The difficult thing here is making use of talent, diverse ideas, and disagreement in a way that is positive and constructive, rather than allowing them to become destructive and divisive. I have a feeling that even in immortal life we will find differences of opinion inseparably linked with free agency.

Despite the many unanswered questions, the scriptural contradictions, and other issues which constantly challenge my religious belief and faith, I find that science, while ably conquering the material universe, has less to offer than my faith concerning what matters most. In fact, anyone involved in continuing research is continually made aware that science only collects evidence. Sometimes, if we are fortunate, this evidence leads to hypotheses, but these are retained only as long as new evidence supports them. Science proves nothing absolutely; something more is needed. While I can certainly empathize with the bleak and lonely existentialist position which concedes only that man exists, it is not enough for me.

This leads to the next major point: how I can reconcile my religious beliefs with a professional tradition that is so indifferent to religion. My present view has taken many years to evolve, so that all I can do is give a synoptic overview. The Christian view (as I saw it early in my life) was that some twenty centuries ago a man was born who was the Son of God, chosen to come to this earth to fulfill not only ancient prophecies but also to introduce a divine plan conceived and developed prior to the organization of this earth.

From the documents available there appeared to be four separate accounts of Christ's life and ministry on this earth, plus the writings of some of his contemporaries such as the apostle Paul. A study of these records ultimately convinced me that, with regard to men and their relationships with each other, the records contained some supremely important truths. However, in matters of this kind, the only sure way of testing their validity (as much as we can ever do) is through the crucible of our own experiences and those of people we know or know about—and in part through a study of our history and literature. Thus, completely apart from the supernatural aspects of the New Testament, the ethical and moral teachings, I came to believe, have validity and significance for men and women of all cultures and ages.

However, from an early age I had felt an obligation to examine the scriptures and literature of other religions. I frequently asked myself how the teachings of Jesus Christ might compare with those of mystics and inspired men of other centuries and cultures. In the process of this study and searching, I found myself experiencing delight and appreciation for the great insights and revelations of Buddha, Zoroaster (in the sacred writings of the Gathas), Mohammed, and Confucius. In fact, I found a common theme running through most of these. However, the more I studied these writings and their various interpretations and commentaries, the more I became impressed that the Christian ethic, as an inspired and magnificent piece of architecture, had no really close competitor.

As I have gained experience and maturity in my profession, an examination of the most intimate and precious aspects of my own personal life and the lives of those individuals who have entered my "life space" has led me to continue my critical appraisal and evaluation of the validity of the teachings of Christ. And I have found myself continually coming to the same conclusion: that, whoever Jesus Christ was or wasn't, the Christian ethic is unmatched anywhere. To deny this, I would be false to myself and those powers of judgment and discernment which I possess. It has seemed quite apparent that of all the billions of intelligences who have existed on this earth, none made such a contribution and impact as this one individual, Jesus Christ. I therefore came to believe that Christ's claim to divinity had to be given serious consideration.

I was deeply impressed by the New Testament account of the teachings and miracles of Jesus, which are certainly appropriate to a divine being. He offered mankind a plan for salvation from sin and error and for self-fulfillment in this life and in a post-mortal existence, and he demonstrated His unique power over sin and death in His crucifixion and resurrection. But, however deeply impressed the investigator and truth-seeker is by this great series of events, one may still wonder if it is really all true. Did Jesus Christ actually conquer death? Or is this merely a legend which has developed around a humble and deeply spiritual mortal being? This question is obviously one of the greatest importance.

It was at this point that the crucial element of faith entered in. I am convinced that from the study of visible evidence men will never have final, certain knowledge about most things in the fields of science or religion. The history of physics, for example, has been one of continuing revolutions in which the "past" has repeatedly been challenged and in which new theories have replaced the not-so-new. We might consider, for example, Yang and Lee's[9] overthrow of "parity" a few years ago, or Werner Heisenberg's introduction in 1927 of the "Uncertainty Principle," which plays a fundamental role in quantum mechanics and which shook physics to its foundations. In fields such as archaeology, there is even less "certainty" (the downfall of the Piltdown man being a dramatic example of this).

I finally concluded that after I had read all the books from Aristotle to Camus and the learned discourses of both the wise and foolish, I would still find no absolute final proof. I would have to reach out into the unknown and seek my Creator through an act of faith. I could have played it safe and refused to do this, preferring to wait for "ultimate evidences," but in so doing I think I would have denied myself peak spiritual experiences and self-actualizing insights. Complete, verifiable evidence will never be available. But I believe that an encounter with the Creator, a vastly more moving and profound experience, is well within the realm of possibility for any human who chooses to seek it.

I am convinced that it is through faith, sometimes by the medium of prayer, that we receive the witness of the Holy Spirit (which Jesus Christ has promised to all men who so wish to avail themselves). And it is the witness of the Holy Spirit which testifies that Christ is the Son of God and that His teachings are true and which indicates whether our judgments and discernments are true. It is this most powerful of religious experiences that burns within people and motivates them to dedicate their lives to the service of their Creator. It can bring about a most dramatic change of personality, creating a sweetness and gentleness of spirit and a tolerance and love for one's fellow man that are amazing to behold.

That this occurs is not to say that members of other religions do not also have experiences of this nature. I cannot believe that God rejects any person who sincerely seeks after truth concerning His reality.

For many years I heard the terms "born anew" and "born again" used frequently in connection with the Christian faith. I found it, frankly, devoid of much meaning. My own religious or spiritual development had been rather gradual and, while there had been moments of deep religious significance, there were never any dramatic changes. However, I have occasionally known people to experience this spiritual rebirth. Sometimes one who has lived "carelessly" and seriously offended family members or others within his or her influence "accepts Christ" and as a result develops an attitude of deep regret and humble repentance. He or she acquires a totally new sweetness of spirit and tolerance toward others, and a very obvious inner light radiates through the person's whole personality. The experience is one of vital spiritual awakening and a transforming faith, and this experience gives great meaning and significance to the term "born anew."

A physician in Scotland who attended Billy Graham's crusade in Edinburgh wrote of this experience in a national (U.S.) publication. He ridiculed the whole affair, particularly the teen-age girls and others who responded to the "call" and were "saved." He cast them in the stereotype that many dormant religionists and agnostics apply to camp-meeting salvation, which amounts to a ridiculous caricature and parody of the real thing. I feel that this reflects only ignorance about a supremely important experience in the lives of legions of men and women. Some of these individuals, through their cynicism and pride in their "emancipated" intellect, have cut themselves off from almost any understanding of or sensitivity to a genuine religious experience.

With regard to my attraction to the Mormon view of Christianity, two factors weigh heavily. I am impressed by the positive impact of its philosophy and remarkable action program on people's lives, an impact akin to what I occasionally witness in psychotherapy. And, secondly, the Book of Mormon has come to have a unique validity for me. This I initially found very hard to relate to myself, but when I eventually studied the book with care, I was very impressed, especially as a psychologist and student of human behavior. I was struck with the universality of its content and its "psychological validity." It was not "religious gibberish," but a remarkable chronicle of challenge and travail of the human spirit. Its history is psychologically true for any age or people.

To thumb through or read a chapter at random does not do justice to the Book of Mormon. It has major rhythms, remarkably similar to those of the Old Testament, in its recounting of cycles of reconciliation and alienation in the relationship between God and his chosen people. It has new names, faces, and geography, but the plot is ageless: the eternal struggle between tyranny and liberty, freedom and bondage, and the flowing tides of a great civilization's rise and fall. Always, however, there is the central unifying theme, the relationship between God and man.

There are some specifics of dogma, theology, and religious history in my church that leave me confused. Somehow they do not seem to fit into the architecture of the Four Gospels. These dissonances are indigestible, sometimes painful to face. My temporary solution, as I mentioned previously, has been to write these discrepancies out on a blank page in the center of my family Bible. My understanding of my religion is like an unfinished tapestry which has an overall pattern that is fairly clear and makes sense to me. On that basis I have decided to exercise a little patience with the dissonances and ambiguities that exist on the unfinished edges of this tapestry. But the same is also true with my profession; there are vast legions of unanswered questions. I have learned to live with this.

In my profession as a clinical psychologist I have a personal and professional interest in ridding my patients of their demons, their unconscious self-destructive impulses, their irrational approaches to problems, and their loss of identity. I try to free them of the pathological preconditionings which hound them so that they can rationally choose their destinies as free men or women. My success has been variable. Some people get well for reasons I do not understand. Others, with rather minor problems (apparently), stay about the same, for reasons that are also hard to understand. The goals of the healthy religion are very similar to those of some aspects of psychiatry and psychology—to enlighten and liberate men and women, not through fear and coercion, but through reason, love, and faith. And as a pragmatist and empiricist I am much impressed by what I see as the fruits of healthy religious development, though I recognize that religious dogma and institutions are sometimes misused with sad and painful results (as are other kinds of dogma and institutions, such as those found in the academic and political worlds).

I must add that I have much appreciated and have highly valued my friends of other faiths, as well as some who have had no involvement with religion. I have found them to be men and women of honor and good will, who have on occasion shown great courage and grace under pressure or in moments of personal sorrow. They have greatly helped me to appreciate the complexity of the human spirit and to recognize other pathways to personal fulfillment. I do not believe that God is sexist or racist. He loves all good people who seek after truth regardless of background.

I have come to know God through Jesus Christ. At the intellectual or rational level I have examined the tenets of my faith against the evidence of my own experiences and those of other individuals I have known and have become personally convinced of the validity of these experiences. A comparison with other faiths, scriptures, and prophets has led repeatedly to this same conclusion. I have seen the tremendous changes that can come into the homes of individuals who have accepted Christ and His ethic into their lives. And this, when all is said and done, may be the most powerful evidence to the outside observer.

The cumulation of these evidences and experiences has enabled me to plant and nurture a germ of faith whose growth in time has led to the witness of the Holy Spirit. It is this "light" which sharpens my spiritual and ethical discernments and leaves me with a burning testimony of the truth of Christ's message and the essential validity of His restored gospel.

Notes

1. J. A. Leuba, "Religious Beliefs of American Scientists," *Harper's Magazine* 169 (Aug. 1934): 291-300.

2. D.M. Riggs, *An Exploratory Study of the Concepts of God Reported by Selected Samples of Physical Scientists, Biologists, Psychologists and Sociologists.* (Unpublished doctoral dissertation, U.S.C., Los Angeles, 1959).

3. Ann Rowe, "A Psychological Study of Eminent Psychologists and Anthropologists and a Comparison with Biological and Physical Scientists," *Psychol. Monogr.* 67.2 (1953): 1-55.

4. Discussed in G. Lenski, *The Religious Factor* (Garden City, N.Y.: Doubleday & Co., 1961).

5. "Science Pauses," *Fortune* 71.5 (May 1965).

6. Romans 7:15 (paraphrase).

7. O. H. Mowrer, "Integrity Therapy," *Faculty Forum* 30 (May 1965).

8. *The Decline and Fall of Sex* (New York: Harcourt Brace & Co., 1957).

9. Drs. Chen Ning Yang and Tsung-Dao Lee (of the Institute of Advanced Studies at Columbia University) won the 1957 Nobel Prize in physics for their work earlier in the year, in which they toppled a corner stone in nuclear physics, the principle of the conservation of parity or space reflection symmetry.

13

Allen R. Barlow

A Personal Revelation

Serious students of Mormon history and doctrine may occasionally encounter difficult and perplexing issues that can tax both mind and spirit. In short story form, Allen Barlow suggests that the "divine life-shaping principles" that lie at the core of the restored gospel can provide a secure guide through this confusion. Although it includes autobiographical elements, the story as a whole is a fictional rendition of spiritual truths acquired during a lengthy personal search. Dr. Barlow's graduate studies were in electronic engineering and physics. He received his Ph.D. from Utah State University. He lives with his wife Cheri and their two children in Tokyo, where he is Director of Engineering at Asahi Kasei Microsystems Co.

When I awoke after the operation, Shelley was sitting on the edge of the hospital bed gently stroking my hand and forearm.

"You're back," she said softly. She paused for a moment, then added: "The doctors say you're going to be just fine." Another pause. "Are you feeling any better?"

I nodded.

"There've been lots of calls," she continued slowly. Everybody from work and the ward. Even more from the Boise office. So many people are asking about you there that they started posting notices of your condition in the front lobby."

That made me chuckle briefly but the pain from the incision in my side cut it short. "I can just imagine that," I whispered hoarsely. "Up on the bulletin board, just below the latest prices for the company stock."

She smiled with me momentarily, then turned away and resumed stroking my arm. There was a long silence and when she looked up again her eyes were moist with tears. "They said that you died. They had to restart your heart."

I nodded again.

She studied my face for a while as if to probe my thoughts. "But you're back," she concluded with quiet emotion. "I'm so glad you're back."

It had been business as usual the previous morning: a shave, a shower, a bowl of Wheat Chex, and off to work. I generally don't see the family in the morning and that day was no exception. Shelley is pregnant and needs extra sleep. Our two-year-old sleeps in too. My commute from southeast San Jose to the heart of "Silicon Valley" takes about forty minutes. I carpool with another fellow in the ward, Dean Grames, who works for the same company. Dean and I were both transferred to the bay area about a year earlier from the company's Boise office. About the time I pulled into his driveway, I first noticed a pain developing in the middle of my back.

"Mornin'," he said. Dean's voice always sounds a little "backwoods" to me. I suppose that's understandable: he's from one of those small southern Utah towns. Parowan?

Panguitch maybe.

We backed out and headed down the street toward the freeway. Our commuting conversations tend to be a little slow getting started. It wasn't until we were past the freeway on-ramp that I broke the silence. "I've got some kind of strange kink in my back this morning." I wiggled in my seat in an attempt to pop it back into place.

"Hmmm. Do you get 'em often?" Dean queried.

"No, not really. Every once in a while I suppose, but just twisting it a bit usually does the trick. This one feels different somehow."

"My cousin Jim used to have back problems," he replied. I could tell that a short medical narrative was forthcoming. It seems that some close relative of his has had every physical disorder I've ever heard of. "When Jim was in high school," he continued, "he and some buddies were out partying in my aunt's station wagon. Ran a red light and got broadsided by a 'two ton.' Knocked his back all out of kilter, and...." While I drove on the pain began to grow; so did Dean's discourse. This was clearly an area where he had considerable knowledge. "...and so you may wanna try a chiropractor. At least Jim had real good success with 'em and. . . ."

I had difficulty attending to his story. The pain was spreading to my chest and all the muscles were locking up. These cramps were starting to feel more like a heart attack than slipped vertabrae. I interrupted Dean's monologue: "I'm feeling this in front now too. What do you make of that?"

"Oh, that's real common with back problems. Had that myself. When I was at the university, I. . ."

The muscles relaxed somewhat as we approached the plant, and by the time we entered the parking lot the pain had become more tolerable. The magnitude of the impending crisis was not yet fully apparent.

"Good morning, Roger," came my secretary's cheery voice as I passed her desk.

"Good morning, Ruth," I responded. "How are you this morning?"

"Great," said she, "and how are you?"

"Well, I'm not sure. I've got some kind of problem with

my back this morning." I paused briefly. "Ruth," I continued, "I think I'd rather not see anyone for a little while. If somebody comes or calls, just take a message, OK?"

"OK. Are you sure you're going to be all right?" she added with characteristic concern.

"Oh yeah. It's no big deal. I just need a little time to shake this thing off."

Stepping into the office, I shut the door and lay down on the floor. That helped for a little while, but then the cramps increased again and I began to have trouble breathing. I tried to sit up, but excruciating pain seized my whole chest and aborted the attempt. Resting briefly, I tried again. (Professional vanity was not going to allow anyone to find me lying down on the job!) A torturous exercise, but this time it was successful. From a sitting position on the floor, I inched my way toward the desk chair, and with a final burst of determination, lifted myself into it. Exhausted and nauseated, I sat and rested until the pain felt manageable. It was the better part of an hour before I regained sufficient composure to allow myself to be seen.

"Ruth," I called on the intercom in feigned calm, "could you come in here for a minute? I need a little help."

An hour later I was admitted to the hospital and not long after that was on the operating table. Spontaneous pneumothorax—lung collapse, they told me, peculiarly accompanied by substantial internal bleeding of unknown origin. I had already lost four units of blood. Immediate exploratory surgery was mandated.

Lying in the ambulance en route to the hospital, it first occurred to me that I might die. A novel thought for me. I had never taken time before to seriously contemplate my own life's end. Maybe it takes a personal trauma to inspire such reflection. But in my thirty years of life, I had never lost a brother or parent or close friend. Not even come close. My reaction to the notion intrigued me somewhat. No regrets. No grief. No clinging to life's last breath. Death entered my mind as a tranquilizer: a sorrow eased, a burden lifted. "Perhaps my prayers have been heard after all," I mused. "Now I shall have some answers."

And I wanted answers. During the previous year Shelley and I had been in great spiritual turmoil. Prior to that, we were the most typical of Utah Mormons. Genealogically, we are both "nth" generation Church members, children of bishops and stake presidents, second-cousins-twice-removed to half of the Wasatch front, it seemed. Like so many of that genus, we were more than a trifle naive about the breadth and depth of the difficulties in the history and doctrine of the Latter-day Saints. Or, perhaps more accurately, we had indulged a semi-conscious determination to remain ignorant of them—a natural and all too common state of mind in a church whose members are regularly admonished to restrict their curiosity to "official sources." But without warning and for no apparent reason, a weak spot developed in our naiveté.

An issue came up in some class or discussion. I cannot even recall now what it was. Since Shelley was not in school that semester, she decided to do some bona fide research on the subject. I joined her. The result was devastating: we found no acceptable answer, but instead encountered a hundred other problems, many of them more serious and fundamental than we could ever have imagined.

The Book of Abraham, for instance. There seemed to be no reasonable explanation for the gross mismatch between the Church's reading of that papyri and the Egyptologists' version, except to assume that Joseph Smith was either a fraud or deluded. The filibusters in the popular apologies on the subject provided no comfort. And why all the lies and denials of polygamy from Joseph? Why would he "spiritually marry" women who had living husbands? And if the Melchizedek priesthood was restored in 1829, why does it not show up in any writings until 1835? Why did the revelations have to be fixed to include it? And why would the true Church continue even now its clandestine editing of talks and history it doesn't like?

The list grew. It was not entirely one-sided, of course. The unimpeachable strength of the Three Witnesses' testimony was confirmed. There is chiasmus in the Book of Mormon. And the Church has flowered into a large and wonderful organization. It is, after all, "by their fruits" that "ye shall know them." Yet somehow the "con" evidence seemed weightier than the "pro." We began to reevaluate our own spiritual experiences. No shortages here; both of us felt that the Lord had answered our prayers many times. There had been moments of inspiration. Direction in times of uncertainty. Comfort in times of despair. Often, we found, we had extended our interpretation of these occasions, letting their existence imply the truthfulness of the Church. And now on closer examination, neither of us could find anything in our private spiritual storehouses that explictly supported Joseph Smith's claim to prophetic authority.

Our first recourse for treating our growing spiritual queasiness was obvious: prayer. I felt like Joseph said he did: "If any person needed wisdom from God, I did...." But unlike him, we obtained no answer from the heavens. We persisted. "Seek and ye shall find, knock and it shall be opened unto you." We knocked. Obstinate silence. We knocked louder. Still no response. The queasiness turned to fear and fear to panic. We began to pound on His door. There were many tears. Throughout the episode we counseled with priesthood leaders and parents and family and trusted friends. Some asserted that only sin could put us in such a state of mind, or that the devil had done this to us and was after our souls. "Even the very elect shall be deceived," they reminded us. Others suggested that we "put all of this negative thinking behind us." A few *demanded* it, and sought promises that we would do so. I found no solace in such counsel—only reminders of Nixon and Watergate. Everyone bore witness to the truthfulness of the Church. I sensed sincerity in each testimony, but felt no inner comfort. And no one could offer adequate answers.

The silence in the heavens grew and grew, and finally I realized it was to be absolute. I learned, too, that panic is a self-limiting phenomenon. Its toll had been extracted: I collapsed in spiritual exhaustion. No more prayers. No more tears. For some months, I stopped going to church as well. But I couldn't make myself do much on those Sundays. Usually I would just sit in a lawn chair in the backyard and stare at the trees and roses and the robins and bluebirds while my golden-haired daughter played in the sunshine. Much of the time my dulled mind would be nearly blank, but every now and then a recurring thought would steal in: "This is surely a beautiful world. How strange that it doesn't mean anything."

My inactivity in the Church was short-lived. It just didn't feel right. But the very thought of total activity brought back the spiritual nausea. So I compromised. I resumed attendance at Sunday meetings and paying tithing, but that was all. Shelley's spiritual status was even less clear to me than my own. We did discuss it, of course, but somehow my mind tended to drift as she spoke. She had been spending her Sundays studying about the Zoroastrians or something, and felt like it was helping her to figure out life. She elected not to return to church with me. I didn't mind.

As I lay in the bed in the intensive care unit I reviewed all of this and sampled the rest of my life. The happy days of academia at Utah State. Tracting hogan to hogan on the Navaho reservation. My childhood in Bountiful. Davis County was a rural area then: mostly farms and open fields and scrub oak forests. I spent a lot of time in the woods near our home making little huts or building bridges across the creek or looking for buried treasure. A wonderful place for a boy to grow up.

Meanwhile, the hospital was buzzing around me with activity. Nurses and doctors kept jabbing me with needles and adjusting the IV and transfusion equipment and calling out status on my heart rate. For a while it disturbed me very little. My ability to ignore had grown tremendously during the last few months. Finally, however, the pain became too intense to permit the luxury of meditation. My chest muscles seemed to be crushing my lungs and only the smallest of breaths were bearable. "I can't breathe," I whispered. It took three gasps to get the sentence out.

"I can see that," a physician patronized. "And I'm just about to give you a little shot of morphine. That should help you relax some. Here we go now." But just as he raised the needle, I felt a ripping sensation over the whole length of my body, like I was being torn in two. Suddenly I was tumbling over and over in a pitch black tunnel. I never felt the injection.

For a moment I felt like a child again, doing somersaults down a hill, except I had the distinct impression that I was being drawn upward. "Golly," I thought, "it's just like the books say: the tunnel, the blackness, the tumbling...." Not wholly unexpected, then, was the intense light at the end of the tunnel that emanated from a heavenly personage, whose "brightness and glory defy all description." (I understand that phrase better now.) But I was a little surprised by the person's identity: not Christ, nor one of the prophets, but rather my own Grandmother Welti. I had never known her in mortality. She died the year that my parents first met. I recognized her instantly, though I'm not certain how. Maybe it was from the two or three gray and blurred photos my mother had of her. Or maybe it was the similarity of her face to my own. I could plainly see now that of all her thirty-seven grandchildren, I did indeed look the most like her, as Mother had so often told me.

At the tunnel's end, my grandmother was the only thing to be seen. Otherwise I seemed to be engulfed in a thick and cold black mist. The intense brightness of her form did not illuminate anything else around us.

"Grandmother," I tried to say, "I am so glad you're here. I have so many questions." Instead I heard a voice—my voice—murmuring, "Now we'll see if they can justify it all." It sounded fierce and demanding. It shocked me. But this sort of thing happened each time I tried to speak in that place. My words and the tone of my voice emerged quite changed from my conscious intent.

My declaration removed a faint smile from Grandmother's face. Concern replaced it. "Why have you come before you are whole, Roger?"

An unnerving question, but I thought it inappropriate to inquire about its meaning just then and instead tried to rephrase my prior statement: "Well, I am hoping to get some questions answered." But my voice was still uncooperative. "I'm as whole as I'm going to get. If I'm less than I should be, it's His fault, not mine, and I mean to tell Him so," it asserted. "I'll see Him now, if you please."

This little speech made me yet more uncomfortable.

Grandmother, on the other hand, seemed amused by it and the smile returned to her lips. "Will you indeed?" she asked. "Brave, if not bright," her eyes told mine. "Come then, Roger," she said. "I'll show the way."

She held out her hand to me, and as I took it, the black mist vanished, revealing a vast celestial "park" (for lack of a better word—at least it seemed to have a generally out-of-doors feeling to it). It was immense and the whole of it was radiant and glorious like my grandmother. The further ahead I looked, the more brilliant it was. After we had walked a while toward the center of the light, my awe of the place was supplanted by concern for the difficulties my speech was causing me: "Grandmother, everything I say is coming out distorted." But alas, what actually emerged was: "Grandmother, I can't protect myself here. There is nowhere to hide."

"Quite true," was her reply. "You are perhaps too used to the facades and veneers of mortality. Here in eternity there can be none of that. Mind and spirit have become one. You are what you are. You say what you feel."

Such an explanation was further cause for concern, I suppose. "What I was" was plainly not much compared to her dazzling radiance. And it was true that my feelings really did match my spoken words. But more than concerned, I was feeling supremely frustrated at the lack of control I had on this conversation. The discussion seemed destined to course entirely beyond my influence.

"Grandmother," I ventured presently, "didn't you find religion confusing down there? The various tenets of the Church. All of them absolute, they assure me, yet so many based on dubious history." Predictably, it didn't come out that way at all. Instead I said: "Freedom is a miserable thing, don't you think? So painful."

"Painful it is, to be sure. To those who really know it, it gives moments more painful than death, and in fact, even more painful than birth. But don't say 'miserable.' Say 'breathtaking,' or better yet, 'exhilarating.' There is not growth without it. And growth is life."

"But did it have to be so confusing?" I futilely attempted

to reply. Instead my irritated voice exclaimed, "Look, all I wanted was to be shown a clear path. I could have managed all the rest just fine."

She laughed. "The rest is virtually nothing. Haven't you seen that? Making a path IS mortality: hacking your way through the brush of temptation and persecution, stumbling up the hills of uncertainty, scaling the cliffs of ignorance, quenching your thirst at the springs of love. These are the very things that bring you to The Goal."

"But even the goal is ill-defined, isn't it?" I tried to counter. But my bitter voice replied instead: "A glib saying. It's so easy, isn't it? 'Make a path.' And where should it go? 'Hey, no problem. We'll send down a hundred prophets (all of them with suspect credentials) to clearly explain it to you. And they will point a hundred different directions and then you take your pick. What? Not enough help? Tough break, Kid. That's all there is. No maps on this trip. No compasses either.' "

"I expected better of you than that," she said, a hint of sadness in her voice. "A person of your advantages. Life's Goal is plainly to draw near to God and to become like Him. That cannot be a novel concept to you. You must have heard it all of your life. Which of the prophets did not teach it? And how shall we accomplish that except by learning and loving? I dare say you're no stranger to that notion either. And what? No compass? Who can doubt the validity of his path when he feels that inner peace that can come in no other way? And of those who earnestly seek Him, who among them does not know his path is pointed wrong when that inner peace is supplanted by lust for pleasure or comfort or fame. Or by apathy. No, my child. The Goal and its direction have always been quite clear."

Forgetting my newly acquired speech impediment, I vainly attempted to defend myself: "Of course I know all that. But what about ordinances and the 'one true Church' and priesthood and such? Why is that so confusing?" But again my words were transformed: "Ah, go on. People don't need some grand philosophy. They need a detailed plan. If they would have just made the steps plain and the leaders' authority unquestionable, we good ones would have unfailingly followed them."

"So, there's the root of it," she said. "You think the answer is more valuable than the ability to work the problem. No, Roger. It's not true. Simple obedience is a necessary element in life, but it is no virtue in and of itself. Only as a forerunner to understanding can it aid the purpose of life. When God asks obedience of His children, it is for their own protection as they begin to explore new and unfamiliar realms. But we must grow beyond it as He did. God's power comes from within. He has learned all things. And so must we.

"This checklist you ask for has not the power of exaltation. An enticing idea, but vain. And you are not the first drawn to it you know. The Rebel espoused it aeons ago and thus lost even his first estate. And a third of the heavenly hosts with him. Perhaps you remember."

With that verbal nudge, I awoke to my memory of the premortal, including that terrible conflict. Its image left me almost speechless. "Oh," I muttered. Or tried to. Even that came out transformed: "Oh, damn!" I heard my troubled voice whisper.

"Yes, I'm afraid so," responded Grandmother.

We said no more for a while, but walked on and on toward the center of the light. Before long, the glory and virtue of the place began to cleanse my aching spirit of such concerns. "Virtue" may be an odd noun to use in describing a physical location, but how else shall I do it? This place was lovely beyond words, and its beauty penetrated me to the core. I cannot describe it except by analogy: Compared to our temporal world, it was as the finest palace to the dankest dungeon. In it, my wounds were healing.

At length I spoke again: "Grandmother, does God really answer the prayers of mortals?" I must have been gradually getting in tune with the place: the irritation in my speech had declined to more modest tones, and the difference between my intended and actual phrasing seemed diminished. "Grandmother," said my voice, "why wouldn't He answer my prayers?"

"Be ever grateful, Roger, that God doesn't base his

interaction with us on our often confused perception of our requirements. He loves too much for that, and gives far greater gifts. To those who truly seek Him, He grants not what they ask, but what they need. But in your specific case? It would be overbold of me to suppose I know His mind, but let me just speculate. He may have felt it time to dispel your confusion about the things in life that matter most. It's a common error among mortals active in organized religion to place allegiance to historical propositions and to organizations above devotion to divine life-shaping principles. Most of them wouldn't admit it, of course, but anyone free of such afflictions can see it easily. But let us suppose He had answered your questions in just the way you wanted. Would it have made you love life and your fellowman more? Increased your integrity? Enlarged your creativity? Improved your ability to discern truth? Deepened your faith in His guarantee that such things as these need never be at the mercy of other things that matter less? Or would you have become yet more narrow with such a revelation, celebrating the correctness of your belief, and becoming ever less empathetic toward your fellow men's struggles with life's perplexities?"

I was learning caution now, and held my silence, fearing what folly my tongue might utter.

"Small wonder then," she continued, "that He seems to favor comforting, strengthening, and inspiring over clarifying factual curiosities."

I asked no more, but pondered all of this as we continued our stroll. Our walk was brief, but it was more delicious and soul-gratifying than all of my previous existence. My spirit had never known such peace. A moment in the bliss of the hereafter is more than compensation for all of mortality's trials. At length we came to a bridge that spanned a wide chasm. Here we stopped and I felt a new and strange and wonderful thing: True Joy. I shall not attempt to describe it. It was more powerful than the human soul can comprehend, and flowed with gale force, beckoning me to cross the bridge.

"Come," said Grandmother. "He dwells on the far side. We will tell Him your tale."

Oh that I had words to describe that place! More than

I've ever wanted anything in my life, I wanted to run across the bridge. Oh that feeling! I wanted to hug it, to drink it, to bathe in it. It was fabulous. Yet just then, more surely than I've ever known anything, I knew that I must not. There was no doubt. I must not. Not yet. And yet I knew the choice was mine alone. That knowledge was more painful than dying had been.

"I understand now, Grandmother," I attempted to say. "Is it not possible for me to return for a while, that I may become whole?" The changes in my phrasing were growing slight: "I'm beginning to understand...," my humbled voice said.

She gazed intently at me, careful to completely understand before answering. "An unusual request, Roger. Most who have glimpsed this place would a thousand times rather stay than return, even if they can but loiter about the edges." She paused. "Still," she added thoughtfully, "since you dare ask...." Turning, she looked long and deep into the center of the brightness before us. After several minutes she faced me again. "It is well. He approves. Go and be thou whole."

I looked one last time at her—at her goodness and radiance, consuming it greedily for a moment before my descent.

"What will you tell them of this place, Child?" she asked in parting.

"I cannot say, Grandmother. But plainly I am no prophet." This time my words emerged unaltered.

When she came to see me on the second morning Shelley seemed to have largely recovered from her prior trauma. "A present from Shelley's Answering Service," she said gaily, and handed me a bouquet of flowers. "The phone is still ringing off the hook, but I'll only bother you with the important ones: First, your folks called and said they're glad you're doing OK and they'll try to come down either this weekend or next. Then Kelly called. He wanted to make sure he was putting the straight scoop about you into the rumor mill at work. Then your big brother Frank called and said that this was a dirty trick you pulled here, and don't you ever do it again or he'll beat you within an inch of your life." She paused, waiting for my smile. I gave it, and she continued. "Let's see. Oh yes. Lastly, your boss called and said don't worry about taking the rest of the day off." She laughed. "No, really, he's very concerned and wanted to know how bad it was, and how long you'd be in the hospital. I told him three to four weeks, like the doctors said."

"There," she added with finality. "I guess I've talked about enough. Now, what have you got for me? Anyone ringing your number?"

I'd slept well during the night and dreamt of other things, but her question brought the whole episode forcibly to mind. "Oh dear," I thought. "It begins already. What indeed shall I tell them?"

Just how does one tell of celestial things in the language of humans? No words of mine could begin to do it justice. How would an aborigine explain a vision of Manhattan to his peers? Or by what means can we teach quantum theory to a pre-school child? And what distortions would compound as the child then explained it to his classmates?

"Well," I said hesitantly, "I spoke with my grandmother the other day." Since those were my first words of the morning, my throat was congested and my voice faltered.

Shelley looked puzzled. "Huh?" she asked. "You don't have a grandmother."

My response was delayed as I pondered a suitable approach. Conveniently, she did not wait. "You're tired," she said. "Just rest now. I'll be back this afternoon."

"Yeah. I think that's best."

Shelley squeezed my hand, and left me.

14

Mary L. Bradford

Pillows Of My Faith

Mary Bradford, lecturer, editor, and author, has structured her essay on belief around "pillows that comfort and heal, bolsters that translate into principles I live by, and sandbags that barricade against the ravages of time and adversity." She also gives attention to women's issues as they relate to her faith and the need for intellectual freedom and integrity. Sister Bradford is the former editor of Dialogue: A Journal of Mormon Thought, *and is currently a member of the Advisory Board of that journal. She is the compiler and editor of* Mormon Women Speak *and is working on a book of her own personal essays which is tentatively called* One Woman's Perspective—*a title that derives from a regular column she writes for* Exponent II. *Since 1969 Sister Bradford has been a writing and speaking consultant for the United States government. She is the mother of three children and resides in Arlington, Virginia, with her husband Charles.*

One day I received a long distance call asking me to participate on a panel called "Pillars of My Faith." Because of a faulty connection, I heard "pillows" of my faith. After a hearty chuckle, I realized that I like "pillows" better. Pillars can crumble in a quake or be toppled by a hirsute Sampson, whereas pillows can comfort, support, and sandbag against disaster. Of course, pillows can be mashed, run over, and otherwise rendered useless by the stresses of life. But faith is not synonymous with certainty. As Lowell L. Bennion puts it, "Faith is not cut and dried, is not fixed and static, but is something as dynamic as life itself."[1] Realizing that a metaphor can break down as quickly as the stuffing of a pillow, I organized my thoughts around *pillows* that comfort and heal; *bolsters* that translate into principles I live by; and *sandbags* that barricade against the ravages of time and adversity.

I was the first child of parents who taught me to believe in miracles and gifts of the Spirit. After all, I was a "miracle baby." Shortly after my birth, I was saved from death by a bishop who arrived after the doctor had given up on my little blue body. Bishop Howick was known for the "gift of healing," and it was understood that I had been spared in order to develop worthwhile gifts of my own. In our comfortable home on an acre of fruit trees with room for cows and chickens, I looked to the ring of mountains beyond our yard for safety and inspiration.

With my parents and siblings—two brothers and a sister—I went to church in a comfortable ward that included a band of cousins who accompanied me all the way through high school. Though my parents had little formal education, they encouraged their children to go as far in school as their austere budget would allow and our own efforts could supplement. My diary records that after working for a year between high school and college, I was barely able to cover the first quarter's tuition at the University of Utah. When I burst into tears at the thought of quitting until more money could be found, my father exclaimed, "You're going back to school if I have to rob a bank!" Then he turned to Mother with the words, "What's fifty dollars if she's going to be unhappy?"

Such a large sum in those days (the '50s)! Such strong family support! This brought me to some remarkable teachers and mentors at the University of Utah and the LDS Institute of Religion across the street. Contrary to the dire rumors I had heard about loss of faith and even loss of life through the influence of supposedly godless professors, my studies only quickened my faith. Later, in graduate school, my thesis chairman would persuade me to choose as my subject Virginia Sorensen, a living Mormon novelist. Though my chairman and Virginia were no longer "active" in the Church, their integrity and high standards of scholarship pointed me toward a career in literature. Virginia, who became a close friend, was courageous enough to write about her Mormon background in a way that helped me to better understand my own. I also came to know the work of other Mormon writers.

As a compulsive reader, I was surprised at myself for reaching college without having read them. But I had been taught to respect the "revelations" of others, and I could see that these writers of Mormon background were revelators in their own way. Through them, I saw that the great pioneers of my cultural and religious history had been struggling human beings. It seemed that even so humble a soul as mine could aspire to good works.

At the Institute I joined the Church fraternity, Lambda Delta Sigma, which was dedicated to the five ideals of "fellowship, leadership, spirituality, intellectuality, and cultural life." I also took classes in everything from world religions to courtship and marriage. In the seven years I spent there, I was exposed to T. Edgar Lyon's unfailing devotion to the cause of honest history, to George Boyd's challenging dedication to scholarship, and to Lowell Bennion's quiet consecration to Christian service. In fact, Lowell (or "Brother B.," as we called him) came to symbolize all the pillows of my faith. Even today, the still, small voice of my conscience often speaks in his voice. Through his teachings, writings, and counseling, his "work parties," his service projects that took us out into the community and beyond ourselves, I began to accept responsibility for my own life. It was in his company, too, that I first began to think of the Church as "my" church, as belonging not only to its leaders, but also to me.

When I finally departed the university and the Institute, it was for another safe place, my first full-time job as an instructor in English at the Brigham Young University where I found another delightfully individualistic circle of teachers and friends. The mostly Mormon students were easy to reach because of shared values, but they were also challenging to teach because of their high expectations of the school and of themselves. I remember feeling fortunate—I was actually being paid when I would have gladly served for nothing!

Also at BYU was a young man I had met at the "U of U"—Charles (Chick) Bradford—just back from a mission and a masters degree. He too had studied at the Institute and could see our relationship as an opportunity to test Brother B.'s courtship and marriage advice. We had already dated according to the Bennion "ABC Method," except that we had traveled all the way to Z and back again. We moved on to a "secret" engagement recommended by Brother B., as a method of allowing couples to make plans before announcing them to the world at large. And we traveled together—with chaperones, of course—so that we might see each another in circumstances apart from the unrealistic dating scene.

The last step was to marry in the temple before parents and friends. The lengthy reception that followed was not part of the method, but the directors gave us the Institute as a wedding gift (for one evening). After teaching one more semester, we departed for Washington, D.C., where he took a position on the staff of Senator Wallace Bennett. My long childhood was over, and the pillows were beginning to harden into the bolsters of my maturity.

I see now that during my "Utah years" my pillows had been mainly people. Joseph Smith's declaration, "If my life is of no value to my friends, it is of no value to me," was my motto. Although the scriptures warned against putting my faith in the arm of flesh, I went ahead and trusted a whole host of people. And I have never been sorry. This trust did not displace my faith in God but reinforced it. Many of my fellow men and women combined the best male-female traits that I have always attributed to God.

Because my father was a nurturing man and because I had been influenced by a number of other nurturing men, I was able to think of God the Father as friendly and understanding, yet demanding high standards of conduct and scholarship. At the Institute, Brother Lyon described Joseph Smith as a father who sometimes missed church meetings to minister to a sick child. My own father had been gentle and responsive to my needs, rising in the night to heat towels for my "croup" and bringing me out of nightmares with segments of oranges.

My teachers at the Institute and at the university were nurturing too. Their message was that God is good, that He isn't the scary all-powerful Calvinist of other religions, that He operates under laws that bind us all. Relationships with my brothers and my boyfriends and then with my husband gave me reason to trust the male of the species.

Later, when I became immersed in women's studies and began to think of myself as a full fledged "Mormon sister," I gained a testimony of the integrity of women who are willing to share their own gifts of the Spirit.

I had so completely "internalized" my mother's influence on me that I was quite grown up before I began to understand her as a separate person. Then I grew to appreciate her unwavering devotion to her family and to her God. Because of this, I moved easily into friendships with female cousins and neighbors and into lasting friendships with women.

The Mormon concept of God as a being "in history" and in some way limited by law led me to a paradox: God is far higher than I, with powers that surpass understanding, and yet He is not responsible for death or any form of evil.

For me, this means that He is not a cosmic real estate broker whose main duty is to dispense kingdoms to the worthy; nor is He like a giant puppeteer who plucks people off the earth at inconvenient times for unclear reasons. Nor is He a kind of entrapment officer working unceasingly to catch the unwary. In fact, I am able to love and worship Him because of my own free agency that grows from my uncreated pre-existent spirit.

As I grow older, I am bolstered by my faith in the Creator of my spirit, and I respect those who are in positions of authority. "We shall always need authorities to guide us," says Brother Bennion, "but we must learn to test their right to lead us. This we can do through thought, experience, and revelation."[2]

Since I truly value my agency, I am comforted by the concept of division of labor. I have my job; you have yours. We are required to seek our own revelation. If your revelation contradicts mine, we must study our differences through prayer, remembering the admonition that unrighteous dominion ends priesthood authority.

Priesthood, in fact, is another name for service and stewardship.

After settling in Arlington, Virginia, and starting our family, I was excited to learn of the founding of a new Mormon quarterly journal, the very one I had volunteered for when it was just a gleam in Gene England's eye. Now he and Wes Johnson, doctoral candidates at Stanford, had gathered a group of former Institute types to work on an independent publication dedicated to the process of "bringing their faith into dialogue with human experience as a whole and fostering artistic and scholarly achievement based on their cultural heritage."[3] I was asked to join the editorial board.

Little did I know that ten years later I would become editor of *Dialogue*, moving it to Virginia where it would become a kind of "cottage industry" in my home. With the office in the basement, I could run the house and the journal together. Volunteers and staff (which sometimes included my bishop-husband and our three children) seemed to meld the five ideals of Lambda Delta Sigma and my professional and family life into one integral whole.

After six-and-a-half years of this, I finally wrote my feelings in my farewell essay: "I feel such a combination of pain, guilt, elation, joy, regret and fatigue that to describe *Dialogue* as just an intellectual scholarly journal is just not good enough. When I consider the passion and the energy that went into the founding of it and its continuance for fifteen years, I can only think of another friend who once cried out,

'I must worship in my mind!' Worship is emotional, spiritual, passionate—and yes, intellectual. So is the enterprise called *Dialogue: A Journal of Mormon Thought*."[4]

During those years, I felt that *Dialogue* was acting in the best volunteer tradition of church and community. We who worked on it were in touch with some of the best minds—and hearts—in the Church. It represented the "examined life" in an increasingly complicated and frightening world.

In working with thinkers throughout the Church, I became convinced that the doctrines and the beliefs of the Church were strong enough to withstand any amount of analysis and discussion. A few years ago, we in Zion East were heartened to learn of the brightly colored sandbags Utahns had banked around their city during spring floods. A disastrous experience the year before had taught them to be prepared. It occurred to me that they would need spiritual and emotional sandbags as well. Brother B. always placed creativity near the top of his stack of sandbags or near the "heart" of his "pyramid of values."

"When we are creative, we are truly in the image of God."[5]

It is the creative self that provides the energy to write poetry, to paint pictures, and, in fact, to learn a new and better way of seeing. In my search for wholeness, I try to excavate the submerged artifacts of my dreaming, creating self.

My diary, which I have kept off and on since the age of thirteen, often records my dreams and waking interpretations. This kind of diary gives me inspiration and support for many of my waking ambitions. Getting to know myself in this way is the beginning of wisdom. The importance of dreams both waking and sleeping in the lives of the Church's founding fathers and mothers supports this.

But dreams remain insubstantial unless work can be found that meets the needs of the whole person. Some have lofty ambitions that lead to fame and fortune. Others are happy simply doing good. I have aspired to be a writer, a teacher, a friend, a mother. All of these jobs have caused me to reach beyond myself. In reaching for what I know is beyond me, I must use creativity, and the other sandbag—courage.

"A saint is someone who is taking a risk," says Dian Saderup, essayist.[6] This fits psychologist Abraham Maslow's definition of a "self-actualizing human being," characterized by the courage to step out of the protective coloration of comfortable retreats to seek frontiers of the self. We do this in our own diverse ways. My husband, who walks with two braces and a cane, must constantly take thought of details that others take for granted. So small a thing as a square of cellophane on the floor can bring him down. But he steps out anyway, welcoming life while, at the same time, encouraging his children to follow their dreams. Because of his constant courage, I have overcome many of my fears and phobias and have avoided the temptation to pass them on to our children.

Pillows, bolsters, sandbags. I suppose it doesn't matter which term I use to describe my faith as long as it helps me to walk uprightly with my God in a world where "the things that matter most" are not ultimately "at the mercy of the things that matter least."[7]

Notes

1. Lowell L. Bennion, *Religion and the Pursuit of Truth* (Salt Lake City: Deseret Book Co., 1959), p. 124.
2. Ibid., p. 29.
3. Paraphrase of Frontispiece in all issues of *Dialogue*.
4. Mary L. Bradford, "Famous Last Words or Through the Correspondence Files," *Dialogue* 15 (Summer 1982): 11.
5. Bennion, *The Things That Matter Most* (Salt Lake City: Bookcraft, 1978), p. 56.
6. Dian Saderup, "The Wall," *Mormon Women Speak* (Salt Lake City: Olympus Publishing Co.), p. 7.
7. A quotation from Goethe, often used by Bennion.

15

William Clayton Kimball

The Habits Of Belief

William "Tony" Kimball has been described as the reigning Mormon authority on C. S. Lewis. A hint of that expertise is evident in his essay, "The Habits of Belief." In it, Dr. Kimball reminds us that any human philosophy is inadequate to comprehend "things as they really are." Like Lewis himself, Kimball argues for the need to resist the reigning cultural and intellectual spirit of this or any age. Brother Kimball was educated at the University of Utah and later at Harvard, where he received his doctorate. He is Professor of Government at Bentley College in Waltham, Massachusetts. An entrancing speaker and teacher, Brother Kimball is something of an intellectual and spiritual legend to two decades of LDS students in the Boston area. He has been on the editorial board of BYU Studies *and is presently on the board of* Dialogue. *He has served in several bishoprics, as a bishop, and as a high councilman.*

There are times when you wish you had kept a journal. I made no record of the night I decided, without question and beyond reason, to remain a Latter-day Saint. But the memory is still very clear. I do not remember just why I was thinking about my grandmother, and about my great-grandfather. But I got out a small pamphlet which Truman Madsen had written for the Heber J. Grant family reunion in 1961 and read it through again. Truman was just blocks away, serving as president of the New England Mission. I was sitting in my room at Harvard. I didn't feel especially spiritual, nor was I in the throes of a crisis of faith. But I knew, very explicitly, that it was my time to choose whether to remain a Latter-day Saint or not. I thought about it for a while, and made the decision. It was affirmative, and it was irrevocable.

There was nothing particularly intellectual or analytical about the whole process. I was, in a sense, immersed in a sea of feelings: tribal identifications, memories of my childhood, frustrations of graduate school...and through it all this question looming. I knew several things. First, it was a very real question. Had my answer been different, my life would have changed. Second, the question was not really mine. It had not really emerged out of the thought patterns I had been following. Third, it solved no immediate problems, and only deepened some long-range ones. I could not account for my decision on rational grounds. I knew that many things had come together suddenly on that cold fall night. I was not elated nor was I depressed, and I think I just went back to my studies.

I thought back on that night a few years ago when I was called as a bishop. The call was a shock because I knew the Handbook and it said that bishops had to be married. Being a bishop was not a consequence I had anticipated when that basic choice was made almost twenty years earlier. As it became clear to me that I would accept the call, I recognized that the same process was at work. My acceptance was not based on rational analysis. I just knew that an agreement had been made, and that I was bound by the consequences.

I

A specific faith is more often ascribed than achieved (that is, more inherited than truly chosen). Trying to explain to another why one still believes in the faith of his childhood is really impossible. In the first place, it is not quite true. At each stage of life, faith changes. While it is correct to say I was born a Latter-day Saint, and that I am still a Latter-day Saint, no real explanation is apparent. I suspect that in the matter of faith, the only connecting threads between childhood and middle-age are the habits of belief. Had I ceased to practice the habits of belief at some stage in my life, no intellectual or spiritual regimen would have preserved me as a Latter-day Saint.

The tribal feelings that tied me to my heritage and home sufficed for years to maintain my faith. My knowledge of scripture was a storybook knowledge. The intense discussions in my teenage years of what I thought were the mysteries could just as easily have focused on cars or any other pubescent passion. I was LDS because of who I was and where I was. I had no need to rationalize my faith.

My first years of college (at the University of Utah) held great challenges. I sought out teachers whose demands excited me. While I compartmentalized easily, the things I was learning in the college classroom were kept in balance by Institute classes from Lowell Bennion, and the "mentoring" and tutoring of several friends. The foundations both of my later questions and my constant balancings were laid during those two years.

I rushed off to the mission field filled with excitement, but motivated by the wrong reasons. However, serving a mission is one of the few acts where doing the right thing can more than counterbalance the wrong reasons. I was brought up short (especially in one leg) by a speeding automobile in Heidelberg, Germany. For the first time I was forced to ask questions about who and where I was, why I'd been hit, and what it meant for my life. Lying in a hospital bed for two months was a catalyst of major import!

As I limped through the rest of my mission, I encountered

several things that had a profound impact on me. For the first time I learned to read scriptures carefully, to pursue references and footnotes, and to follow the theology and not the story. I got a letter from one of my mentors that was, in an explicit sense, scripture for me. And I ran across a copy of Sterling McMurrin's little lecture, "The Philosophical Foundations of Mormon Theology."

I returned from my mission with my habits intact, but my faith in tatters. This was more a result of seeing the human side of the Church than any real disenchantment with doctrine. But in terms of commitment to the Church during the next two years, it often came down to a reliance on the testimonies of others.

Spurred on by the McMurrin pamphlet, I took all the philosophy I was able to fit into my schedule during my last two years of college. I took Church history classes at the Institute from T. Edgar Lyon. And, early in the summer before I left for graduate work at Harvard, I started to read C. S. Lewis. This was a new beginning, although when I made the commitment to remain LDS some months later, it hardly seemed to be such.

II

When I noted earlier that my choice to remain committed to the Church was "beyond reason," I did not mean it was irrational. It was a decision that was made beyond the places where reason can take us. We cannot ground a statement of faith on a set of facts. Nor can we follow a logical chain which will lead us to a position of faith. The very way we view a set of facts or employ logic is determined by an interpretive, often impressionistic, framework. It is this framework which allows us to fit the raw data into some understandable pattern.

In order to build a framework that can support a structure of faith, one must resist the prevailing spirit of the age. I have found that second only to the practice of the habits of belief, which is the foundation upon which my framework is grounded, a critical state of mind is necessary. Many would object that a critical state of mind is precisely that which will destroy one's faith. I disagree. Without effective ways to test reality, we fall victim to the unstated assumptions of the world around us. Only an unthinking practice of the habits of faith will prevent a decay of belief, but I learned long ago that in my life I cannot fall back on a faith without intellectual works.

The most important parts of my framework I learned from C. S. Lewis and some of his associates. The second year of graduate school was the time I went wild over Lewis's works. I focused as much or more on his scholarly essays and books as on his Christian apologetics. Much of my enjoyment came from the sheer pleasure of his style. As one of his colleagues said, he "put every nib right." But much of what I learned from Lewis was underscored by things I was learning in my professional studies.

An example of the sort of thing I mean, and one of the major intellectual tools I find essential in judging what I encounter, has to do with what has been called the "sociology of knowledge." The finest and most stimulating class I encountered at Harvard focused on the development and delineation of models in the social sciences. The lectures ranged from the development of models and analogies in science to theories of how the brain organized knowledge. The next semester I sat in on a master teacher's class on epistemology. For one whose primary experience had come in "survey" classes, this was heady stuff. Had I absorbed those topics, and many others I was discovering, in isolation, I am not sure what the result would have been. But my exposure was tempered by the constant reading of Lewis's works and the realization (before I knew that he had taught philosophy at Oxford in addition to being a tutor in English literature) that his writing reflected a deep knowledge of many of these things I was now learning.

In *The Discarded Image*, a work finished just before his ill health brought most of his writing to a halt, Lewis sought to acquaint students of literature with the beauty and complexity of the medieval model of the universe, the model which stood behind the works and thoughts of both giants and average men. In the Epilogue, he sought to warn his readers to be conscious of the power of intellectual models, and to appreciate them for what they are. We should respect all models, said Lewis, and never accept any of them fully. He also noted that there is a two-way traffic here. The intellectual model of an age is not only the product of the prevailing temper of mind; it alters that temper as it influences the thoughts and explorations of those who accept it. No model, he warned, is a "catalogue of ultimate realities." Each reflects the prevalent psychology of an age as much as it reflects the state of knowledge at that time.

Thus armed, I found it much easier to isolate, in other works I was reading, axiomatic elements which were stated as absolutes, but were not in actual fact. Two examples must suffice. In the late 1960's, the Gospel Doctrine lessons were based on the writings of John A. Widtsoe. It fell my lot to teach the lesson on politics and religion. In reading the lesson I discovered that Elder Widtsoe's concepts about government were neither distinctly Mormon, nor derived from scripture. He drew upon the ideas of English Idealism, the very sort of philosophy popular at Harvard when Widtsoe was a student. His ideas of the state were far more Hegelian than Madisonian. I also read Robert Bellah's evolutionary classification of religious development. Here was an application of the "idea" of evolution to a subject which was inappropriate. (I was interested to note that more recently Bellah has, in light of the rise of religious fundamentalism in America and in Islam, which violated his "progressive" schema, modified his theory. It is no longer so explicitly evolutionary.)

In both cases, Widtsoe's organic theory of the state and Bellah's use of evolutionary frameworks (equated with "progression"), intellectual models were used that were inappropriate to the subject matter. Lewis recommended the reading of old books to keep our perspective. Everyone writing in our time shares the essentials of the intellectual model we unconsciously accept. Since we cannot study the books of the future, we are forced to study the books of the past to get a different model's perspective. That way we might be able to appreciate the power and limitations of our own current models on our thought patterns.

It was only a small step to the realization that I had been reading "old" books of the best sort for years: the scriptures. I realized, however, that I must be very careful about imputing meaning into the Bible or Book of Mormon. They were written by men with radically different models behind their cultures. But at the same time, I found them testifying of the reality of a living God, of the divinity of Jesus Christ, and of the existence of a realm of spirit which my "native" model in the twentieth century did not allow. If I read meaning from my mid-twentieth-century model back into those books, I would never be able to understand completely what they were trying to say. At this point the "de-mythologizing" of Rudolf Bultmann, which seemed quite threatening to my beliefs some years earlier when I first encountered "higher criticism" of the Bible, now fell apart and was revealed as a fairly unsophisticated attempt to read a twentieth-century world view back into the time of Christ. It was both inappropriate and unfair.

To solidify this suspicion of "accepted" models, my reading in the philosophy of science emphasized that a theory is not a fact. Theories are ways of organizing facts in some meaningful way. Beyond that, the very idea of what a fact *is* depends on the theory we bring *to* the raw data. Theories do not emerge out of a collection of facts. There *is* no collection until there is a theory. I saw countless violations of that simple truth in the theories I was encountering in both secular and religious reading.

The most influential book I read on this idea was by Lewis's closest friend for most of his life. Owen Barfield became an Anthroposophist early on, and most of his writings reflect that peculiar slant. But I found much of what he said to be useful and full of insight. During my second year of graduate school I ran across his book *Saving the Appearances: A Study in Idolatry*. It was difficult reading, but I found it tremendously rich in ideas. Barfield makes short work of those who believe that a certain collection of facts dictates a certain sort of theory to "explain" them. To suppose that the latest explanation or theory is, finally, the perfect explanation is to engage in "chronological snobbery": the belief that the most recent formulation is better than what came before just because the proofs now seemed so conclusive.

But it seemed very clear to me as I read that nature yields up most of the hard evidence we obtain in response to the questions we ask. The quality of the evidence will depend on the perceptiveness of the questions and, lacking omniscience, we must always assume that no model or explanation has given us total truth. Science, history, psychology, and all other human endeavors must always be content with approximations. When those approximations are represented as total truth, they become idols to worship.

Two other elements from Lewis, supported by my own experience and much of what I was reading elsewhere, have remained highly useful to me. In his autobiography, Lewis refers to a distinction he ran across in the work of a now-forgotten philosopher. In essence he says that you cannot experience something and at the same time examine that experience. If you are being transported by a passage in a Mahler symphony and you decide you want to see what is happening to you that produces your feelings of ecstasy, those feelings will stop immediately. As soon as you turn your attention away from the music to focus on the feelings, you are no longer paying attention to the music. You are paying attention to you. All that will be left are traces of the feelings, mere physical remnants. And, usually, once you have interrupted the initial experience, you cannot recapture it.

I found this especially useful in the realm of spiritual experience. When you are deeply moved by the testimony of another, if you try to examine what is happening, the act of examination more or less unplugs the spiritual current which turned you on, and the whole thing is gone. I learned myself that what we call the confirmation of the Spirit comes unbidden and can be blocked by too much introspection as well as inattention.

The other major element in my framework that I learned primarily from Lewis has to do with what he calls "debunking," or seeing through things. In his argument against debunking he is making a case for the existence of objective knowledge. His argument is open to challenge because it rests, finally, on the acceptance of the very thing he is trying to demonstrate: objective knowledge. But his description of the consequences of a disbelief in objective knowledge cannot be challenged. If we go on seeing through things forever, the whole world will become transparent. At some point each person must accept something as real, and not susceptible to being seen through.

III

There are other elements in the framework I've built, but the general thrust of the effort is to construct ways of thinking about the world and the gospel which permit the constant play of perspective. I noticed many years ago that challenges to the "model" of an eternal gospel arise constantly. The directions from which the challenge comes change as the fashions of the secular culture change. For me, the only way to preserve a testimony of the truth of the gospel as proclaimed by The Church of Jesus Christ is to give those challenges access to my testimony. Each new element of knowledge must be considered and then integrated or rejected.

At bottom, the framework can only be sustained if it is grounded, as I said at the beginning of this essay, on a continual practice of the habits of belief. These habits are the old tried and true things: regular attendance, tithe paying, observing the Word of Wisdom, participation, and the more difficult matters—prayer, scripture reading, fasting, contemplation, and patience. In my experience, the first four will keep you afloat when the others are lacking. But when these habits change, belief cannot often be sustained. The rule is simple: if we wish to know the Father, we must do His will.

In this account of my faith, it should be obvious that I have left more things out than I have included. What I have called the "framework" which supports my continued faith in the gospel of Jesus Christ and my membership and activity in The Church of Jesus Christ of Latter-day Saints is a structure I have built consciously. And the intellectual outlook or model which rests on that framework has one other major component which cannot be analyzed. It is the emotional or affective dimension of my testimony. It would require another essay to explore that topic. The building blocks have not been rational or even intellectual. Music, which has always been my first love, plays a major role. Things I have read, experiences I have had, all sorts of things go into this affective component of my testimony.

In recent years I have found that this emotional part of my witness has played havoc with my ability to express to others the things I hold most deeply. I no longer can sing "Lead, Kindly Light," without being moved. The same is true of singing or even hearing "Come, Come, Ye Saints." I found too often as a bishop that in the middle of unprepared remarks a thought or an image would creep up on me in such a way that I could not continue until I regained my composure. (I could never understand how Marion D. Hanks could get through the telling of some of his heart-wrenching experiences without batting an eye.)

While I can bear witness to others, I am more and more limited in the range of symbols and expressions I can use. I see this as a weakness of sorts. I mention it only because it is tied in with the particular manifestation in my own life of the "burning of the bosom" with which we identify the touch of the Spirit. I could not sustain the intellectual model I have erected on my framework without the constant nourishment of the touch of the Spirit.

To conclude, I refer back to a distinction made earlier. My faith in the gospel of Jesus Christ as preached by the Latter-day Saints was at first ascribed; it was my heritage. But through the experiences I have had, and the challenges my faith has faced, it is now completely my own. I have chosen to remain a Mormon and to use the lens of Mormonism to view the world.

My favorite quotation from C. S. Lewis, slightly modified, expresses it all. I know that the gospel is true as I know that the sun has risen, not only because I see it but because by it I see everything else.

16

Laurel Thatcher Ulrich

Lusterware

There are a great many forms of false or misplaced faith. Such pseudo-faith may be based on ignorance or factual error and may sometimes seem—temporarily—to be a safe, comfortable protection. Unfortunately, though, such "faith" responds to growth or to new knowledge either by revealing its essential brittleness and breaking, or by retreating even further into illusion and falsity. A more genuine faith, by contrast, is subject to expansion, change, and occasionally painful adjustment. However, it is ultimately much less vulnerable than pseudo-faith, precisely because it is honest, malleable, and open even to unpleasant or unfamiliar truth. Laurel Ulrich helps us to see the difference between the two kinds of faith with her borrowed image of "Lusterware." Sister Ulrich received her Ph.D. from the University of New Hampshire, where she is now Assistant Professor of History. She writes a regular column for Exponent II, *of which she is a Senior Editor. She is the mother of five, and with her husband Gael resides in Durham, New Hampshire. She is the author of* Good Wives: Image and Reality in the Lives of Women in Northern New England, 1650-1750. *Her essay is reprinted by permission of* Exponent II.

I have been thinking lately about an Emily Dickinson poem I first heard twenty-five years ago in an American literature class at the University of Utah. I remember feeling intrigued and somewhat troubled as the professor read the poem since he was reported to be a lapsed Mormon. "Was that how it felt to lose faith?" I thought.

> It dropped so low—in my Regard—
> I heard it hit the Ground—
> And go to pieces on the Stones
> At bottom of my Mind—
> Yet blamed the Fate that flung it—less
> Than I denounced Myself,
> For entertaining Plated Wares
> Upon my Silver Shelf—

Since then I have lost faith in many things, among them Olympia typewriters, *New York Times* book reviews, and texturized vegetable protein; and yes, like most Latter-day Saints I have had to reconsider some of my deepest religious beliefs. I have always been a somewhat skeptical person. I can remember raising my arm in Beehive class in the Sugar City Ward and telling my teacher that regardless of what she said I did *not* think that polygamy was sent by God. That kind of behavior may have had something to do with the palm reading I received from another teacher at an MIA gypsy party. She traced the lines on my upturned hand and told me my "head" line was longer and better developed than my "heart" line. For a while I worried about that.

As I have grown older, I have become less fearful of those "stones at the bottom of my mind." In fact, I am convinced that a willingness to admit disbelief is often essential to spiritual growth. All of us meet challenges to our faith—persons who fail to measure up, doctrines that refuse to settle comfortably into our minds, books that contain troubling ideas or disorienting information. The temptation is strong to "Blame the fate that flung it" or to ignore the crash as it hits the ground, pretending that nothing has changed. Neither technique is very useful. Though a few people seem to have been blessed with foam rubber rather than stones at the bottom of their minds (may they rest in peace), sooner or later most of us are forced to confront our shattered beliefs.

I find Emily Dickinson's little poem helpful. Some things fall off the shelf because they did not belong there in the first place; they were "Plated Wares" rather than genuine silver. At first I didn't fully grasp the image. The only "Plated Wares" I knew anything about were made by Oneida or Wm. Rogers. Although less valuable than sterling, that sort of silverplate hardly falls to pieces when dropped. Then I learned about lusterware, the most popular "Plated Wares" of Emily Dickinson's time. In the late eighteenth century, British manufacturers developed a technique for decorating ceramic ware with a gold or platinum film. In one variety, a platinum luster was applied to the entire surface of the object to produce what contemporaries called "poor man's silver." Shiny, inexpensive, and easy to get, it was also fragile, as breakable as any other piece of pottery or china. Only a gullible or very inexperienced person would mistake it for true silver.

All of us have lusterware as well as silver on that shelf we keep at the top of our minds. A lusterware Joseph Smith, for instance, is unfailingly young, handsome, and spiritually radiant; unschooled but never superstitious, persecuted but never vengeful, human but never mistaken. A lusterware image fulfills our need for an ideal without demanding a great deal from us. There are lusterware missions and marriages, lusterware friendships, lusterware histories, and yes, lusterware visions of ourselves. Most of these will be tested at some point on the stones at the bottom of our minds.

A number of years ago I read a letter from a young woman who had recently discovered some lusterware on her own shelf. "I used to think of the Church as one-hundred percent true," she wrote. "But now I realize it is probably ten percent human and only ninety percent divine." I gasped, wanting to write back immediately, "If you find any earthly institution that is *ten percent* divine, embrace it with all your heart!" Actually ten percent is probably too high an estimate. Jesus spoke of grains of salt and bits of leaven, and He told His disciples that "the kingdom of heaven is like unto treasure hid in a field; the which when a man hath found, he hideth, and for joy thereof goeth and selleth all that he hath, and buyeth that field" (Matthew 13:44). Thus a small speck of divinity—the salt in the earth, the leaven in the lump of dough, the treasure hidden in the field—gives value and life to the whole. Now the question is, where in the Church of Jesus Christ of Latter-day Saints do we go to find the leaven? To the bishop? To the prophet? To the lesson manuals? Do we find it in Relief Society? In sacrament meeting? And if we fail to discover it in any of these places shall we declare the lump worthless? Jesus' answer was clear. The leaven must be found in one's own heart or not at all: "...the kingdom of God is within you" (Luke 17:21).

Many years ago a blunt bishop countered one of my earnest complaints with a statement I have never forgotten: "The Church is a good place to practice the Christian virtues of forgiveness, mercy, and love unfeigned." That was a revelation to me. The Church was not a place that exemplified Christian virtues so much as a place that required them. I suppose I had always thought of it as a nice cushion, a source of warmth and comfort if ever things got tough (which they seldom had in my life). It hadn't occurred to me that the Church could *make* things tough.

Eliza R. Snow expressed it this way in a hymn that seems to be missing from the new book:

> Think not when you gather to Zion,
> Your troubles and trials are through,
> That nothing but comfort and pleasure
> Are waiting in Zion for you:
> No, no, 'tis designed as a furnace,
> All substance, all textures to try,
> To burn all the "wood, hay, and stubble,"
> The gold from the dross purify.

Probably the hymn deserved to be dropped from the book. The third stanza suggests that the author, like more than one Relief Society president since, had made too many welfare visits and had listened to too many sad stories. Her charity failing, she told the complainers in her ward to shape up and solve their own problems:

> Think not when you gather to Zion,
> The Saints here have nothing to do
> But to look to your personal welfare,
> And always be comforting you.

In the Church, as in our own families, we have the worst and the best of times.

A young missionary on a lonely bus ride somewhere in Bolivia thinks he is equal to what lies ahead. He can endure hard work, strange food, and a confusing dialect. But nothing in the Mission Training Center has prepared him for the filthiness of the apartment, for the cynicism of his first companion, or for the parakeet who lives, with all its droppings, under the other man's bed.

A young bride, ready to enter the temple, feels herself spiritually prepared. By choosing a simple white gown useable later as a temple dress she has already shown her preference for religious commitment over fantasy. She has discussed the covenants with her stake president and she feels she understands them. Yet sitting in the endowment room in ritual clothing no one had thought to show her, saying words she does not understand, she turns to her mother in dismay. "Am I supposed to enjoy this?" she says.

An elders quorum president, pleased that his firm has won the contract for the ward remodeling project, prepares for the hard work ahead. He knows the job will be demanding. He expects some tension between his responsibilities as project manager and his commitment to the Church, but he is ready to consecrate his time and talents for the upbuilding of the Kingdom. What he doesn't expect is the anger and the humiliation that follow his year-long encounter with the Church bureaucracy. "I wonder how far up this sort of thing goes?" he asks, and contemplates leaving the Church.

A middle-aged woman reads deeply in the scriptures, sharing her insights with friends individually and in a small study group. She feels secure in her quest for greater light and truth until she begins to examine certain troubling episodes in Church history. The discrepancy between the official accounts and the new accounts distresses her. Has she been lied to? And if in one issue, why not many? Confiding her doubts to her friends, she feels them back away.

"And the rain descended, and the floods came, and the winds blew, and beat upon that house; and it fell not: for it was founded upon a rock" (Matthew 7:24-25). What rock can secure us against such storms? Occasionally some gentle soul, perhaps as puzzled as my Beehive teacher by my outspoken ways, will ask, "What keeps you in the Church?" "My skepticism," I answer, only half in jest. Over the years I have noticed that Saints with doubts often outlast "true believers." But of course the answer is inadequate. I don't stay in the Church because of what I don't know, but because of what I do.

The Church I believe in is not an ascending hierarchy of the holy. It is millions of ordinary people calling one another "brother" and "sister" and trying to make it true. Not so long ago I had one of those terrible-wonderful experiences that I have been talking about. It started in an innocuous way, then built to a genuine crisis, a classic Liahona-Iron Rod conflict between me and my bishop. After a week of sleepless nights I went into his office feeling threatened and fragile. What followed was an astonishingly open and healing discussion, a small miracle. As I told a friend later, "If we hadn't been Mormons, we would have embraced!" Our opinions didn't change much; our attitudes toward one another did. I give him credit for having the humility to listen, and I give myself credit for trusting him enough to say what I really felt. The leaven in our lump was a common reaching for the Spirit.

I am not always comfortable in my ward. There are weeks when I wonder if I can sit through another Relief Society lesson delivered straight from the manual or endure another meandering discussion in Gospel Doctrine class. Yet there are also moments when, surprised by my own silence, I am able to hear what a speaker only half says. Several months ago as I was bracing myself for a Fast and Testimony meeting, a member of the bishopric approached me and asked if I would give the closing prayer. I said, "Yes," feeling like a hypocrite, yet at the same time silently accepting some responsibility for the success of the meeting. Were the testimonies really better? When I stood to pray I was moved to the point of tears.

For me the issue is not whether The Church of Jesus Christ of Latter-day Saints is the One True Church Upon the Face of the Earth. That sounds to me like a particularly Zoramite brand of lusterware:

> Now the place was called by them Rameumptom, which, being interpreted, is the holy stand. Now, from this stand they did offer up, every man, the self-same prayer.... We thank thee, O God, for we are a chosen people unto thee, while others shall perish. (Alma 31:22,28)

The really crucial issue for me is that the Spirit of Christ is alive in the Church, and that it continues to touch and redeem the lives of the individual members. The young man survived his mission, returning with a stronger, more sober sense of what it meant to serve. The bride returned to the temple and enjoyed it more. The elders quorum president, though still struggling with his anger, knows it is his problem to face and to solve. The middle-aged woman grew through her loss of faith into a richer, deeper spirituality.

As I study the scriptures very few contemporary problems seem new. I wonder how men in tune with the divine can appear to be so complacent and self-righteous in their dealings with women. Then I read Luke's account of the visit of the angel to the women at the tomb on the first day of the week: "It was Mary Magdalene, and Joanna, and Mary the mother of James, and other women that were with them, which told these things unto the apostles. And their words seemed to them as idle tales, and they believed them not" (Luke 24:10-11). I wonder how a church purportedly devoted to eternal values can invest so much energy in issues that strike me as unimportant. Then I read the nineteenth chapter of Leviticus and find the second greatest commandment, "thou shalt love thy neighbour as thyself," side by side with a sober command that "neither shall a garment mingled of linen and woolen come upon thee" (Leviticus 19:18-19). Every dispensation has had its silver and its lusterware. God speaks to His children, as Moroni taught us, in our own language, and in our own narrow and culture-bound condition.

To me that is a cause for joy rather than cynicism. I love Joseph Smith's ecstatic recital in Doctrine and Covenants 128:

> Now, what do we hear in the gospel which we have received? A voice of gladness! a voice of mercy from heaven; and a voice of truth out of the earth....
>
> A voice of the Lord in the wilderness of Fayette, Seneca county....
>
> The voice of Michael on the banks of the Susquehanna....
>
> The voice of Peter, James, and John in the wilderness between Harmony, Susquehanna county, and Colesville, Broome county....
>
> And again, the voice of God in the chamber of old Father Whitmer, in Fayette, Seneca county, and at sundry times, and in divers places through all the travels and tribulations of this Church of Jesus Christ of Latter-day Saints! (D&C 128:19-21)

Joseph's litany of homely place names, his insistence that the voice of God could indeed be heard on the banks of an ordinary American river or in the chamber of a common farmer, gives his message an audacity and a power that cannot be ignored. For me Joseph Smith's witness that the divine can strike through the immediate is more important than any of the particulars enshrined in the church he established. If other people want to reduce D&C 128 to a data processing program for handling family group sheets, that's fine. I am far more interested in that "whole and complete and perfect union, and welding together of dispensations" that Joseph wrote about.

Two or three years ago I attended a small unofficial women's conference in Nauvoo. The ostensible purpose was to celebrate the founding of the Relief Society, but the real agenda was to come to terms with the position of women in the contemporary Church. The participants came from many places, a few of us known to each other, many of us strangers, the only common bond being some connection with the three organizers, all of whom remained maddeningly opaque as to their motives. I cannot describe what happened to me during those three days. Let me just say that after emptying myself of any hope for peace and change in the Church I heard the voice of the Lord on the banks of the Mississippi River. It was a voice of gladness, telling me that the gospel had indeed been restored. It was a voice of truth, assuring me that my concerns were just, that much was still amiss in the Church. It was a voice of mercy, giving me the courage to continue my uneasy dialogue between doubt and faith. I am not talking here about a literal voice but about an infusion of the Spirit, a kind of Pentecost that for a moment dissolved the boundaries between heaven and earth and between present and past. I felt as though I were re-experiencing the events the early Saints had described.

I am not a mystical person. In ordinary decisions in my family I am far more likely to call for a vote than a prayer, and when other people proclaim their "spiritual experiences" I am generally cautious. But I would gladly sift through a great trough of meal for even a little bit of that leaven.

The temptations of skepticism are real. Sweeping up the lusterware, we sometimes forget to polish and cherish the silver, not knowing that the power of discernment is one of the gifts of the Spirit, that the ability to discover counterfeit wares also gives us the power to recognize the genuine.

17

Noel B. Reynolds

Reason And Revelation

In the following essay, Noel Reynolds considers the relation between reason and revelation. He invites students of human thought to carefully consider the limitations of philosophy or of any intellectual discipline in their attempt to apprehend reality. He also urges that we discern between authentic spirituality and the sentimentalism that sometimes poses as spirituality. Brother Reynolds received his Ph.D. from Harvard. He is Professor of Political Science at Brigham Young University where he recently completed a term of office as Associate Academic Vice-President. He is the editor of Book of Mormon Authorship *and continues to write articles on religious topics, in addition to his professional publications in legal and political philosophy. He has served in numerous Church callings, including scout master, bishop, and counselor in a stake presidency. He, his wife Sydney, and their eleven children reside in Orem, Utah. The paper here presented is a revision of a Brigham Young University devotional address given on 30 June 1981.*

I believe the gospel of Jesus Christ because I know it is true. One way of characterizing our mortal probation is to describe it as a test of whether we will choose to believe the truths we encounter in this life and conform our lives to them, or whether we will pick and choose, modify and revise, and shape a set of beliefs which are more convenient to a lifestyle which suits our desires. The challenge the gospel presents to us is whether we will be willing to believe this fundamental truth, which will require a radical revision of our lives, or whether we will choose to rationalize it away as a means of protecting our commitment to our sinful ways.

But this way of explaining faith leads to a discussion that is complicated and not immediately helpful for the purposes of this volume. I will therefore approach the discussion by a side route and consider the role of reason in the process of learning from revelation. And I propose to begin that discussion negatively through a look at purported forms of religious understanding which deny any important role to reason or critical inquiry.

We live in an age plagued with false gospels and pseudospiritual modes of life. As our young people are confronted with one or more of these, their own spiritual maturity will be repeatedly put to the test. However, this is not new. From the most ancient times, there have been religious traditions which insisted that true revelatory experiences involving the gods were always characterized by ecstasy or frenzy of the mind. In some of these traditions, wines or drugs were used to induce the frenzied state in which one could become the mouthpiece of the gods. Certain Christian and Jewish variants of these traditions have taught that the ancient prophets wrote in excited or frenzied states in which they were not in full control of their own minds.

Stated in these stark terms, this tradition is easily recognized as something alien to the teachings and practices of the restored gospel. We know the spirit of revelation as a spirit of peace. Notice the contrast between these mystical traditions and the scriptural references describing the voice of God as it comes to men. In the book of Helaman, we are told that it is "a still voice of perfect mildness," like "a whisper," and it pierces "even to the very soul" (Helaman 5:30). As reported in 3 Nephi 11:3,

> it was not a harsh voice, neither was it a loud voice; nevertheless, and not withstanding its being a small voice it did pierce them that did hear to the center, insomuch that there was no part of their frame that it did not cause to quake; yea, it did pierce them to the very soul, and did cause their hearts to burn.

Because of the variety of emotional extravagances that prevailed among the Christian sects of his time, Joseph Smith often warned the Saints against these things and showed them the way that they might avoid coming under these same influences. He commented once that "nothing is a greater injury to the children of men than to be under the influence of a false spirit when they think they have the Spirit of God" (*Teachings*, p. 205). It is extremely important that, as Latter-day Saints grow, they learn to develop their ability to discern the difference between the voice of the Spirit and the many alternatives available in this world.

On another occasion Joseph Smith taught the Saints how they might learn the true spirit of revelation:

> A person may profit by noticing the first intimation of the spirit of revelation; for instance, when you feel pure intelligence flowing into you, it may give you sudden strokes of ideas, so that by noticing it, you may find it fulfilled the same day or soon; (i.e.) those things that were presented unto your minds by the Spirit of God, will come to pass; and thus by learning the Spirit of God and understanding it, you may grow into the principle of revelation, until you become perfect in Christ Jesus. (*Teachings*, p. 151)

Perhaps it is because the Spirit does cause feelings such as a burning of the heart that it seems to be easily mistaken for other emotions. I would like to begin by pointing out some of the kinds of false spirits or emotions that seem to produce some spiritual confusion among our young people when they mistake their feelings for manifestations of the true Spirit.

Sentimentalism vs. Spirit

My first example may be a simple hazard of youth, though I suspect it is a general problem of our times. We are witnessing a widespread inability to distinguish between sentimentalism and true spiritual experience. Unfortunately, some of the literature used in the Church today is too much like the popular sentimental trash which is designed to pull our heartstrings or moisten our eyes, but which does not communicate true spiritual experience.

The tendency of our youth to use sentimental stories in Church talks creates a culture of spiritual misunderstanding in which thinking and learning are discouraged. When I was a bishop years ago in an Orem ward, I felt strongly the need to counsel the youth not to use the compilations of sentimental stories that were available. I feel that our failure to immerse these young people in the scriptures and other high-quality literature makes them vulnerable to the cheap tactics of every moralistic movement which they encounter. Every teacher of youth knows what a challenge it is to make every lesson into a spiritual experience. Because youth respond positively to sentimentalism, there is a danger that we might come to rely on it as a more dependable way of getting their attention and creating an intensfied classroom atmosphere. Genuine spiritual experience is not mechanically available to us. Both teacher and students must work together in a thoughtful and humble way for it to occur. This must be a particularly difficult challenge for seminary teachers who meet daily and for long hours with many young people who would prefer to be somewhere else.

But is it possible to imagine that Nephi was brought up on such sentimentalism? On the contrary, as he informs us in the first verse of his record, he was carefully instructed in all the learning of his father. And that learning was of no small effect, for, as he encountered the real problems of real life, he responded in a supremely intelligent and powerful way, quickly learning the Spirit of God and obtaining its guidance in the most difficult tasks.

It may be that some sentimentality is a good and necessary thing, and certainly there is a place for it in our relationships with our loved ones. But it should never be leaned upon as a substitute for spirituality. Reliance on sentimentality will stunt our spiritual growth by robbing us of the spiritual gift of discernment and filling our understanding with false experiences.

Our spiritual immaturity can also be revealed through our choice of books. I was dismayed several years ago as editors of major LDS publishing houses apologetically explained to me that they are primarily interested in books which can either feature a well-known Latter-day Saint author or are written on a very simplistic level and in such a way as to give people a warm, comfortable feeling without any challenging ideas. Anything more demanding of the reader, I was informed, will not sell enough to justify publication. As a Latter-day Saint I was chagrined. But as I took more occasion to observe what is selling well in our bookstores, I could see they had only been candid with me.

Spiritual confusion may also manifest itself when we are invited to invest in expensive items which we do not really need but which can somehow be related by the salesman to goals we develop in church. College women frequently find themselves buying extremely expensive cookware sets, so they will have first-class equipment when they get married. Somehow the purchase is supposed to improve the young woman's prospects of successful marriage.

At the same time, her parents may be investing precious savings in some sure-fire get-rich scheme without seeking sound financial advice—relying instead on trusted friends or relatives who have no better judgment. The vast majority of these investors lose everything, and usually only the scheme perpetrators get rich. In fact, many such schemes turn out after the fact simply to be frauds. But instead of heeding spiritual warnings, we are lulled by other feelings into actually believing that we have spiritual reassurance and that we are going to get rich, so we can help the Church or spend all our time with our children or some other worthy endeavor.

I firmly believe the Lord will give us the guidance we need in our financial affairs if we will think it all through carefully and responsibly and seek him in prayer. But when He speaks, it will be by the same still, small voice He uses on other occasions and not through a burning feeling of excitement at the prospects of having more wealth than our neighbors, nicer clothes or cars, or not having to work for a living. I believe we are much more likely to receive spiritual guidance in our business affairs when we ask the Lord what we can do or produce in this life that will be of real value to our fellow men. Can any man risk offending the Lord by seeking His blessing for any less noble scheme?

It is therefore extremely important that as Latter-day Saints grow, mature, and seek an education, they learn to develop their ability to discern the difference between the voice of the Spirit and the many alternative voices available in this world. We must be clean in every way that we might be receptive to the true Spirit. We must come to know the Spirit that we might not be misled by the imposter varieties. And we must learn to think clearly and to recognize the ways of good and evil in their many forms, that we may avoid evil early and help others to do the same.

Most Latter-day Saints probably assume that an education should help them develop the kind of judgment and thinking ability needed to be able to recognize these kinds of dangers. Yet they may also have some ambivalence about the tools of analysis taught in philosophy and science and may wonder how these tools can help them rather than becoming an obstacle to their testimonies and to personal revelation. I would like to suggest an approach to education that will help one derive strength from it without letting it develop into a spiritual stumbling block, as it undoubtedly has done for many, many people.

An Approach to Education

As infants, every one of us came into this world faced with the same general problem. We knew nothing of this world, and we did not know how to find out the truth about it. So we started from ignorance, but we were given some basic tools. We had senses with which we could establish contact with the world around us. We had minds with which we could reflect on the things we observed in the development of our understanding. There are people and a culture which will help each of us deal with the problems of life and will also pass on to us a variety of beliefs about the world in which we have found ourselves—some true, some false. And we have a basic spiritual gift. By learning to use these God-given faculties well, we can come to grips with this world more or less successfully.

As we mature and grow in our knowledge of the world, we can also begin to develop our knowledge of God and His ways. And just as with our knowledge of the world, our knowledge of Him comes through the things told to us by others and through our personal experiences. But how do we know what is true and what to believe? Is it not reasonable to expect that our knowledge of God and His ways, though it reaches into the spiritual sphere, is built up by use of the same thinking skills and honest self-criticism that we have learned from infancy in mastering the world around us? Would it make sense for the Lord to design this world in such a way that a devotion to learning the truth about the world in which we live would make it more difficult for us to learn the truth about its creator? Are the hard won skills of honest and diligent inquiry to be rendered irrelevant in the quest to know our God?

Countless scriptures promise us that we will be rewarded for the faith that we develop in God. We would not expect to be rewarded for faith in false things, so what basis or merit is there in our having faith in the true God? Why should we be rewarded for that? The only answer would seem to be that there is some meritorious action on our part which prepares us for the gift of faith. There must be available to every one of us some reliable means of finding a measure of truth and knowing when we have found it.

We are all of necessity developing a broad system of beliefs which we will use to determine our daily conduct.

Through trial and error, we discover which ones are good, and we reject the bad. We can use this same method for testing our religious beliefs and the teachings given to us by others. But the problem which always confronts us is the difficulty of being rigorously honest in this process. Beliefs have implications. We cannot help wanting some things to be true and others to be false. If we love our sins, we will likely not want the gospel to be true, because it commands us to forsake them utterly.

So our integrity is constantly on the line, and only God knows when we actually sacrifice for the truth or when we harbor error willingly. To gain increasing knowledge of Him, we must learn not to promote ourselves by manipulating others, by intimidating, lying, or cheating—by exploiting others or deceiving ourselves—because none of these will work with Him. And our knowledge of Him comes through the revelations of the Spirit, which we receive only at His pleasure.

Light of Christ

The Spirit, or Light of Christ, is given to all men to provide guidance and encouragement in those important domains of moral action where reason and experience are demonstrably inadequate guides. It is a simple fact of modern philosophy that unaided human reason has not even come close to providing us with a single true and persuasive set of moral principles. And even if we had such a complete set of ethical guidelines, our reasoning abilities would not be adequate to use them in particular situations to determine what we should do. We are therefore all in need of an omniscient friend who knows what courses of action will have the best implications for the future. The great good news of the gospel is that there is such a friend who has prepared the way whereby we can receive and use such assistance. As this friend gives us spiritual guidance and tells us what is right, we will come to rely on him, if we are honest in heart and as we recognize the reliability of that guidance. Thus by being rigorously honest in pursuing what is right and true, even when it requires sacrifice on our part, we can come to have faith—to act as Christ directs without knowing how or why, but knowing that His is the only reliable direction we have ever discovered.

All of this assumes that His voice is distinctive, that it is recognizable by us and not readily confused with other sources of ideas. It also assumes that we have a commitment to what is right, that we will be able to respond to that spiritual guidance as we learn about it. The suggestion is, of course, that it is this very commitment to the right and our sensitivity to direction from the Lord, as well as our honesty of heart, that are being tested in this probationary state.

Usefulness of Reason

This analysis suggests that the Lord expects us to use all the tools He has given us in a diligent and rigorously honest way in the pursuit of truth. Although I have already indicated that reason is inadequate to insure the discovery of truth, it is extremely useful in identifying error. There are many ways in which reason can be used to reveal erroneous or problematic claims to the truth. We can identify contradictions or gaps in our own system of beliefs as we examine them rationally. Reason will also help us to identify inconsistencies which need repair that might occur between our own beliefs or ideas and the beliefs of the prophets as recorded in scripture. And it will help us compare alternative courses of action. That is, it will help us if we have developed our ability to think and to use our rational capacity.

But reason is not adequate to show us definitively which answers are true. We will always be in need of an omniscient friend to point out the way, to let light through the clouds and darkness, to open our understanding to truths and explanations we could never have thought of from our positions of ignorance. And no doubt, many of our problems of understanding will result from partial or inadequate interpretations of the scriptures or the prophets, something that the Spirit will also help us to overcome.

Two scriptures illustrate some ways in which the Lord

expects our reason to be involved in the process of receiving revelation. To explain Oliver Cowdery's failure to translate the Book of Mormon, the Lord said:

> Behold, you have not understood; you have supposed that I would give it unto you, when you took no thought save it was to ask me.
>
> But, behold, I say unto you, that you must study it out in your mind; then you must ask me if it be right, and if it is right I will cause that your bosom shall burn within you; therefore, you shall feel that it is right. (D&C 9: 7-8)

On a later occasion, it appears that Edward Partridge and others may have inquired of the Prophet as to how they should travel to the land appointed for their new residence. Seeking direction on this point, the Prophet was instructed:

> Wherefore, let them bring their families to this land, as they shall counsel between themselves and me.
>
> For behold, it is not meet that I should command in all things; for he that is compelled in all things, the same is a slothful and not a wise servant; wherefore he receiveth no reward. Verily I say, men should be anxiously engaged in a good cause, and do many things of their own free will, and bring to pass much righteousness;
>
> For the power is in them, wherein they are agents unto themselves. And inasmuch as men do good they shall in nowise lose their reward.
>
> But he that doeth not anything until he is commanded, and receiveth a commandment with doubtful heart, and keepeth it with slothfulness, the same is damned. (D&C 58:25-29)

The point of this second scripture seems to be that these people could have counseled directly with the Lord and among themselves in seeking an answer to this question without troubling the Prophet for direction. The power was in them wherein they were agents unto themselves. It was only by exercising that agency that they could gain a reward. And yet the exercise of that agency clearly included counseling with the Lord.

The Lord delights to bless His children, and when we need answers quickly to questions where we cannot help ourselves, He does not hesitate to give us the guidance we need. But where we can help ourselves, He does not take from us that opportunity of coming to our own decisions. We are promised the guidance of the Holy Ghost in all things. It is my belief that as we exercise our agency in humility and righteousness, the Lord will warn us spiritually should we begin to go astray. I also believe that at every stage of the process of analyzing a problem and formulating a decision, those gentle promptings are available to help us find our way and come to the proper course of action.

This process is illustrated rather well in the development of the Welfare Program of the Church. This program was not revealed full blown to the prophet or even to the brethren in the presiding councils of the Church. Rather the need for such a program became evident to these leaders. Through inspiration they selected the individuals who would be instrumental in developing the program. After a rather long, prayerful period of counseling together and experimenting with various possible forms of a program, a final proposal was prepared and brought before the presiding councils of the Church. William E. Berrett has given us one account of that event. He says he was in the first meeting in which the Welfare Program was announced to the members of the Church in 1936:

> President Grant related that individuals had asked him whether he had been talking to Heavenly Beings, whether the Lord had given him a vision. His answer was, "No, I have not talked to angels; I have not had a vision." And he recounted that the word of the Lord on such matters was already given. A plan was worked out in accordance to earlier revelations....

> President Grant said that...he went before the Lord in prayer to ask him if the plan was acceptable, and he got the feeling from the crown of his head to the soles of his feet that the Lord was pleased. ("Teaching by the Spirit," BYU, 27 June 1966)

Our decisions to follow revealed guidance will always require faith. In this life, we can never act in full knowledge until we come to "see as we are seen," and "know as we are known"—undoubtedly a miraculous gift which is not widely enjoyed.

The Role of Sin

The iron rod goes along a straight and narrow path. There are many ways in which we can stumble and lose our footing. The most frequent cause of our wandering from that path is sin, which clouds our vision and dries up our access to spiritual guidance, leaving us alone to wander with our own dim light and weakened resolve.

Pride is an obstacle for almost all of us. Somehow the requirements of faith seem to threaten our identity. This is probably true only because we choose to identify with things of this world, things which the Lord will ask us to give up. Anticipating that demand, we often find reasons in advance to steer clear of Him and His guidance, thereby losing precious opportunities and stunting our own spiritual growth.

Some of us make the mistake of imposing on the Lord our conceptions of Him and what He is like, what is good and right, and what is true. He may just let us have our pet beliefs and suffer the consequences. I am reminded of that great sermon in which Moses discussed this matter with the ancient Israelites. Before leaving them, he said:

> Take ye therefore good heed unto yourselves; for ye saw no manner of similitude on the day that the Lord spake unto you in Horeb out of the midst of the fire:
>
> Lest ye corrupt yourselves, and make you a

> graven image, the similitude of any figure, the likeness of male or female.
>
> And the Lord spake unto you out of the midst of the fire: ye heard the voice of the words, but saw no similitude; only ye heard a voice. (Deuteronomy 4:15-16, 12)

Moses was at pains to stress to the Israelites that they did not know what God looked like, because he feared that they would tend to make images of God for the purposes of idol worship. Rather he stressed with them that all they knew about God was that He has a voice. That, of course, is the most important thing to know, because the God of Israel can speak to man and tell him what to do. Later in the same sermon, Moses warned the Israelites that in the last days their descendants could be saved from their dispersion only if they would forsake their evil ways and hearken to the voice of God once more (Deuteronomy 4:30).

We could also err by blindly trusting in others who seem to be more spiritual than we are. But in so doing, we must remember that if they lead us astray it will be no excuse for us at the judgment day. At that time we must each stand on our own feet, on our own performance. We will be judged on what we did with the opportunities and talents given to us. Brigham Young is reported to have warned the Saints many times not to simply rely on his word but to get confirmation of that word for themselves, that they might know his directions were from God.

We need to be sure that our testimonies and gospel understanding keep pace with our learning of the world. Having lived many years in university communities, I have had that sad experience of working with members who have grown too sophisticated, in their own view of themselves, to remain faithful to a gospel which they really only understand on a grade-school level. There is always a great danger that faithful members of the Church will find their testimonies threatened by the doctrines of men as they extend their education.

But should our reaction be simply to shield ourselves

from exposure to the teachings and theories of the world? Such a posture communicates a lack of confidence in the gospel itself, or possibly too much faith in reason or science, or both. For either, on the one hand, we do not really believe that all truth can ultimately be circumscribed in one great whole with Jesus Christ at the center, or, on the other, we do not appreciate the fundamental limitations on the power of man's reason and science to discover truth about the world, and especially about God.

Confidence in the Lord

I believe that one day we will be able to understand all things, that we will rejoice to see how all things are in the Lord's hands, and that all things in the final analysis will work together for our good. But that vision is beyond human science, and I look forward to it as a matter of faith—faith based on invaluable personal experience with the Lord and His revelations. So I believe we must approach the learning of the world with open minds and with confidence that the Lord can and will protect us from error if our hearts are pure—and not lifted up in pride.

I am thinking of the kind of confidence expressed by President Tanner in a story he told in General Conference several years ago. I will relate it in his own words:

> Some years ago in Canada I was driving along and had two young men with me in my car, and a young man thumbed a ride with us. I asked the boys who were with me if we should take him with us, and they said yes. I picked him up, and after we had driven along a little way he said, "Do you mind if I smoke in your car?"
>
> I said, "No, not at all, if you can give me any good reason why you should smoke." And I said, "I will go farther than that." (I was stake president at this time.) "If you can give me a good reason why you should smoke, I will smoke with you." Well, my two young friends looked at me and wondered.

> We drove on for some distance, about twenty minutes, I think, and I turned around and said, "Aren't you going to smoke?"
>
> And he said, "No."
>
> I said, "Why not?"
>
> And he said, "I can't think of a good reason why I should." (CR, April 1965, p. 93)

This is not to suggest that I believe there is any procedure by which we can compel the Lord to reveal to us the fullness of the truths for which scientists seek. I have heard well-intentioned LDS scholars announce such projects, but I have not seen them reach the promised end. The Lord has His own timetable—and His own ways. He has given us all the direction we need to get access to the most important opportunities of life. And He will quickly and constantly provide the daily personal guidance we all need to keep our feet on that straight and narrow path which leads to life eternal. Beyond that, I do not believe He objects to our further inquiry if we can keep all things in perspective. But we have no assurance of receiving early or full answers to our questions. These other matters wait on His good pleasure.

Guidelines to Keep Faith

We need not fear losing our testimonies or our faith through scholarly pursuits if we will observe a few basic guidelines:

1. Keep the commandments. I have heard many stories about intellectual apostasy, but I am not convinced I have ever seen a genuine case. More often, intellectual dissent serves as a handy rationale to justify one's sins. Intellectuals who are morally clean, who pay their tithing, and who are not lifted up in pride find no intellectual motives to apostatize.

2. Study the scriptures. The prophets were men of great understanding and inspiration. As we grow and struggle with the problems and questions of life, we will continually find higher levels of wisdom and guidance in their writings. And the Lord will often use our thoughtful scripture study as the

opportunity to illuminate and expand our understanding through the Spirit.

3. Pay careful attention to the assumptions and limitations of the various forms of human intellectual endeavor. Do not be intimidated by irresponsible claims that some scientists or scholars might make. Develop a responsible awareness of the foundations of any discipline you choose to pursue, so that you can assess for yourself the strength of the theories and evidences that are under discussion.

One of the most disappointing things I sometimes find as I interview students who are graduating from the university where I teach is an inability to discuss the assumptions and the limitations of the particular science or discipline that they have been studying for four years. How can you appreciate the strengths and use those strengths appropriately if you do not understand the limitations? It may be true that these limitations are most easily understood by the most advanced practitioners of a discipline. But there is no reason that university level students in any discipline cannot develop a significant appreciation of these matters.

Intellect and Faith

There is a strong sense in which genuine intellectual apostasy is not even a possibility for someone who has had much personal spiritual experience and has obeyed the first principles and ordinances of the gospel by repenting of his sins and receiving the Lord's forgiveness through the baptism of fire. Those are clear and undeniable firsthand experiences with the Lord. An honest intellectual knows that none of the moral or scientific theories of man are nearly so certain to be true. These can never transcend tentative hypotheses. So how should he respond to a theory or doctrine, however attractive, that does not seem to square with his spiritual experience or understanding of the scriptures? He will very naturally decide to shelve the matter until such time as his understanding of the world or the prophets or both progresses to the point that the two will fit together. But he would be a fool to reject that which is most certain and valuable for theories which he knows are likely to be revised or refuted by future scholars.

Another way of putting the problem of reason and revelation is to ask if revelation must give the same results as philosophical or scientific inquiry to be valid. Because of the narrowness of these two, as conceived by contemporary practitioners, the answer must be negative. For example, contemporary philosophers and scientists must accept certain ground rules—such as the principle of naturalism—which restrict in advance the range of possible explanations that can be given for our observations. Specifically, no explanations are acceptable which refer to gods, other supernatural beings or forces, or even purposes.

It may well be that such a principle has been necessary for secular science to make any headway when its practitioners represent so many different beliefs about the existence of gods. But it is also clearly true that to the extent that the supernatural world does exist and does interact causally with the world of our ordinary experience, science has arbitarily erected a barrier against its own free explorations of that essential feature of reality—and has condemned itself permanently to a partial and defective understanding of the truth.

I know some members of the Church have chosen to get very excited about the conflicts they see between the theories of science and the teachings of the prophets. But it seems to me that most of this is unnecessary and only provides the devil with another tool for introducing pointless division among the Lord's people. Take, for example, theories about the origins of the universe and of life on this earth, a subject on which the scriptures do seem to say something. The scriptural accounts seem to impose at least two limits on any theories we might choose to develop. The classical Christian doctrine that the earth and the life forms were created *ex nihilo* (from nothing) is rejected. On that score Latter-day Saints agree with modern scientists. But the other clear teaching of the scriptural account is that the creation was the work of the gods, that they did it in a carefully ordered way to accomplish their eternal objectives. But science by its own game rules cannot include any gods or purposes in its explanations and theories. So the scientific theories *cannot* use anything beyond chance and nature to explain our origins. Should we be surprised, or even concerned, that scientific theory does not recognize the role of the gods? Science operates under that handicap. But once we see that difference, there is a world of interesting facts that scientists have turned up which invite our analysis from a much broader point of view, a view which allows far more than chance and nature in our theories and explanations.

Conclusions

What will happen if we can repent, overcome sin and pride, and humbly seek truth and right at the Lord's hand? He will always expect us to use our own resources to the fullest—our reason, our experience, the scriptures, inspired guidance of our leaders, and the gift of the Spirit which gives new guidance and confirmation as necessary. We will come to know of His never varying goodness. We will learn that He always promotes good and warns us from evil. We will become convinced of His great love and mercy for us. How else could He tolerate us and labor with us so long and patiently and forgive our sins? We will learn that He will exalt us above our own weaknesses to the extent that we allow it. We will gain an increasingly adequate understanding of the real world. We will learn to see the hand of God in all things. This will enable us to get both ourselves and others into perspective. On the one hand, we will see the divine potential of each individual as a son or a daughter of God. On the other hand, we will recognize that as vile sinners we are forever doomed to misery if we repent not and cultivate not the heavenly gift.

Mormonism is a distinctively intellectual faith. From the very beginning, great importance has been placed on giving a full picture of the world and its relation to God to the humblest member. Our members pride themselves on the ability to explain in detail the reasons for the interesting and different doctrines of this restored gospel. We can explain why we are commanded to be baptized for the dead and why the Word of Wisdom was given. Doubtless, we carry this too far, sometimes providing semi-authoritative explanations for things we really do not understand at all. But we have a much higher tolerance for that speculative error than for the attitude which tells us we should rejoice in inconsistencies when they are discovered, that we should rejoice in the apparent lack of logic or wisdom in the commandments of God. Such claims are foreign to scriptural and prophetic views. When we object to someone's teachings on the grounds that they do not make sense, it is a false spirit that replies, "That is the beauty of it."

This is not to say that the Lord provides us with the explanations for all things. Some of the most basic teachings of the gospel are left unexplained, and we do accept them simply on the basis of faith. But overall, the Lord has provided us with a coherent picture of Him and our relationship to Him. He has blessed us with the ability to see continuity in our experience with Him and all our daily experiences. It is because of this continuity and coherence that we are able, day by day, to separate out truth from error, that we might grow to know and understand Him and His commandments better.

Education and Opportunity

As I look back on my educational experiences, the two most important things I learned at BYU were, first, a knowledge of the Lord and His gospel and of His expectations of me, and second, an ability to read good books, to understand the views of others, and to think independently in evaluating those views. We constantly remind ourselves that our bodies are the temples of God, that we should keep them fit and clean. Our morning streets are crowded with people jogging to maintain fit bodies. I am concerned that we are not jogging our minds sufficiently. Paul has remarked in the epistle to Timothy that the exercise of the mind and the spirit is far more important than the exercise of the body (see 1 Timothy 4:8). How can God reveal sublime truth to muddled minds? We must prepare an ordered mind so that He can say to us as He said on many occasions to His children anciently, "Come, let us reason together." As President Lee is reported to have said, "It is good to be faithful, but it is better to be faithful and competent."

The youth of today face the greatest challenge that has ever been presented by the Lord to His servants—that of preparing the world for His return. Their ability to handle the challenges they will face will in large measure be a function of the seriousness with which they have taken their educational opportunities. I would plead with young people everywhere not to be misled by those who would have them believe that spirituality is simply an emotional state. I would urge them to prepare themselves appropriately to approach the Lord with clear and open minds that they might be able to understand and follow His word when they receive it. Doing this, they will be able to speak and act in the name of Jesus Christ and do His works. And they will know that the gospel is true.

18

Leonard J. Arrington

Why I Am A Believer

Leonard Arrington writes that he feels "very comfortable with poetry, music, art, drama, testimony, ritual, ceremony, and other expressions of religious feeling and thought." He nevertheless insists on the crucial role of the intellect in his religious outlook. In the following pages he structures his witness around four basic issues: whether God exists, whether Jesus is a divine teacher worthy of our worship, whether Joseph Smith was a prophet, and whether LDS culture bears fruit worth defending and supporting. Brother Arrington is perhaps the most prolific of all historians of Mormonism. He is, in the words of Richard Bushman, "the patron of virtually all contemporary scholarship in the field of Mormon history." Educated at the universities of Idaho and North Carolina, he has taught at North Carolina State, UCLA, Utah State, and Brigham Young University. He is the former Director of the History Division of the Church. Among his many significant books are Great Basin Kingdom: An Ecomonic History of the Latter-Day Saints, 1830-1900; The Mormon Experience: A History of the Latter-Day Saints *(co-authored with Davis Bitton); and* Brigham Young: American Moses. *He and his wife Harriet reside in Salt Lake City. A slightly abbreviated version of this paper was previously published in* Sunstone. *It is reprinted by permission.*

My path of commitment to and belief in The Church of Jesus Christ of Latter-day Saints developed around four basic religious questions I encountered as I grew up. First, is there a living God? Second, was Jesus a teacher worthy to be worshipped? Third, was Joseph Smith a prophet deserving of allegiance? And fourth, is our Latter-day Saint culture meritorious—worth defending and working for?

As these questions may reveal, I believed the intellect to be enormously important—more important than the heart, more important than tradition. If my mind could not confirm the truth of my religion, I felt I would be unsettled and apprehensive. Nevertheless, I felt very comfortable with poetry, music, art, drama, testimony, ritual, ceremony, and other expressions of religious feeling and thought. I was also comfortable with people who contended that religion was a matter of spirit, not mind, and that testimonies could come only through the assurance of the Holy Ghost.

My struggle with the first question began when I was a freshman at the University of Idaho and continued until the third year of graduate school. I acted as a believer, willing to assume there was a loving and powerful Creator. But I was not satisfied until I had studied the matter through and came to a conviction that my intellect could defend. My first satisfying experience was with Lowell Bennion's *What about Religion*? This manual, used in the MIA, taught a crucial truth, namely that the restored gospel represents truth and enlightenment, not superstition and ignorance. Scholarship and education are part of the gospel; Mormonism undertakes to foster the discovery and spread of truth; God has commanded that we study and learn and become acquainted with all good books; the glory of God is intelligence; and it is impossible for a man or woman to be saved in ignorance (D&C 90:15, 93:36, 88:118, 131:6). The manual also quoted with approval Brigham Young's statement in the *Journal of Discourses* that we accept truth no matter where it comes from, that Mormonism comprises all truth, and that there is an indissoluble relationship between religion and learning (*JD* 1:334, 11:375, 15:160). These became articles of my religious faith and continue to remain so.

When I went to the University, my roommate, anxious to test my mettle, provoked me into reading *Why We Behave Like Human Beings* by George A. Dorsey. This widely read treatise by a noted anthropologist and behavioral scientist gave a rather mechanistic interpretation of the ultimate questions and was not intended to inculcate faith in religion. Man was little more than a complete biophysical machine. The book did not make me cynical, as it apparently had done to my roommate, but it did help to keep alive within me a quest for certainty. I vividly remember one phrase from it. Dorsey quoted Dr. John B. Watson, the famous behaviorist, as saying that thinking was no more than "laryngeal itch." That stimulated me to read several books on evolution, including *On the Origin of Species* and *The Descent of Man* by Charles Darwin.

Dissatisfied with the superficial and uninformed views that were being conveyed in certain publications to which I was referred, I concentrated on the works of philosophers. First, I read *The Story of Philosophy* by Will Durant, which introduced to me the names of the most prominent persons who had pondered the great issues. For the same purpose I read C. E. M. Joad, *Guide to Philosophy*, and Windelband's brilliant but tedious *History of Philosophy*. I then systematically read some of the great thinkers—Plato, Aristotle, Thomas Aquinas, Spinoza, Immanuel Kant, Josiah Royce, and William James. I read some philosophical novels: Somerset Maugham's *Of Human Bondage* and George Santayana's *The Last Puritan*. I read Robert Shafer's *Christianity and Naturalism* and George Santayana's *Reason in Religion*. I read the autobiographies of St. Augustine, John Henry Newman, and John Stuart Mill. I read several books that reviewed what the great thinkers had said about God, man, and the universe, and had personal experiences that confirmed their views in an intimate way. By the time I began my third year of graduate work, I had satisfied myself about the existence of God. And my religious experiences in my more mature years have merely served to corroborate what I had then come to believe. While philosophers have not always argued that the existence of God is demonstrable, they have presented arguments that have been persuasive to me. My experience suggests that

Francis Bacon was correct when he contended that "a little philosophy inclineth man's mind to atheism; but depth in philosophy bringeth men's minds about to religion."

My conceptions of Jesus emerged when I was still in high school. I must confess that I read the Bible through when I was thirteen but, country boy that I was, I was turned off by the King James Version, which was to me a strange and unfamiliar idiom. When I went to the University, George Tanner, my LDS Institute instructor, gave direction to my search for Jesus as a person, as a leader. He introduced me to new translations of the Bible and I read through the New Testament versions of James Moffatt and Edgar Goodspeed, and Richard G. Moulton's *Modern Reader's Bible*. These were very helpful and I still often use them. At his suggestion I also read Shirley Jackson Case, *Jesus: A New Biography*; Ernest Renan, *The Life of Jesus*; Albert Schweitzer, *The Quest for the Historical Jesus*; and James E. Talmage, *Jesus the Christ*. All of these persuaded me that Jesus was, indeed, a historical figure (some historians had expressed doubt on this point), that the values He taught were superior to anything mankind had ever devised, that Jesus was indeed a divine person; and that His life provided a model worth imitating in meeting today's difficult problems.

As to Joseph Smith, I am grateful that I was not introduced to some of the views of his philosophy and theology that are being advocated today—views of his life and thought that clash with the impressions I have acquired and confirmed in my years of research in the Church Historian's Office. I was very fortunate in having been given, as a teenager, John Henry Evans's book *Joseph Smith, An American Prophet*. I read the book while still in high school and was very impressed with the Prophet. I remember giving some two-and-one-half minute talks that were based on the book. Unquestionably Joseph had a marvelous intellect and also acute spiritual sensitivity. He honestly sought to resolve the many intellectual, spiritual, social, and personal problems that arose in his lifetime. He was an imaginative thinker and leader. He accepted truth from many sources. And he had good values: people were more important than money, and the law of eternal progression pointed us all in the right direction.

What about the Prophet's accounts of his own experiences: the First Vision? the visit of the Angel Moroni to tell him about the golden plates? the return of John the Baptist to confer the Aaronic Priesthood and of Peter, James, and John to confer the Melchizedek? Can one accept all of the miraculous events that surrounded the restoration of the gospel? I was very fortunate to have read George Santayana's *Reason in Religion* before confronting these historical problems. I do not say that I fully understood it or that I agreed with his basic premise, but the book gave me a concept that has been helpful ever since—that truth may be expressed not only through science and abstract reason, but also through stories, testimonies, and narratives of personal experience; not only through erudite scholarship, but also through poetry, drama, and historical novels. Santayana used the term "myth"—a term well understood in recent religious literature—to refer to the expression of religious and moral truths in symbolic language.

The word "myth" has some pejorative connotations in modern English. It can mean a story or belief asserted to be true but without any basis in fact. It can be an invented explanation of some natural or historical phenomenon or a wholly fictitious supposition or belief. However, this is not what Santayana had in mind. What he called myth was a traditional account of events and happenings that have religious significance. To say that something is a myth is not to say that it was deliberately fabricated, but to identify it as an account that may or may not have a determinable basis of fact or natural explanation. The truth of a myth is beyond empirical or historical accessibility. Examples are the Christian story of the Resurrection, the Virgin Birth, and the creation of the world as described in the Book of Genesis. These are ways of explaining events or truths having religious significance that may be either symbolical or historical.

To go one step further, even in a Shakespearean tragedy where, unlike the episodes of Mormon and Christian history, the characters and events are wholly fictional, one can find philosophical and religious truth. Examples of novels disclosing religious truths that I had read during the formative stages of my religious beliefs include: Pearl Buck, *The Good Earth*; Knut Hamsun, *Growth of the Soil*; William Henry Hudson, *Green Mansions*; Fyodor Dostoyevsky, *Brothers Karamazov* and *Crime and Punishment*; and Leo Tolstoy, *Anna Karenina* and *War and Peace*. And, for that matter, the philosophical drama in the Old Testament, the Book of Job.

Because of my introduction to the concept of symbolism as a means of expressing religious truth, I was never preoccupied with the question of the historicity of the First Vision—though the evidence is overwhelming that it did occur—or of the many reported epiphanies in Mormon, Christian, and Hebrew history. I am prepared to accept them as historical or as metaphorical, as symbolical or as precisely what happened. That they convey religious truth is the essential issue, and of this I have never had any doubt. Ineffable experiences, messages, and value affirmations do not always lend themselves to scientific or literal or precise articulation. It does not bother me at all that, in describing a religious experience that transcends his ability to express it, a narrator, a testimony-giver, often resorts to traditional phrases in presenting it. Indeed, I do it myself, as those who have heard me speak in testimony meeting can vouch. The Italians have a useful expression for this sort of thing: "*Se non e vero, e ben trovato,*" which means, roughly: "Whether it is literally true or not, it's still true."

This brings me to my fourth basic question: Are Mormon values, policies, practices, and leadership sufficiently superior to justify a lifetime of devotion? Can one work as effectively in furthering the work of God through Mormonism as through other causes? I came to the conclusion that Mormonism was indeed a positive influence worth contributing to and perpetuating.

In 1985, Alfred Knopf published *Brigham Young: American Moses*. In preparing that biography, I learned that Brigham saw and read the Book of Mormon in 1830, when he was twenty-nine. Why then did he wait almost two years before joining the infant Church of Christ, as it was then called? When asked to explain this, he replied that he wanted time to observe the character of those who were leading the movement. "I watched," he said, "to see whether good common sense was manifest" (*JD* 8:38). After twenty-two months of observation and investigation, he decided that the movement did indeed manifest "good sense." He joined in 1832 and spent the rest of his life laboring on its behalf.

My examination of Mormon cultural institutions did not begin until 1941, when I was twenty-three and in my second year of graduate work. This study was the result of my surprising discovery at that time that there was a historically based Mormon culture. I had grown up on a farm in a non-Mormon community in southwestern Idaho, the son of parents who had grown up in North Carolina, Tennessee, southern Indiana, and Oklahoma. Neither parent had had any experience with the Mormon way of life. There were no Mormon schoolteachers or administrators in our local school system, and none of our close neighbors was a Mormon.

Then I went to the University of Idaho, where there were few Mormons in attendance. (At that time, most Idaho Mormons went to BYU or to Utah State University in Logan.) After four years in Moscow, Idaho, I went to the University of North Carolina in Chapel Hill where I was the only Latter-day Saint in the University and in the community. So all these years I was outside the Mormon cultural community.

My major at the University of North Carolina was economic theory. While doing some teaching at North Carolina State University in Raleigh, I took a minor in agricultural economics and rural sociology. One day, as I was perusing some books for a class, I happened to come across a description of the Mormon village in a new book on *The Sociology of Rural Life* by the young sociologist T. Lynn Smith. I did not know at the time that T. Lynn was a Latter-day Saint and a graduate of BYU, but I was absolutely fascinated with his pages on the Mormon village—something I had never heard of before. I hunted for discussions on the subject in other texts and was delighted to find that Mormon rural life was of great interest to sociologists.

About the same time, partly as the result of the curiosity

aroused by discovery that there was a recognized Mormon rural life pattern, I ran across an article by Bernard DeVoto in *Harper's Magazine* which was about his grandfather, a Mormon farmer who had lived at Uinta, southeast of Ogden; and also two articles by Juanita Brooks, whom I had not heard of before, that were also in *Harper's*: "The Water's In" and "A Close-Up of Polygamy." These introduced me to the literature on Mormon culture—something I had not been aware of because I had not grown up in Utah or in a Mormon village. Basically, I have spent the rest of my life trying to keep abreast of this literature and trying to make some contributions myself to that body of writing.

My study of this literature very quickly told me that Mormon culture was praiseworthy—that my people did indeed believe in education and were willing to sacrifice to put their children through college; that Mormon educators were remarkably loyal to the Church, were well respected, and sought to preserve the best values of the culture; that the people were not provincial but, partly because of missionary contacts, had an interest in the peoples of the world; and among the influential leaders of the faith were a number of impressive intellectuals. This was a great church, I came to believe. It perpetuated fine ideals of home, school, and community life; its approach and philosophy enabled its members to reconcile religion with science and higher learning; its strong social tradition taught its members to be caring and compassionate; and its strong organizational capability empowered its people to build better communities. As Brigham Young said, a central doctrine of Mormonism is that God's primary work is through people, and so our principal concern was with the here and now.

In short, it *was* a religion and a church worth working for. I went into the American armed services soon after reaching these conclusions, and upon my return at the end of World War II, I expected to live in a Mormon village to rear my children and to perform my life's labor.

After three years overseas in North Africa and Italy, I did return, obtained a professorship at Utah State University in the Mormon village of Logan, and remained there to rear our family in what Grace and I always regarded as sacred space, because in Logan we actually experienced the way of life we had read and dreamed about. Except for three sabbaticals, we did not leave our beloved Cache Valley until I was called to be Church Historian in 1972. In that capacity I was able to examine over a period of several years the most intimate records of the Church—records that are replete with faith-promoting incidents that served to strengthen my belief in the divinity of the latter-day work. Particularly meaningful to me was my private knowledge of the divine circumstances that led up to the announcement by the First Presidency that the priesthood might be conferred on all worthy males without regard to race or color.

Although now released from the position of Church Historian, I am still devoted to carrying out responsibilities which I trust continue to help build the Kingdom of God on earth. Many satisfying spiritual experiences, as well as my continued study of the Saints and their leaders throughout our history, have intellectually and emotionally validated my decision to serve the faith that I committed myself to many years ago, and that I believe to be based on true principles. "Blessed is he who has found his work," wrote Thomas Carlyle; "he needs to ask no other blessedness."

19

Philip L. Barlow

The Uniquely True Church

Philip Barlow has attempted to shape not only his faith, but his entire adult life around the question: "How am I to live with meaning, integration, and authenticity?" He finds that first, Christ, and second, the Church, are crucial elements in answering that question. Brother Barlow is the compiler and editor of A Thoughtful Faith. *He holds a masters degree in theological studies from the Harvard Divinity School, and for several years he taught at the Institute of Religion in Cambridge, Massachusetts. He is completing doctoral work at Harvard in American Religion and Culture with a dissertation on the history of the Mormon use of the Bible. He has authored a number of articles in professional journals, and is currently writing a philosophical novel:* War Against the Gods. *Brother Barlow has worked in the Church in many capacities, including service in a bishopric and on a high council. He is the father of two children.*

I

"The morals of our people," wrote Boston's John Adams, favorably comparing his own home ground to everywhere else,

> are much better; [our] manners are more polite and agreeable; ...our language is better; our taste is better; our persons are handsomer; our spirit is greater; our laws are wiser; our religion is superior.[1]

Such chauvinism may, I think, have a certain charm—provided it does not seem too near in time or space or content. However, a more specifically religious example may hit closer to home and feel less comfortable. A character in one of Henry Fielding's novels, the good Parson Thwackum, insists that

> When I mention religion, I mean the Christian religion; and not only the Christian religion, but the Protestant religion; and not only the Protestant religion, but the Church of England. And when I mention honor, I mean that mode of Divine grace which is not only consistent with, but dependent upon, this religion; and is consistent with and dependent upon no other.[2]

As with John Adams, Thwackum's confidence has its quaint side. In real life, though, such thinking has sometimes been coupled with power and influence, and the results have proven unfortunate.

But religious conceit can strike nearer yet. For example, I have a well-traveled friend who insists that Salt Lake City—though for quite different reasons—ranks with Boston, New York, Paris, and perhaps a dozen other elite cities around the world, each of which half-believes itself to be the hub of the solar system (never mind the Copernican theory).

We are easily possessed by our surroundings.

I have drunk deeply of this cultural confidence, for I was raised near Salt Lake City, a Mormon in a Mormon town. Partly to explore my own religious chauvinism, I decided some years ago to move to New England to attend the Harvard Divinity School. This was not "to train for the ministry," as my LDS friends jokingly described it; I went to better understand my faith in the light of other faiths.

Across the street from what was once my office in Cambridge lies the campus of the Episcopal Divinity School. On this campus, discreetly placed behind the chapel, kneels a life-sized statue. By all appearances he has knelt there a great while. His head is raised, his back is arched, his palms are lifted to his face, perhaps stopping tears. His posture is one of profound despair.

The statue has occasionally been my companion. I have spent hours alone with him, responding to or identifying with him. He remains unnamed, to the best of my knowledge, so I call him "Anguish." To me he means the abyss of Not Knowing, or the agony of personal or global sin. He means Fear. He means participation in estrangement and unjustified suffering—comprehension of the human condition. My brother, more observant than I, once pointed out to me that did the statue's hand not obscure his eyes, he might be staring at the cross on the pinnacle of the steeple high above him. Perhaps, then, he also means compassion for the suffering Christ—compassion signifying not merely "sympathy for," but "suffering with."

I have considered the odds of such a troubled statue finding a home on Temple Square or on some other distinctly Mormon ground. The prospect seems unlikely. I do not mean a "look-how-much-the-pioneers-suffered-for-us" statue. We have that kind already and they are important tributes to valiant people. But I mean art that reflects my stake in the universal plight of the race.

It is hardly surprising that our public places house no such art, for Mormonism is an optimistic and proselyting faith, which desires—appropriately—to convey its optimism to others. Yet anguish is part of my reality, and Mormons are left largely without a profound public mechanism to convey and share that reality. As a result, when I desire to explore personal or religious feelings, there are times when where I most want to be is behind the chapel of the Episcopal Divinity School, or worshipping in silence with my Quaker friends, or meditating in certain Catholic cathedrals whose interiors so well reflect the transcendent mystery of God. One of the things that I learned in Cambridge, therefore, was that I ought not to merely *tolerate* non-Mormon religions; I found that each of them had truths to teach me. My chauvinism, I hope, has since retreated a bit. My religious faith must now be expressed in the context of a more serious appreciation for the genuine worth of other people's religion.

I learned a few other things while in divinity school. I learned a little about modern biblical criticism—it was not what I had been led to expect. I learned something of Mormon history, and of Christian and non-Christian and secular history. I studied theology, ethics, epistemology, and metaphysics. In the process of this exposure, I experienced pain. My beliefs underwent significant changes, redefinition, and sometimes suspension. During more than one extended period, I had to consider leaving the Mormon Church. That would have been a mistake.

II

Eventually, I left Massachusetts with a more fully textured faith than I had taken there with me. My commitment to the gospel has grown more keen and better informed. The allegiance that I feel to The Church of Jesus Christ of Latter-day Saints is now based upon a highly personal recipe that includes simple affection, spiritual intuition, "direct awareness," experience, faith, and logic. I would like to describe the nature of this allegiance by offering fifteen observations.

Before volunteering those observations I wish to admit an assumption and to offer a confession. The assumption is this: I think it is a mistake to attempt to elevate religion by disparaging reason. I believe my mind to be more a friend than a foe to my spirit, and that God gave me my intellect in the same sense that He gave me my soul. I believe that "spirit" and "faith" and "revelation" and "reason" can be related, compatible terms. Joseph Smith implied as much when he said that his revelatory experiences often consisted of receiving "sudden strokes of ideas" from the Spirit and that the "Holy Ghost has no other effect than pure intelligence."[3] Although it is of course possible to err by intellectual arrogance or to misunderstand rationality as the only important kind of intelligence, I do not believe that it is possible to think too well. Even if one feels himself to have received inspiration, a mature faith ought to be a thoughtful faith.

My confession is to acknowledge my awareness of the many linguistic, historical, and theological difficulties that arise as one attempts to analyze such documents as the Book of Abraham and the Book of Mormon, and also as one tries to take account of the Mormon (or any faith's) past. Both my professional study and my continuing attempts to conform my private life to the requirements of the scriptures have led me to this awareness. I have reconciled many of these difficulties, not reconciled others, and have suspended judgment on certain of them. Most are explicable if one approaches them not from the perspective that the Church is essentially divine, marred only by the weaknesses of human administrators, but rather that the Church on earth consists entirely of human beings (with all of their limitations) who are trying to respond to the divine with which they have been touched. The distinction is crucial, for the second conception is an inversion of the first. In any case, I believe that to explore issues of Mormon theology and history is entirely appropriate for those who feel the inclination; I do. But since my faith lies essentially on other grounds, since other more appropriate forums exist for technical theological and historical explorations, and since in any case space does not allow it, I will not be dealing with these issues here. With that preface, I offer fifteen thoughts.

III

1. *I exist.* History has seen the rise of philosophic schools of considerable influence which have denied that human beings can be certain of *anything.* Naturally, other philosophers have opposed them. Thus, in the seventeenth century René Descartes insisted that mortal knowledge can begin here: "I think, therefore I am." Augustine anticipated his logic by a millennium: "Who doubts that he lives and thinks?...For if he doubts, he lives." Although psychological objections could be raised, the logic is not without merit.

Still, like most human beings, I feel no need to depend on this kind of thinking, and the fact that I do not is relevant to my religious faith. I believe that I exist primarily by means that are more direct than sheer logic could demonstrate. I *experience* my existence—by direct, intuitive awareness. I feel no pressing need for an exterior revelation, or for a logic outside of my own consciousness, to convince myself of the fact. Certainly this involves a modest faith in my "sense of awareness," for perceptions are fallible. Yet I find that I am cheerfully willing to take that small step of faith; doing so does not feel like a frightening, Kierkegaardian "leap." Thus, by a combination of faith, "direct awareness," and logic, I believe that I exist.

2. *God exists.* Over the centuries a number of arguments have been formulated which attempt to prove or to disprove God's existence. However, it is notoriously true that these arguments tend to convince only those who are already predisposed to belief or to disbelief. Rational persuasion simply does not seem to be crucial in this arena.

Nevertheless, even from the modest vantage of logic I have a strong belief in God, while knowing that such logic is not always cogent for others. Since I believe that I exist, I believe that I got here somehow—and I sense a personal, higher intelligence behind that fact. I do not believe that theories which attempt to account for the universe while omitting God's existence can bear the full weight of reality. Although I allow for the evolving nature of things, and while I recognize the "cruelties of nature," I find that when I contemplate the beauty and intelligence displayed almost everywhere in the world, particularly as manifest in another human face, I find it altogether more natural to believe that these wonders reflect the presence of an unseen creative intelligence than to believe that they originated by non-intelligent forces.

Again, however, experience and instinct seem prior to logic as the genuine base of my faith. I believe because I want to believe. Yet this does not feel like Freud's description of "wish-fulfillment." It feels, instead, *natural*—like breathing.

Though I was brought up to believe in God by godly parents, I have had many opportunities to test this belief. I have tried to imagine God's absence; I have read books on both sides of the issue; I have sometimes felt forsaken by God; and I have observed at close hand the evils and suffering of this world. Yet my simple trust in God's being remains firm.

I do not wish to imply that it is absolute. Over the years I have heard a number of people declare their faith in terms such as these: "If I stood in God's presence tomorrow and He were to embrace me with tears of joy, no more would I know then than I know now that He lives and loves me." That statement contrasts with my own faith (though I do not discount its possibility for others). My belief in God does admit of degrees, and if tomorrow I stood in His presence and were embraced by Him, I would know then in a way that I now do not.

But even though I am aware that I want to believe, even though I am suspicious of states of mind that sometimes cloud my perceptions, and even though I am not a mystic by nature, I believe that I have felt God's influence. I have been comforted and healed and directed by this God. He has reassured me at crucial junctures in my life. I do not understand Him well, but I believe that He has held my hand.

3. *The world and I have purpose.* Since I exist and since I believe that God sent me here, I am comfortable in the trust that He did so with wise and useful intent. Though I have had occasions to doubt, I have a resilient faith in the worth of human existence.

4. *But I am ignorant, and existence on earth bewilders.* Life bubbles about me in confusing variety. It frightens; should I be petrified? It is beautiful; should I be awe-struck? It is contradictory; should I refuse to participate?

5. My ignorance notwithstanding, *I find that I am nevertheless equipped with tools for learning.* For example, I possess a moral sense, and I recognize it as deeper than the particular form impressed upon it by parents and teachers. I have the ability, within limits, to choose. I have a growth impulse. I am given memory, intuition, and reason. Perhaps the heavens whisper to me. I can see and hear and touch and taste and smell. I possess a "homing" instinct: there are things to which I am drawn and things by which I am repelled. I have fears: as I mature, I am able tentatively to distinguish some as healthy and natural, others as pathologic or destructive. Given these tools, I gradually learn and make decisions. I begin to "be"—more and more, in deeper and higher ways. I think, feel, respond, and act.

6. As I develop, I am taught much: "Be nice." "Be good." Values. Incidentals. Which church is "true." "Don't swear." Communists are bad.

My teachers may be wiser than I, but they are also passers of the cultural torch. I inherit their culture. As I grow, I respond to it. Parts of it I will disavow, parts of it I will consciously embrace. Still other parts I may outflank, rearrange, enlarge, or ignore. But I will not escape my culture. I assume it. I *breathe* it. Yet all this must be acknowledged by the God who sent me here. "Culture" may be an ambiguous blessing, but it is inescapable and necessary to human existence.

7. As my life unfolds, I question things. I do so by the very nature of my being. What is "goodness"? How does "niceness" relate to other virtues? Was Nietzsche's ethic more realistic than that of Jesus? Which church *is* true? Or is the question absurd? I have known men that I hold as prophets to swear, and a few of my most thoughtful friends are Marxists. *I adjust and restructure my reality and value systems, perhaps many times.*

8. *I learn universality.* Perhaps I learn it painfully. Whatever I am to make of this life, all human beings are in it

together. Other persons and other cultures must be valued by God; surely they matter no less than I. Yet their beliefs and values in some ways conflict with mine. I must deal with this. I have a great bias toward my own local culture, but I become increasingly suspicious of it as I make contact with the wider world. I grow wary of such terms as "chosen people." I begin to understand that genuine truth may have many vantages. My home town is less unique in God's eyes than I had assumed. *I learn and assimilate relativism.*

9. The relativism grows in direct proportion to my knowledge. Life is unfathomably complex. There is pain and joy, mind and body, creation and procreation. There is time and space, black holes and quasars, truth, deception, and sin. There is meaning—and its absence; there is unity—and estrangement; there is existence—and there is death.

I am left with the same queries with which, in pre-articulate form, I began this life: What *is*? What *matters*? How ought I respond to all of this? What does God intend for me? How am I to conquer the alienation I feel within, the alienation from God and self and others? At length a question emerges around which I must shape my faith, indeed, around which I must shape my being. The question is this: *Amid the complexities of human existence, how am I to live with meaning, integration, and authenticity?*

10. A brave few have dared proffer answers to this question, sometimes with substantial insight. Some have thought that science is the key, or at least that no higher knowledge than that accessible through science is possible. Freud, for instance, was sure that it would be "an illusion...to suppose that what science cannot give us we can get elsewhere."[4] Today, however, philosophers of science would regard that as a naive assertion of an earlier era, and no longer defensible. Indeed, many contemporary philosophers and scientists are rediscovering an elemental fact that was temporarily obscured by the eighteenth-century Enlightenment and the exciting scientific revolution that has flourished in its wake. It is again becoming evident that the "certainties" of science are not so certain; the advances in mortal knowledge are impressive only against the backdrop of basic existential

ignorance; the celebrated powers of human intelligence invite, before all else, a profound modesty. As one thoughtful writer has recently put it: "The culmination of a liberal-arts education ought to include, among other matters, the news that we do not understand a flea, much less the making of a thought."[5] At least officially, science is an empirical *method.* Its empiricism, though essential in its place, restricts itself by definition to ways of knowing that are infinitely too crude to adequately address the question, "How do I live with meaning and authenticity?" The findings of science must inform but can never give or be the final answer. For me, as for the Modernist leader Harry Fosdick earlier in this century, it is something of an embarrassment that our society has "sometimes gotten so low that we talked as though the highest compliment that could be paid to God was that a few scientists believed in Him."

Some responses to my question are even more inadequate than the claims of science (inadequate, that is, as answers to my question). For example, I remember sitting in a graduate ethics class in Boston and listening with fascination to an articulate woman argue, "Sometimes I think that the only hope we have left [on earth] is Feminism." This type of answer is fractional even in its most dignified form. I must explore and transcend my own bigotries, certainly, but this cannot pass as my ultimate end in life.

Other answers are mutually competitive and contradictory, though perhaps not mutually exclusive. The religious or quasi-religious claims of the world's great faiths and of certain philosophical systems are of this sort.

Among the religious philosophies of the world, I can discover no completely universal answer to my question, "How am I to live with meaning and authenticity?" However, the three responses that seem to come nearest are these: *human beings are invited to love, to render service to their fellows, and to pursue the acquisition of knowledge.* Though I do not believe these constitute a complete answer to my question, and while I feel no obligation to make my private faith a kind of "lowest common denominator" among all the world's religions, I nevertheless take these near-universal responses seriously. These three answers to my question resonate within; they "feel" true instinctively, like worthy answers. Numerous prophetic figures have given varying emphases to these goals and have themselves pursued them with varying degrees of success.

Now, through all of the conflicting claims and bewildering confusion on the planet earth, *one known thing completely captures my soul and imagination as an actual, historical incarnation of "meaningful and authentic existence"—and that "thing" is Christ*. To me, Christ represents a complete manifestation of love, of the will to serve, and of wisdom. By a combination of faith and reason and direct intuition of "the Good," I find that I have a deep and joyful awareness of Christ alone as both authoritative embodiment and authoritative articulator of the meaning of authenticity.

"What manner of man ought I to be?" Like Him—in courage, in intelligence, in morality, spirituality, and love. By His own claim He serves not only as the revelation of what I ought to be, but also as the revelation of what God's essence is, thus embodying a literal at-one-ment of the divine and human natures. He showed submission at all costs to His understanding of the divine will. He faced fully the tragic element in human existence, while at the same time revealing the majesty of human possibility. "The potential evil of a human is of such a depth that the Son of God died in the flesh to confront it; the potential good of a human is of such a height that the Son of God lived in the flesh to reveal it."[6]

I identify with Dostoevski's perception of the meaning of Christ. In 1858, from his agonized exile in Siberia, Dostoevski penned a letter to Mme. Natalya Fonvizina:

> I will tell you that I am a child of the century, a child of disbelief and doubt. I am that today and will remain so until the grave. How much terrible torture this thirst for faith has cost me and costs me even now, which is all the stronger in my soul the more arguments I can find against it. And yet, God sends me sometimes instants when I am completely calm;

> at those instants I love and I feel loved by others, and it is at these instants that I have shaped for myself a Credo where everything is clear and sacred for me. This Credo is very simple, here it is: to believe that nothing is more beautiful, profound, sympathetic, reasonable, manly and more perfect than Christ; and I tell myself with a jealous love not only that there is nothing but that there cannot be anything higher. Even more, if someone proved to me that Christ is outside the truth, and that *in reality* the truth were outside of Christ, then I should prefer to remain with Christ rather than with the truth.[7]

Without doubt we could engage in an interesting discussion of Dostoevski's last statement, but that conversation would be complex and is unnecessary here. My point is simply that it is possible to recognize, like Dostoevski did, the unique, divine qualities of light and excellence that emanate from the figure of Christ. And I believe this recognition can emerge not merely in the interest of protecting some previously occupied theological turf, but because one is genuinely searching for a legitimate ground of existence. Futhermore, I believe that this recoginition can and ought to come not only from the rational intellect, but also from something more basic and direct. Intuition? *Spiritual* intuition? Whatever one calls the medium, Franz Kafka recognized the medium's message when he warned, in characteristically disconcerting style, that one may not wish to look too closely at Jesus, "that abyss of light," lest one "fall in." The light that issues from the Christ, whether considered from the angle of His life and teachings or from that of His death and resurrection, is magnetic.

And this unique manifestation of divine excellence, worthy of our worship, is clearly discernible in Jesus despite the imperfect filter of the New Testament documents and other scriptures. As even the agnostic Will Durant was willing to observe:

> That a few simple men [the writers of the New Testament] should in one generation have invented so powerful and appealing a personality, so lofty an ethic and so inspiring a vision of human brotherhood [as Jesus did], would be a miracle far more incredible than any recorded in the Gospels. After two centuries of Higher Criticism the outlines of the life, character, and teaching of Christ remain reasonably clear, and constitute the most fascinating feature in the history of Western man.[8]

Of course, I have come to believe other things about Jesus Christ, things about His grace, about the nature of His atonement, about His relationship to God. But these beliefs lie beyond the scope of my topic. All I wish to convey here is the process by which I began, in my adult years, to reaffirm Christ as an object worthy of faith and worship.

11. Given the universality of the human situation, *I could choose to live more or less authentically with or without a belief in Christ*. That is, Hindus and atheists lead lives of varying degrees of nobility and meaningfulness, just as Christians do. Moreover, I know of no completely satisfying solution to a difficult fact (though Mormonism suggests some): all persons do not have real access to knowledge of Christ. But the fact that I do not have all the answers has not altered my faith in Him, nor my belief that He is the fullest embodiment of an authentic response to "the human predicament," nor my belief that every person who *has* had the opportunity to know of Him, and thereafter chooses to follow Him, is better off with the light of His image.

12. Given my faith in Christ, *I nevertheless could live more or less authentically with or without an organized church*. This, I think, is self-evident. Joseph Smith's own family for long periods chose to remain nondenominational Christians. Yet I have come to believe that for most of the people most of the time (perhaps all of the people most of the time) it is better to belong than not to belong to an organized (Christian) church.

I recognize that this is a large assertion, for the institutionalization of *anything* brings with it certain potential liabilities, because of the very nature of institutions. In any organized church, for example, (just as in any secular organization) there may develop unseemly pressures to conform to a misconceived "orthodoxy." There may develop an unspoken etiquette, implying that one may rarely talk in public about what he actually feels or thinks, but only about what he *ought* to feel or think—thereby straining "authenticity." As in any organization, unnecessary and unhelpful restrictions of autonomy may accrue. There may be complacency or exasperating bureaucratic entanglements. Moreover, formal, institutionalized religion may sometimes function as an ironic, distracting buffer between God and His worshippers; the focus may unconsciously shift from "serving God and man" to "doing things correctly." One will inevitably witness occasional instances of pettiness, unfairness, distasteful personalities—"people problems." Since such difficulties will exist in any large organization that involves human beings, one may therefore be tempted at times to live one's religion apart from other persons, in the peace of solitude.

The profound error in this course of action is demonstrated by the Savior's example. Jesus did not choose to remain above and apart from human beings. Instead, He condescended to our condition in order to heal, teach, and serve us. Indeed, it was precisely in the midst of our imperfections that He found opportunity to accomplish His redeeming work.

With modest effort, after all, one can largely avoid letting a church become a buffer between oneself and God. And with a little strength of character one need only believe what he or she believes. Moreover, some of the "problems" of religious organizations are themselves ultimately a part of the answer to my central question—"How do I live with meaning and authenticity?" Indeed, "people problems," not sanitized isolation, are precisely what genuine disciples of Jesus are invited to engage. Anyone (including a robot) can unthinkingly conform, and anyone (including a dog) can rebel and withdraw. The more difficult and worthy accomplishment lies in the Way of Jesus—in meek, but courageous service, in constructive interaction with God's children.

In extended isolation from the worshipping community one is especially susceptible to conceit, to forgetting how much one may learn from other human beings, whatever their station. Apart from the congregation, one has radically fewer opportunities to serve. One's ability to love becomes abstract, remote from the life-giving power of real human contact. One's sense of responsibility grows constricted, academic, emasculated. In this isolation one is in danger of losing a sharp awareness of collective sin, of group power, and of the resources of community ritual. It is clear that *love, service, and the acquisition of knowledge are better worked out in regular contact with a community to which one feels responsible than in comfortable, unadulterated solitude.*

13. *Yet I could live more or less authentically in most of the churches.* So which Christian church? For me, the answer to that question is The Church of Jesus Christ of Latter-day Saints. I really do believe that Joseph Smith was called of God and that the world would be blessed to hear the Mormon message. I believe the Church to be uniquely "true"—that is, that it possesses certain divinely framed resources which are singularly well suited to foster love, service, and the guided pursuit of the most important knowledge.

Nevertheless, I am aware that Latter-day Saints have no monopoly on truth and goodness. I no longer believe, as I may have assumed in my youth, that the planet earth is little more than a cumbersome footnote to Mormonism. Experience and the prophets have amended some of my former preconceptions. I am pleased that as a member of the Church I am invited to seek after anything that is virtuous, lovely, or of good report, whatever its source. The Book of Mormon, among other things, has taught me that God is God to all of His children, not just to those of my faith. Nephi, for example, condemns a narrow, self-satisfied posture that is unanxious to welcome God's word wherever it might surface. "Know ye not that there are more nations than one?" he asks.

> Know ye not that I, the Lord your God, have created all men, and that I remember those who are upon the isles of the sea; and that I rule in the heavens above and in the earth beneath; and I bring forth my word unto the children of men, yea, even upon all the nations of the earth?...I command all men, both in the east and in the west, and in the north, and in the south, and in the islands of the sea, that they shall write the words which I speak....I shall speak unto the Jews...and I shall also speak unto the Nephites...and I shall also speak unto the other tribes of the house of Israel...and I shall also speak unto all nations of the earth....[9]

I have come to understand that Joseph Smith's expression of the Lord's mind to the effect that the restored Church is "the only true and living church upon the face of the whole earth, with which I, the Lord, am well pleased,"[10] must be balanced and integrated with other statements of the Lord through the prophets. For example, the First Presidency has officially observed that such great religious and philosophical leaders of the world as Mohammed, Confucius, the Reformers, Socrates, Plato, and others received God's light. "Moral truths were given to them by God to enlighten whole nations. . . ."[11] The Doctrine and Covenants similarly asserts that God works not only through prophets, but also through secular leaders, such as America's founding fathers.

None of this, of course, is a threat to the unique role and stature of The Church of Jesus Christ. It simply reinforces the obvious notion that God loves all people and influences them through many channels. I have come to see that as a Latter-day Saint I can allow the term "chosen people" to have no room for an elitist tinge. The deepest meaning of this difficult term is revealed for me in the image of the Christ who washed the feet of His disciples. Perhaps we are a people chosen to serve people.

14. *But why the Mormon Church?* As I have indicated, I

am the child of LDS parents. This will not sound to anyone else like a convincing reason to remain a Mormon; it simply explains my early orientation. Yet, as with my faith in God, I have had many opportunities to test my faith in the Church. As I have matured and experienced the world, I have slowly and increasingly come to recognize the depth of the advantages of my Mormon-nurtured upbringing.

I am sure that I could not find a more apt analogy for the way my faith has grown than the famous one by Alma in the Book of Mormon comparing faith to a nourished seed. As a matter of fact, the overall structure of my faith seems closer to the pattern carefully laid out by Alma (Alma 32:21-43) than it does to the now current popular interpretation of the later prophet, Moroni (Moroni 10:3-6). The words of the two inspired men are not necessarily in conflict. Indeed, Moroni's promise has been fulfilled for me by the very process Alma describes. But the two passages may also represent two different kinds of experience; as commonly understood, they are at least distinct, one from the other. When I have prayerfully and diligently been engaged in magnifying the assignments I have accepted in the Church, when I have striven to transcend the superficial or conventional approaches to those assignments that sometimes have mired me, when I have earnestly and consistently wrestled with the scriptures, and when I have actively lived rather than merely analyzed passively the various principles of the gospel, I have found that there is a sense of growth, "aliveness," and inspiration—indeed, a sense of meaning and authenticity—that is absent when I do not do those things. This process has proceeded so far as to yield *knowledge* in some areas; certain principles of the gospel have assumed a life of their own.

Moreover, I have participated in bishoprics and quorum presidencies when wisdom beyond our own was given and applied, with results that altered lives for the better. To cite a small and impersonal example, I remember when as a college student in Ogden, Utah, my roommate and life-long friend, who was also the man to whom I served as counselor in the elders quorum presidency, unexpectedly stood in the middle of a quorum meeting to speak. I was seated next to him. As he rose, he leaned in my direction, slowly shook his head, and whispered under his breath, "I don't know why I'm doing this." He then proceeded to ask the quorum if there was an "Adult Aaronic" brother present who would like to participate in an ordinance we were about to perform. A man near the back of the room immediately stood and came forward. For some reason he had been waiting that morning for just such an invitation. I was subsequently assigned as a home teaching companion to this brother, whom I came to know well. I can verify that a life had been changed, partly by this small bit of inspiration. Another example is my own partriarchal blessing, whose accuracy and insight cannot, in my case, be dismissed in the same way that vague astrological predictions can be dismissed. I submit such private and modest examples not because they are particularly dramatic and calculated to convince, but precisely because they are simple and widely accessible.

I have known people who have rejected the Church because they have overestimated its nature and purpose, and have grown disappointed when the Church did not satisfy the functions that they have privately imposed on it. Is it possible to overestimate the Church if it truly derives from God? In my judgment, yes. Some have misunderstood the Church as an end to be served for its own sake, which is in essence a kind of idolatry. The Church exists, instead, as an *instrument* through which together we may serve God and His children. I have heard others express their disappointment by making the unremarkable observation that, "I don't get anything out of it anymore." Though it is certain that most Latter-day Saints could strive more earnestly to reach for the profundities that are accessible through the gospel, it seems to me that such comments as "I don't get anything out of it anymore" in part reflect a loss of vision on the part of the speaker. When Church members assemble, the idea is at least as much to *give* as to "get," to contribute as to be spoon fed.

It is even more common, however, for people to underestimate the blessings of the Church. For some, this is because they have never had or truly embraced the opportunity to participate in them. Others, though, have felt the blessings of the Church, but have for diverse reasons become unappreciative or condescending, then apathetic, and finally blind to these blessings. This is tragic, because the Church's resources are many and fundamental.

In my life as a Latter-day Saint, I have been directed, edified, and given solace by scriptures to which all do not enjoy access. I have been inspired by the lives and counsel of prophets who have pointed me to Christ. I have been loved and taught by bishops and teachers who had plenty of other things to occupy their time, whose efforts were motivated simply by a desire to serve, to fulfill their voluntarily accepted Church responsibilities.

Notwithstanding the inevitable foibles of Church administrators (usually acknowledged by the administrators themselves) and despite my belief that the priesthood and the Church will function somewhat differently in the future (just as they have in the past), I detect God's involvement in the unique polity of the Church. I sense great wisdom in a strong, hierarchical, prophetic leadership. Though this leadership may occasionally insist on policies with which I take exception, sometimes firmly, I am aware that their position is delicate and difficult; I remain loyal to them and am grateful for their generous, able service. This strong central leadership conserves order, protects sacred ritual, preserves the wisdom of tradition and experience, and offers inspired guidance that has many times proved a blessing to my life.

What is especially distinctive about Mormon polity, however, is the fact that this strong, prophetic leadership works so well in rare—unique—combination with what is essentially the Church's lay orientation: its local, congregational focus, and the personal responsibility felt by each of its involved members. For example—and though we do not accomplish the task so well as we might—many organizations even much smaller than the Church stand all amazed that such things as lay "home teaching" and "visiting teaching" are actualities. I am impressed that very busy individuals whom I do not necessarily know well will assume the difficult responsibility of establishing regular contact with my family, standing ready to serve them. Similarly, I recognize important truths and blessings in the assignment I have accepted to home teach persons with whom I might not otherwise naturally associate. The effort to penetrate "social distance" and superficial politeness has humbled and bettered me.[12]

I am happy that I was not raised with the implied and deadening delusion that a professional clergyman can vicariously live my religion for me, while I go blithely about my "real business." I am thankful that while the Church normally enforces no creeds, as Joseph Smith insisted it does not, yet it has not been allowed to lose its sense of direction and purpose, like so many other well-meaning, broad-minded faiths. I love Mormonism's vitality, its positive acceptance of life. I appreciate its inspired insights into the importance of the physical realm, the relation of the physical to the spiritual, and the temporal to the eternal.

I think that even many believing Mormons may not be aware how distinctive and important much of their theology is. To give a philosophic parallel, the famous Friedrich Nietzsche once declared it to be his goal to condense what the greatest thinkers had taken volumes to write into a mere ten pages, "nay, into ten lines." Now if a thoughtful person were to consider the monumental accomplishment that such an ambition, if it were successful, would imply, such a person might also begin to comprehend something of the magnitude of the inspired wisdom that has been compressed into a passage like Moses 1:39 in the Pearl of Great Price: "For behold, this is my work and my glory—to bring to pass the immortality and eternal life of man." To so define God's primary work in the universe (in twenty words!) is a cosmically broad and important assertion. Yet the Mormon scriptures are full of such things.

The restored gospel contains the most satisfying and inspiring perspectives on the nature of God and humans, their relations, the meaning of Christ, and the very purpose of human existence. I intuit truth in Joseph Smith's pronouncements concerning the self-existent, eternal nature of intelligence and certain physical and metaphysical laws. Faith in such truths enables me to trust in God despite the evil and suffering I see all about me.

Although expressions of LDS theology sometimes come out sounding as though the speaker is advocating faith in middle class American culture, I nevertheless discern—beneath the veneer of popular conservatism—genuine, inspired insight in the Church's stance on the redemptive, creative role of marriage and family. Likewise, I find genuine worth in the efforts the Church makes to support those institutions. I am guided by the gospel's insistence on the sacred nature of all aspects of life, and by the demand of total consecration, without which Joseph taught that sufficient power toward salvation cannot be generated.

For reasons that I cannot develop here, I think that Mormon theology is uniquely successful at holding together the concepts of individual freedom (over which a war was reportedly waged in Heaven) and community cohesion (Zion, marriage and family, "We cannot be made perfect without [the dead] nor they without us...," etc.). By contrast, the successful union of individual freedom (with the atomization of society that it tends to foster) and social cohesion (with the infringements on personal freedom that it breeds) eludes humanity generally, and this failure prevents profound understanding between large portions of the eastern and western hemispheres.

The Church of Jesus Christ of Latter-day Saints is not a "perfect" church, if by that one means a church in which no changes could be profitably made (they are being made all the time), or a church without problems and tensions. No organization that involves human beings could be perfect in that sense. But I find God's inspiration in the Church. Mormonism has produced a set of symbols, a theology, and a practical structure that provides a wonderful mechanism through which I can respond authentically and meaningfully to mortal life, and through which I have hope of immortal life. I do not believe the Church has a monopolistic hold on truth in some absolute sense; the scriptures themselves deny that. But I do believe that its power and worth far transcend Joseph Smith's native wisdom. I have served in the Church, and while I have served I have experienced first-hand God's inspiration. The Lord's influence is here; I believe the Church to be uniquely true.

15. In Lewis Carroll's *Alice in Wonderland*, the White Queen told Alice, "I'm just one-hundred and one, five months and a day." Alice replied, "I can't believe *that*!" Said the Queen, pityingly, "Can't you? Try again: draw a long breath, and shut your eyes." I would suggest that the White Queen's idea of faith as self-hypnosis is not the sort of faith the Lord had in mind when He invited us to "be believing." The Lord, I imagine, wants teachability, openness, and intelligent trust—not gullibility. I cannot think that God sent me to this world to determine my eternal "salvation" or "damnation" on the basis of a correct or false guess—arrived at either by rational ability or by a kind of spiritualized "blind man's bluff"—about the truthfulness of, say, the gold plates and the angel Moroni. I do not believe the crucial issue is finally, "Will I be sitting in the correct pew when the archangel sounds his trump?" Rather, I believe God sent me to earth to respond freely, with faith, to the conditions of a sometimes dark and difficult world. My choices here can either promote ("save") or inhibit ("damn") my progress and well-being. I believe my highest response to these conditions is to learn something about myself, to learn to love blindly, to serve my fellow beings, to acquire a kind of wisdom that is apparently best communicated through human experience. I feel as though I am invited by a spirit above me to follow what light I am given, to live productively and authentically, with honor and vigor. I further believe that the most profound expression of the honor and vigor that I seek is manifest in the figure of Jesus Christ. I yearn to emulate and grow closer to Him and am reverently grateful to whoever and whatever fosters that end. It is precisely for these reasons that the Church was founded. As Paul put it, Christ gave apostles, prophets, and other officers of the Church for the perfection of, ministering to, and edification of the members of "the body of Christ," to promote a unity of the faith, that we may "grow up into [Christ] in all things."[13]

My religious tenets operate at two distinct levels: that of

literal truth and that of metaphorical truth. I *believe* that God, Christ, and the Church are literally "true," yet I do not have direct access to these things in the ordinary sense of the term. Rather, I experience them intuitively, spiritually, "through a glass darkly." I *know*, however, that they are true metaphorically, for they function successfully in my everyday life. This combination of believing and knowing (both of which are relative terms) amounts to a trust that I call my faith. I readily acknowledge that my faith *is* a faith; it is not a perfect knowledge. Indeed, I am content that it is so. The informed trust that comes with faith can, if it is genuine and well placed, produce a strength and a goodness that could not grow from literal, absolute knowledge. An earthly example is the power and peace that is a byproduct of a friendship or marriage based on love and trust (faith) rather than on a constant, empirical, and absolute knowledge that theoretically would verify that the friend or spouse is being "true." Although there are in fact such things as unworthy friends or disloyal spouses, it is nevertheless impossible to build a healthy friendship or marriage without a deep and lively faith.

I am painfully aware that my conceptions are human, finite, hopelessly crude. If I should pass to another world and discover the limitations of my spiritual framework, I shall be grateful but unashamed. My belief will still have been authentic. I will have attempted to live in "good faith," trying to respond to what light I had, seeking to shed by the grace of God the folly of my ways.

Notes

1. Quoted in Laurel Ulrich, *A Beginner's Boston* (Boston: Cambridge Ward, The Church of Jesus Christ of Latter-day Saints, 1973), p. 32.

2. Henry Fielding, *The History of Tom Jones* (London: George G. Harrap & Co., Ltd., 1925), p. 96.

3. *History of the Church of Jesus Christ of Latter-day Saints* (Salt Lake City: The Deseret Book Company, 1967 reprint), III: 381, 380.

4. Sigmund Freud, *The Future of An Illusion*, trans. and

ed. James Strachey (New York: W.W Norton and Co., 1961), p. 56.

5. The entire essay by Lewis Thomas, "On the Uncertainty of Science," *Harvard Magazine*, Sept.-Oct. 1980, is worth consulting. Another interesting source on the limitations of current science which is easily available to general readers is *The Road Less Traveled* by the psychiatrist M. Scott Peck (New York: Simon and Schuster, Inc., 1976).

6. Philip L. Barlow, "Unorthodox Orthodoxy: The Idea of Deification in Christian History," *Sunstone* 8.5 (1983): 13-18.

7. *New York Times*, 1 Jan. 1984, Book Review section, p. 33.

8. Will Durant, *The Story of Civilization*, Vol. III: *Caesar and Christ* (New York: Simon and Schuster, Inc., 1944), p. 557.

9. II Nephi 29: 7,11,12.

10. D&C 1:30.

11. Official statement of the First Presidency, Feb. 15, 1978.

12. The point that the Church's distinctive structure and radical lay orientation is uniquely effective in promoting the process of redemption is well developed in Eugene England's essay, "Why the Church is as True as the Gospel," *Sunstone* 10.10 (1986): 30-36.

13. Ephesians 4:11-15.

20

Bruce W. Young

The Miracle Of Faith, The Miracle Of Love: Some Personal Reflections

Bruce Young is the father of two children and husband to Margaret Blair Young. Those facts are significant not only in their own right, but because in the essay below he discovers (with biblical precedent) a profound analogy between the religious life and the experience of marriage and family. Dr. Young was educated at BYU, Columbia, and Harvard. He has published articles on a number of subjects including Shakespeare, on whom he is an expert. He teaches English literature and literary criticism at Brigham Young University. Brother Young's Church experience is broad and includes service as a teacher and in a bishopric.

I start this essay concerned that my title may keep some readers from reading what I have to say. Seeing the word "miracle" and the seeming equation of "faith" and "love," some of those I most want to reach may quickly assume that this is an essay on "faith as wish-fulfillment" or "faith, love, and bliss in five easy steps." And so I want to emphasize at the outset that I do not see either faith or love as easy. In fact, my "personal reflections," as I call them, include the history of my difficulties in accepting love and exercising faith, two difficulties I believe to be closely related. But I want to stick with the word "miracle," even with the misunderstandings it may provoke, because it expresses what I believe to be a vital truth: that faith and love are means by which we may draw on and exercise divine powers, including the power of personal transformation. The word "miracle" also suggests to me that faith and love, though beyond our present ability fully to understand, can become beautifully and intensely real to those who experience them. Yet they and their fruits are so different from the grim routine (so-called) of everyday, that it is the inclination of almost everyone—even of those who see and know the fruits—to question the evidence of their own experience. It is hard to accept as real what may become two of the most powerful realities in our lives.

I will be discussing the role faith and love have played both in my religious life and in my recent courtship and marriage. I am certainly not the first to have seen a profound analogy—indeed, an inescapable link—between these two aspects of life. The Bible speaks of God's relation with His people in the language of marriage. Shakespeare, in *The Winter's Tale*, shows a marriage break apart when a husband cannot believe his wife to be as good and gracious as she seems to be. Before the marriage can be redeemed, he must learn the principle that will guarantee its redemption: First, he is told, "it is required you do awake your faith." Hawthorne wrote several stories demonstrating the destructive power of doubt, whether religious or marital. In one, Young Goodman Brown loses (or thinks he loses) his wife, whose name is Faith, and chooses to live thereafter a life of suspicion and gloom. More recently, Eugene England has applied Michael

Novak's perceptions about marriage to life in the Church. I will be doing much the same thing, but focusing on the nature of faith and on insights peculiar to my own experience.

Getting married has been, for me, a miracle, and the marriage itself continues to be miraculous. For my wife, the marriage has been (so she and her parents tell me) a process of healing and restoration; for me, a process of revelation about myself and of personal change. I say this recognizing that for some of my best friends, including my wife in her previous marriage, things have not turned out happily or well. In fact, for years it was the fear of just such disasters that kept me from getting married. Would I marry the wrong person? Would she eventually—perhaps immediately—stop loving me? I found after falling in love with someone who, unaccountably, was also in love with me, that the fears and anxieties of at least two decades surfaced, and these played on my imagination and feelings with a terrifying intensity, suggesting to me, when I was able to think about it, that I had been resisting marriage, resisting intimacy and love, for years, despite my conscious and sincere protestations that I wanted to be married.

My thesis is that most people are putting up just this kind of resistance to their own happiness, to the possible transformation of their lives, and to their perception of the realities on which the gospel is based. And like me, most have somehow kept themselves from seeing that they are putting up this resistance. They honestly believe they would accept happiness and personal change and evidence for the existence and power of God if it were offered. And so they take the absence of these things from their lives as an indication that such things probably do not exist and that hope and faith directed toward them are futile and illusory.

Shortly before my marriage, still amazed that something so good and real and unbelievable was happening to me, I gave a talk on "how to have good things happen in your life." It might have been called "how to overcome your resistance to your own happiness." The first step, I claimed, is to see and believe in the possibility of good things. Drawing on my difficulties in moving toward marriage, I noted that this first step of seeing and believing is often the most difficult. What I had learned was that for years, without realizing it, I had chosen to see things in such a way as to make marriage impossible. First of all, no mortal woman could possibly have convinced me she was the "right one." It wasn't that I had a list of required talents and character traits. I had given that up some years earlier. Rather, I simply found every woman I met unacceptable because imperfect; there was always one thing or another I felt was not ideal or that I feared I couldn't handle. Even more serious was my perception of myself: Bruce Young, lonely, awkward, socially inept, romantically unappetizing, fated (it seemed) to be forever rejected by women. I had no idea how much self-pity was interwoven into my perceptions. I didn't see that I was choosing to see myself as I did in order to avoid dealing with experiences that frightened me.

My perceptions underwent radical changes near the start of my courtship, but the changes are still ongoing. Somehow those pictures of myself have left traces that keep returning from time to time. But the first changes happened something like this: I let go, for a while, of my great burden of preconceptions, judgments, anticipations, and concerns, and became—in at least one respect—as a little child. I willingly opened myself to what was there before me, specifically to a person named Margaret. I had known her for several months before and had interpreted what I saw and heard with what I thought was a desire to understand and see clearly. But it turned out that I had, in fact, by viewing her through my complicated and overactive mental apparatus, produced an illusion of understanding based on negligible evidence. That mental apparatus, that set of judgments, categorizings, and interpretations, had become a dense, tangled barrier between me and her, keeping me from experiencing her as she was. And, for reasons I now can guess, the judgments I made mostly tended in the direction of seeing her as "not my type": bright, yes, even brilliant—but also too high-strung, confusing, leapingly intuitive. I later found that, though some of these perceptions were accurate in part, by my resistance to her I was helping to create the very nervousness and confusion that bothered me. When I opened myself to her, I experienced something akin to revelation: this person, this woman, was someone I felt I recognized. I felt so close to her, once I dropped the barriers, that I found it hard to keep from feeling I had always known her. I recognized a deep kinship as if we already had in common a reservoir of shared experiences, perceptions, and values. In the great calmness that came with this recognition, I saw her as someone I could share myself with fully, someone I could love and understand and who could love and understand me.

This rather shocking experience of finding myself in love with someone I had deeply misunderstood led me to some general insights about faith and love. One is that we all create most of our own burdens—worries, fears, anxieties, self-torment, self-pity, self-hatred. These, along with our preconceptions, our entrenched notions about how things are and how they must be, set up barriers between us and the world outside ourselves. These barriers keep us from seeing and experiencing the world as it is. They keep us from experiencing the greatest of realities—other persons, including the mortals around us and others we do not (in the usual order of things) see with our physical eyes, but whose existence we can know of, whose personal presence we may in some instances know and feel, if we let ourselves. On the day I was married I felt such a presence as distinctly as I ever have, and my nervousness temporarily dissolved as I became aware of the great love that was, and had been for some months, extended toward me by many, on both sides of the veil. I have become convinced that such love is constantly available to us, but that we usually do our best to keep it out. Besides the love of friends and relatives, living and dead, I have come to know in some measure the personal reality of our heavenly Father and of Jesus Christ, two beings whose love for us is unwavering. That love is always there for us to experience, and it can have a transforming effect on us if we will open ourselves to it and not allow our fears and preconceptions to shut it out.

We have been invited to take off our burdens, including those of fear and self-doubt, and come to one who can take them from us: "Come unto me," said Jesus, "all ye that labor and are heavy laden and I will give you rest. Take my yoke upon you and learn of me. For my yoke is easy and my burden is light, and ye shall find rest unto your souls" (Matthew 11:28). The scriptures describe this process of unburdening when they say, "Become as a little child," meek, submissive, open, ignorant, willing to receive and experience, freed from preconceptions and judgments, putting off the natural man in order to yield to the enticings of the Holy Spirit (see Mosiah 3:18-19). For adults, of course, this state does not come automatically. "Yielding" is often a painful, long-term process requiring us to take responsibility for the confusion, fears, and resentment we feel, realizing they are largely of our own making, and give them up—a hard thing for all of us who want to cling to everything we have created.

Somehow I managed to achieve this kind of unburdening, at least for a time, and opened my eyes in a way they had not been opened before. But the next step I faced—trusting in the goodness and reality of what I saw with those opened eyes—again proved exceptionally hard for me. I wanted certainty, but had long found it difficult to trust my feelings about the truth or goodness of what I experienced. And so I had developed the habit of thinking things out in intricate, endless detail. I suffered from the illusion that a system of mental images, of notations on the scroll of my brain, carefully created and held consciously before my mental eyes, connected and organized and manipulated in every way I could imagine, was the best or perhaps the only way to attain certainty about a thing. I eventually saw that I was "thinking things out" mainly as a way of delaying the inevitable final step of choice—Should I give this paper an A or a B? Should I pick up the phone and make a call? Should I say to someone, "I love you"? I learned, and am still learning, that all of my choices must finally be based on the trust I am willing to put in my perceptions and feelings. Ideas, mental images, and logical connections all can serve a useful purpose. But the mind preoccupied with its own ideas and filled with preconceptions and ready-made decisions, with narrow notions about what is and what is not, will often be blind to realities that are obviously and immediately present. I am convinced—and experience has repeatedly confirmed my conviction—that true certainty comes, not from mental system-spinning, but from learning to identify and trust those feelings and insights that are worthy of trust.

Indeed, I found "thinking things out" utterly inadequate in my progress toward marriage. Thinking helped clarify a few things; it helped retrieve a few past insights when I needed them. But for the most part I found "knowledge" to have a character quite different from what I was accustomed to. I found myself having to open myself to and experience the reality of another person. That meant recognizing the existence of things other than myself, not only this other person, but the relations—strangely neither wholly inside nor outside of me—developing between us. I found that I needed to trust in and remember the reality of what I was experiencing.

Even then, the analogy of this experience to religious life seemed obvious to me. Like my progress toward marriage, my progress in religious faith has required me to remember and trust in the reality of experiences I do not fully understand. Faith, like love, has had much more to do with knowing persons than with understanding concepts. It has meant learning to hear the voice and feel the personal presence of God and to trust the reality of His voice. After coming to know a mortal woman, I found myself seeing more clearly what might be meant by knowing the voice of the Lord. In both instances, an opening of the heart and mind is required. In Alma's words, we must "awake and arouse [our] faculties" and let the "desire to believe" work in us until we are willing to "give place for a portion" of what the Lord would have us see or hear. Then comes the experience of knowing:

> ...Now, if ye give place, that a seed may be planted in your heart, behold, if it be a true seed, or a good seed, if you do not cast it out by your unbelief, that ye will resist the Spirit of the Lord, behold, it will begin to swell within your breasts; and when you

> feel these swelling motions, ye will begin to say within yourselves—It must needs be that this is a good seed, or that the word is good, for it beginneth to enlarge my soul; yea, it beginneth to enlighten my understanding, yea, it beginneth to be delicious to me. (Alma 32:27-28)

In our experience with God, as in our experience with mortals, it is possible to know that what we have found is not a phantom in the mind, not a desire turned into an illusion, but a reality that the desire to know has given us power to see. Alma goes on to describe this kind of experiential knowledge:

> And now, behold, because ye have tried the experiment, and planted the seed, and it swelleth and sprouteth, and beginneth to grow, ye must needs know that the seed is good....(verse 33)
>
> O then, is not this real? I say unto you, Yea, because it is light; and whatsoever is light, is good, because it is descernible, therefore ye must know that it is good....(verse 35)

I knew that what I was experiencing was real. But the emotion of doubt still surfaced from time to time—not because matters of fact were really in question, but because I found it difficult, with my history of self-questioning and of existential uncertainty, to accept as real what so obviously was real. I was finding it difficult, as the courtship progressed, to sustain the power to see and accept and believe—the power I call "faith." As I went through the ups and downs of confidence, trust, and belief, I came to see that doubt is essentially an emotional state and not necessarily—not usually—a response to real evidence. What sustained me through these ups and downs was the recognition—undeniable despite my feelings of doubt—that what I was seeing and experiencing was good and real.

But however helpful and even necessary this recognition was, the next step—that of *choosing* the good things I had found—did not turn out to be easy. There was still the haunting fear that I might not be choosing the "right" thing. What if someone else, even closer to the ideal than this woman I knew and loved, existed somewhere? What if I was somehow wrong about this woman I thought I knew? I recognized, first of all, the inevitable imperfection in my knowledge, an imperfection characteristic of all mortal knowledge, since we must act now, in the present moment, if we are ever going to act and since we cannot see and know more fully unless we act. I also recognized that I was again trying to find some way of escaping from experiences too good, too beautiful, it seemed, to be true—or at least to be comfortable. And though I could see that what I wanted was good, I feared that somehow I would make the wrong choice and so prove unacceptable to God, who would leave me (I feared) forever existentially abandoned. I was like the fearful servant who hid his talent because he knew his Lord was a hard master. Perhaps I was also like the Saints of Joseph Smith's time who wanted to be told the exact route they should travel for fear of making a wrong choice if they trusted their own judgment. Indeed, as I read the familiar scripture where the Lord tells these Saints to do "as they shall counsel between themselves and me," it came to me like a revelation how similar my situation was to theirs. I too needed to be "anxiously engaged in a good cause" and dare to do things of my "own free will." The promises made to them applied also to me:

> For the power is in them, wherein they are agents unto themselves. And inasmuch as men do good they shall in nowise lose their reward. (D&C 58:25,27-28)

Reading these words, I felt assured, despite my fear and

uncertainty, that as long as I did good—and I knew that this thing, this possible marriage, was good—I would "in no wise lose [my] reward." And I saw also the horror of failing to choose anything, failing to do anything, failing to exercise the power in me to do and create good.

And so I came to see my odyssey as simpler in its overall design than the complicated process I had been making it. It was a matter simply of seeing something good and choosing it: stepping forward in faith to make real what was not yet fully real for me. Because I had to step beyond what I could see with my physical eyes, beyond what already existed and was therefore familiar and comfortable, I was afraid. One reason for the fear was that this process of stepping forward did not leave me fully in control, self-sufficient, safely in charge. It did not feel so much like "making" a thing happen as "letting" it happen, my active role being mostly that of choice, of stepping forward. This process—this stepping forward in faith—seemed to me at the time, and still does, a kind of miracle. Something came to be real which before was only desired, and yet I had no doubt of its reality as it came into being.

Now I have been married for over a year, and I find myself trying with some difficulty to explain truths I thought I understood before marriage. I was not aware then how deeply ingrained my strategies of resistance were. Before marriage I found it beyond my intellectual capacity to imagine myself happily, comfortably married. Sharing my life with another person—a woman, a wife—seemed inconceivably fearful and beyond my ability to cope with. It has turned out to be far easier than I had imagined. I feel comfortable, fulfilled, and confident in my role as husband and father (when I married, I was blessed with a four-year-old as well as a wife). But marriage has also included moments of such agonizing straining of the heartstrings, such humiliation and exposure, that I am not sure I would have wanted to choose marriage if I had known it would bring such moments. Yet I also see that, though I chose freely, I could not have chosen otherwise and still been true to myself. And again I recognize my responsibility for creating the experience I have had. Marriage has brought feelings of happiness and of belonging and completeness greater than any I have had before. But I have continued, for some reason, to resist my own happiness.

Indeed, besides resisting happiness, I have sometimes chosen to make myself and others miserable. Why I should choose to create the very thing I think I want to avoid is hard to understand. But whatever the reasons, I've struggled far more often, both in marriage and before, with fear-fulfillment than wish-fulfillment. Bright fantasies, no matter how luminous, have never proved satisfying for long. But I have always seemed able to make my life miserable and then say to myself, "At least *this* is real." I suspect that everyone has felt the fear of failure, of abandonment, even of personal annihilation or unremitting misery. And for some reason it seems easier to create what we fear and be done with it than to wait in awful suspense until what we fear comes of its own volition.

An example from my marriage: Both my wife and I have been haunted by the fear that we would wake up one morning to discover that our spouse never really loved us after all. I have sometimes acted on this fear by interpreting my wife's moods—her frustration with herself, her physical discomfort, even sometimes her preoccupation with other matters—as disapproval of me. Weakened and disturbed by this "rejection," by the feeling that my inadequacy and unworthiness have been exposed, I have responded with self-pity (which my wife particularly dislikes) or with irritation and gloominess (which usually draw from her responses in kind). And so I create, through my perceived failure, additional evidence for such failure. Again and again I have overreacted to any sign of disapproval because something in me fears that the great depth and solidity of love my wife has offered me must be an illusion. How could anything so good have come into *my* life? Sometimes I even provoke conflict without any excuse at all, simply because I want confirmation for my fears.

I have some guesses as to why I and others sometimes choose misery in this way and especially why people have such difficulty in accepting love. First, we feel unworthy and inadequate. And this feeling is self-perpetuating, for it is impossible for us to become good or happy unless we believe we can. A second reason is that love hurts; happiness hurts. What I mean is that the experiences of love and joy are intense, soul-transforming, and therefore not comfortable. They require some letting go and giving up, and so most people are afraid of them. They expose us to highs and lows too strong, we are afraid, for us to bear. I am reminded of T. S. Eliot's words: "Human kind cannot bear very much reality."

A third reason is that there is something attractive about the idea of being totally self-sufficient and self-contained. It seems safer and easier. If our world is self-created and self-contained, nothing seems beyond our understanding or control. Hence, many of us relate, not to other people, but to our mental images of other people. This tendency also explains, I believe, why so many people have preferred theories about the world to the world itself—have preferred, that is, to develop philosophical systems rather than to step out into the real world, vast and beautiful and terrifying as it is, with all that they do not understand about it, and grow step by step in their understanding. I believe this is also one reason many people have preferred to worship a conceptual God—a God in their minds—rather than the true and living God whose voice, though it pierces to the very center, comes from outside themselves.

A fourth reason for our resistance to love and happiness (and to God and His revelations) is that to open ourselves to these things requires effort and commitment on our part. If I accept love from another person, I know, from the moment I acknowledge the possibility of accepting the love, that I cannot willingly be loved without loving in return. I cannot receive without giving. And in anticipation, the commitment to love can seem uncomfortably binding. The daily effort of love can seem unbearably difficult. Likewise, to accept God's love and the revelation of His desires for us is to see the rightness of responding to His love and being obedient to His revelations. Even if we recognize the transforming effect of a right response, we may feel the commitment to God to be a burden, a restriction of our freedom, a cramping of our ego. In order to be free of this self-created burden, we must do something difficult: we must recognize that this vision of a demanding and immensely weighty future is indeed our own creation and then let go of it. Love never ceases to be demanding, but when freely accepted, it becomes a source of energy and hope, rather than a burdensome and paralyzing weight.

A final reason for our lack of faith, if it can be separated from the rest, is that we are afraid our hopes will be disappointed. We don't want to be fooled, and so we create a life or a way of viewing life that is "fool-proof"—so limited, so empty of vision, that there is nothing to be disillusioned about. Sometimes we even choose to offend those who could be our friends, or we choose to demonstrate our incompetence or irresponsibility, or we choose to imagine a life of intractable pressures, conflicts, and miseries, because we would rather lose everything we can and choose the worst we can imagine than hope for anything and have our hopes disappointed.

What does all of this have to do with religious faith? If we define faith as the power to see things that are real and good and then to have those things become fully real in our lives, then our images of ourselves—often of ourselves as inadequate, unloveable, and ugly—are perhaps the greatest obstacle to our exercising faith. Our relations with mortals and our difficulties accepting love from them do not differ greatly, in their essential character, from our relations with those beyond the veil. We resist love from God, and from others—friends and relatives—who have gone through death before us, for the same reasons we resist love from each other: we are afraid we won't be loved when we are known for what we are; we are unwilling to accept the effort and commitment that come with receiving love; we want to be self-contained and not have to deal with the living and not wholly understood realities we find outside ourselves; we are afraid of being disappointed; and we are afraid of the intensity of love, especially of perfect, divine love. We too often would prefer the illusion of a bleak and miserable "certainty" to difficult and uncertain progress toward real knowledge.

Another striking parallel between marriage and religious experience is the antagonism that too often mars both. In both instances, the antagonism usually springs from fears and dark fantasies which, as they lead to resentment and hostility, create the very evidence they claim to be based on. Having experienced such self-created conflict, I am struck by how closely critics of the Church resemble people upset with their marriage partners. There is, for both the critics and the dissatisfied spouses, the same combination of inexorable logic and essential blindness. Everything they see seems obvious to them, and indeed, even with the heavy role played by imagination, there is usually some evidence that can bear the interpretation they give. But anesthetized to their own faults, hypersensitive to the imperfections of others, they do not see the real and potential splendor in the one (or the many) with whom they are yoked. The dark things they see are too often the products of their own hearts. And the evidence of a spouse's willingness to love and give, like the abundant evidence of God's love and active presence in His Church, is easily ignored or forgotten.

All of us, I suppose, are susceptible to doubts and antagonism of this kind. By our fears and our insistent unbelief we set up barriers through which no knowledge can enter, and we blind ourselves at times to those fragments of knowledge we have received, even when we knew, with all our faculties of heart and mind, that what we were experiencing was real when we received it.

But if we are willing to receive and remember it, there is always an abundance of evidence to sustain our faith, not only in a husband or wife, but in the reality and love of God. The precise sort of evidence will differ from one person to another, but the examples I give here are perhaps representative. First, there are many reliable witnesses, men and women, who have seen, known, and spoken with God and His messengers or who have otherwise witnessed the effects of God's love and power in exceptional ways. Besides the widely known experiences, there are countless less well-known instances, recorded in journals, letters, and elsewhere, of the intervention of immortals in our lives. Many of the accounts I know of are far too precise and straightforward to suffer any real danger of being dismantled by the skeptical intellect. If we have faith—if we have open and willing minds and hearts—we can respond to the truth of such testimonies as these.

Another kind of evidence is that brought by our own experiences: our encounter, for instance, with the power to heal or to be healed or with the power to foresee or to understand beyond our natural understanding. What we call "promptings" can come to have a reliability akin to that of our five senses. Experience can give us the assurance that the influence we feel comes from outside ourselves and is a trustworthy guide. Witness David O. McKay's telling his brethren standing on a ledge inside a volcano, "I feel impressed we should leave this place immediately," moments before the ledge crumbled and fell. My own experience, though it has brought nothing as yet so spectacular, has included times of similar guidance. One that I find particularly impressive, but in ways that are hard for me to convey to anyone else, is the insistent prompting I felt one Sunday morning to accept my future wife's hesitant invitation to a reception at her parents' home, when I knew I would have only ten minutes of a crowded schedule to spare for it. That prompting (which helped lead to a then unimagined courtship) reminded me of nothing so much, even at the time, as the handcart pioneers' bone-deep feeling that they must gather to Utah.

I could describe other incidents, from my own experience and that of others, that might seem more impressive, more compelling as evidence, when viewed from the outside. But once the openness to such evidence is there, some of the quietest experiences can be the most reassuring. I have mentioned here only a handful among the possible sources of assurance. I repeat that what is lacking is not evidence. What is lacking is faith.

Most people are at once attracted to and suspicious of happy endings. I certainly wanted and hoped for a happy marriage. But it seemed to me only an imaginary ideal. It did not fit into my mental category of "the real." I could see no way to connect it with my present experience. I feel much the same way about the celestial world. It sounds beautiful, like some country of the imagination, yet solidly and tangibly real as described by witnesses worthy (I believe) of trust. But its very beauty makes it difficult for me to think of it as really existing. I expect to be somewhat shocked when I enter that world—if the desires of my heart are fulfilled and I am found worthy to do so—shocked, at least mildly, to find it to be real after all: tangible, visible, surrounding me, I part of it. That is something like what I feel when I arrive in a foreign country, leave the plane, and find that this strange, unimaginable place is at last real and before me. That is also how I felt about marriage. Something I had dreamed about and wanted came with a strange suddenness into being. And it both fulfilled and upset my expectations. It was so much more real and satisfying than I had been able to imagine (that is always one of the deficiencies of the imagination). But the toughness of its reality also made it harder and more challenging, not than I had feared, but (with my innate love of ease) than I thought I might have liked. Yet here I am, living it, enjoying it, even now.

But perhaps I have made faith sound too easy. I have failed to mention that one reason we find it hard to believe in good things either on a personal or on a cosmic scale is that sometimes the good things we want don't happen. Our hopes are not always fulfilled. That, we have been told, is the nature of our existence here. And though good things can happen to us, though peace and joy are assured us according to our faith, the good things must often come through a process of struggle and disappointment and patient waiting. Some things some of us desire will not come at all in this life. But we have been assured by someone who knew the Lord well that "all our losses will be made up in the resurrection from the dead." Faith must finally be faith like that of Abraham or of Job, who affirmed, "Though He should slay me, yet will I trust in Him."

I'm not sure that this aspect of our experience is really susceptible to being "figured out." The idea that life's trials and deprivations are purposeful seems reasonable to me and has proved true in my own experience. Yet I know too little of life's trials to speak with real authority about them. What I know is that God and His Son, whose suffering was beyond all human measure, have assured us that our trials have purpose and can have a positive outcome if we remain faithful through them. I have experienced the reality of that divine voice, and despite the limits of my understanding, the wisest choice in every way I can make is to put my trust in the assurance that voice gives.

Fortunately, marriage has given me new insight into both the difficult and the glorious aspects of life in the Church and of my personal growth in spiritual things. I see how much responsibility I bear for the quality of my spiritual life. I see that my tendencies to criticize and complain are essentially an expression of my own doubts and fears. Shakespeare and Hawthorne portrayed husbands who could see nothing good about the most loving and virtuous of wives, and so it should not be surprising that the Church of God, glorious to those who see the Spirit at work in it, should have its share of critics. Those in and out of the Church tormented with doubt and feelings of inadequacy remind me now of myself as a sometimes doubting marriage partner, finding it hard to believe I am loved as I am, hungry for assurance, but unsatisfied with any I could be given. Marriage daily reminds me that faith is the power to see, to choose, to act, and to enjoy, and that it requires an abandonment of narrow certainties, preconceptions, defenses, and fears. I am also reminded of the need for work—a necessary partner of faith in marriage as well as in our spiritual lives, for in both, it is "thc willing and obedient" who will "eat the good of the land of Zion" (D&C 64:34). I continue to see, as I experience married life, how easy it is—through laziness or fear—to resist whatever my own mind does not make, whatever is offered from the outside, to resist happiness, to reject the feast of joy laid before me by insisting that my dark fantasies are real or by failing to act, as I must, to help turn my brighter beliefs into realities. I have seen, in my own life and that of others, how substantial that feast of joy can be when it is willingly accepted.

Faith has thus come to take the key role I might have expected it should. Without it—without this willingness to accept and power to give and create—love is not possible, happiness is not possible, none of the things I have wanted can become truly real for me. With it, nothing is impossible. There can enter into my life, through the process of time, even things my eyes have not seen nor my heart conceived, things I have hardly dared to imagine.

21

Richard Lloyd Anderson

A Tested Testimony

For a generation Richard Anderson has been among the most able and learned defenders of Joseph Smith's divine calling. In "A Tested Testimony," he temporarily sets aside the mechanics of scholarship to consider the strengths and weaknesses of scholarship itself; he probes what is beyond scholarship and suggests why religious convictions are consistent with it. Brother Anderson is Professor of Ancient Scripture at Brigham Young University, where he has taught since 1955. Among his many writings are Investigating the Book of Mormon Witnesses *and* Understanding Paul. *His long anticipated biography of Joseph and Emma Smith,* Dear Joseph—Dear Emma, *is nearing completion. Brother Anderson has served the Church as a bishop, in a stake presidency, and, most enduringly, as a Gospel Doctrine instructor. He and Carma de Jong Anderson are parents of four children.*

A first-person essay is a healthy aid to honesty, for reasoning about evidence may be peripheral to central religious decisions. The most telling strategy of pure academics against faith may be forcing a retreat to factual trivia. Indeed, there is often an inverse ratio between the provability of an issue in humanities and social sciences, and its relevance to the core questions that every thinking person must decide about values, goals, and ultimate truth. So I welcome a chance to speak as a human being to other human beings. The occasion is definitely not a lecture, for this conversation asks to what extent books and classrooms are stepping stones to religious judgments. After technical training and professional writing, perspectives can surely be expressed without jargon, without heavy footnoting, without the goal of producing another article for advancement. In short, I am trying to set aside the mechanics of scholarship and discuss its strengths and limitations in an informed and sympathetic way, asking what is beyond it, or why deep religious convictions are consistent with it. For integrity of method is not enough without examining one's motives in using those skills.

If this intended conversation is more than a literary device, the reader must size up the speaker. Every person has an angle of vision. How tested is this testimony? I changed from an intense missionary to an intense college student when 22, and now write at age 60, a turning point that would endow one in ancient Judaism with the wisdom of an elder statesman. I majored in European history as an undergraduate, took graduate degrees in law, Greek, and ancient history. My generation knew the democracy of military service in World War II, and I also served in the ranks of construction projects while school proceeded. The result is my deepest commitment to learning and aversion to academic snobbery. Moreover, my most significant personal education (as distinguished from gathering facts) came in my marriage to Carma de Jong, who was trained by her educator-father in a full range of analytic skills. Four individualistic children have added intense interaction. Since I consider the Ph.D. a tool and not an end, I have read widely in fields with promise of explaining reality, such as literature and psychology. Ward and stake positions have let me see the Church in action, but I wear battle ribbons from two decades of Gospel Doctrine teaching, where adult dialogue demands adult answers. Professionally, I have spent three busy and exciting decades in researching, writing, and teaching, mainly in the fields of New Testament and Church history.

I am qualifying myself as a witness. Most people do not connect that term to testimony. But the latter word came from Latin, where the word for witness is *testis*, whose narrated experience under legal oath was *testimonium*. Since we use the terms "testimony" and "testify" in both legal and religious situations, we should remember that "testimony" in both settings reports firsthand knowledge. The courtroom witness is monitored by judge and lawyers to stay on the subject, and Latter-day Saints are generally aware that their testimonies speak to the issues of the truth of the gospel and its principles. Whether in court or church, only firsthand knowledge is wanted.

In a final sense, Doctrine and Covenants 46 and 1 Corinthians 12 join to say that a testimony comes directly from the Holy Ghost. But truth can often be double-checked by multiple methods. The most satisfying approach in my historical research has been supplementary validation, where an incident could be verified and defined through distinct types of sources, such as recollections, personal journals, letters, newspapers, and public records. Some equivalent of this should produce common sense in religious judgments. Just as I see that medical studies correlate with the Word of Wisdom, there are many historical validations for the restored gospel. The Restoration also meets tests of consistency that Elder Widtsoe expressed by entitling a book *A Rational Faith*. The scriptures have a special place as a tool for truth in many dimensions—for one, they contain the historical record of God's revelations and programs of the past, standards that any religion claiming divine authority must meet. There are also sweeping principles of human development and maturity at work when the gospel is correctly applied. Thus I discern that gospel truths variously pass spiritual, rational, scriptural, factual, and pragmatic tests. As a newly returned missionary,

I could bear testimony from the Spirit, reason, and scripture, but nearly three decades later I can also testify that my study of history and of life firmly support the gospel on historical and practical grounds. Nor is my spiritual testimony diminished, for that remains the undergirding reality for all else.

If all do not easily see such harmonies, that does not automatically invalidate the insight of those who do. A talented graduate student recently interrupted my work to ask for help in deciphering the handwriting of an early journal at the LDS Historical Department. I read it aloud without hesitation, since it was regular cursive script of the period. My graduate student friend could recognize the words only after he knew what to look for. I then remembered that when I was a young researcher such script was difficult to read. The process is paradoxical, for the historian wants an objective reading, but until he imaginatively envisions what his document should be saying, he never adapts to its strange script.

Testimony is discovery. Perhaps it came to me early because love of discovery has been my central drive from boyhood to the present. I scouted out the foothills around my northeast Salt Lake home before the age of ten, and later ranged through places, books, and even professions, never ceasing to be an explorer, until I settled on historical investigation as a career. Does the very process of institutional education give the false impression of knowing all that is important? Anyone who moves to frontiers in the prepackaged university classes immediately sees the unknown and undiscovered looming high over little valleys of knowledge. There are universes beyond solar systems and microsystems within systems. In "mastering" a few fields and sampling many others, I have two main impressions—the tentativeness of much that passes for knowledge, and the broad consistency of the gospel with what is known. A testimony begins with humility, admitting that God's perspective is not earthbound, nor enclosed within voluminous "definitive" studies of the twentieth century. The gospel is true not only on its many correlations with specific factual data, but in its overall consistency with the nature of knowledge. Its teachings of expanding universes, eternal progression, and endless creativity all fit the scope of truth in secular fields. This is not the world of religious creeds and councils, legalistically wrapping principles and Divinity itself into neat bundles. Mormonism offers a theology of unlimited vistas that human study probes.

My overall impressions of the gospel are of dimension, depth, and direction. All valid research first identifies its base or sources. For the gospel these are the teachings of the prophets, especially those formally canonized as scripture. Thus Mormon sources start with the "standard works." Because of their fundamental nature, I have long crossed off much secondary literature in favor of knowing these intensively, just as I choose the earliest historical documents over later commentary. The standard works are true classics, containing principles so profound that one can study them a lifetime without achieving full understanding. Why are you bored if you hear a joke twice but are continually stimulated by the repetition of a quotation from an important mind? There is nothing superficial in the scriptures. The words may be eloquent or unsophisticated, but the content, as Paul said, is often divine treasure in earthen vessels. Few world religions claim such direct revelation. The major ones who do are Judaism, Islam, and Christianity, which are largely in agreement on the inspiration of the pre-Christian prophets. Mormonism is the inheritor of a prophetic tradition that other religions have stifled. As Jesus said, it is easy to enshrine past prophets but hard to accept current ones who criticize your easy ways in the name of the Lord. For me, the main reasons that support the mission of ancient prophets are the same ones that support the additional scriptures of the Restoration. I have a testimony of an unshackled God, with power to speak fully in all ages of the world, including our own.

Historical correlations? Approach this subject with modesty and discernment. A pioneer book on the archaeology of the Book of Mormon began its dust-jacket pitch with, "archaeologists generally agree that," followed by a dozen neat supports of the American scripture. As a bystander, I don't see American archaeologists nicely agreeing on much, and I certainly know that historians are always revising each other. If historians cannot agree when there are records, how can archaeology come up with easy supports when all is inference and deduction? My point is that we should not expect the intellectual world to prove the gospel true. Since knowledge of the past comes in bits and pieces, run what tests are possible and be realistic. Indeed, modern revelation gives a convincing answer on why God does not display overwhelming evidence of Himself and His work to mortals. Our purpose is to learn faith and develop qualities of independence and judgment to qualify us personally for eternal leadership. Jesus said that an adulterous generation seeks signs, and it is also a generation without moral courage that demands total intellectual proof.

Discussion of historical correlations becomes meaningful in this context. Gaining true firsthand knowledge takes so long that one can speak of few things from personal experience, but I have worked to place some things in that category. I have trailed the witnesses of the Book of Mormon to every county of residence, in every source available to me in newspapers, public records, and personal interviews. My small book on this subject is the tip of an iceberg of knowledge, for the lives and testimonies of these witnesses are bursting out of six legal-sized file drawers. I know these eleven men as rugged individualists not likely to be brainwashed by the Prophet or anyone else—that is why most of them left the Church in protest over policies. Disagreement on the truth of the work? There is no evidence of that, for their private discussions always supported the coming of the angel and the physical existence of the ancient record. I find no evidence of conspiracy with Joseph nor any reasonable theory of self-deception to explain their convictions. Just as Paul argued that the apostles were capable men of truth and had seen Jesus in the resurrection, I am convinced that the Book of Mormon witnesses were capable men of truth and saw the angel and the plates.

Hugh Nibley convinced me as an undergraduate that the Book of Mormon consistently displayed Jewish patterns, and he was then only halfway into the massive evidence that he has since published on that subject. My Jewish reading has reinforced that conclusion, but studies in ancient sources have impressed me further. For instance, love of history has led me to examine the major Greek and Roman historians and their explanations of the decline of their civilizations. Like many writers today, they possessed an intense moral sense, and they saw the cycle of modesty, industry, prosperity, luxury, and pride as the pattern of history. The Old Testament chronicles do the same, but on a far more simplistic level. The Book of Mormon has the fuller form of this self-explanation of ancient historiographers. And this is but one of scores of structural intricacies within the Book of Mormon. It has the marks of authentic, ancient historical writing. In a very recent general priesthood meeting, former state judge and Yale Divinity School student Bill Sheffield reflected my testimony of the Book of Mormon content: "complex, sophisticated, doctrinally profound, and beautiful."[1]

Behind events are personalities. The two that really count for Latter-day Saints are Joseph Smith and Jesus Christ, who the Prophet said appeared to him from time to time and directed his words in the revelations. For me the New Testament Gospels come through solidly as ancient sources of quality. And their composite picture of Jesus is coherent and convincing. Of course there are those who think the opposite, but the entire field of New Testament studies is chaotic in method and demands responsible, individual judgment. The student of personality should find superb characteristics in Jesus, one who was loving but morally challenging, courageous, filled with recognition of human selfishness but willing to give unselfish devotion to the Father who sent him and to his brothers and sisters whom he came to teach and for whom he willingly was sacrificed. In an alert life, one constantly learns more about the incredible dimensions of personality. I cannot read Third Nephi without increased appreciation for the powerful empathy of Christ's atonement, nor can I read the earliest account of the First Vision and the revelations of 1829 without feeling Christ's deepest concern. Here one moves from reasons for believing to a religious relationship. How could a young, inexperienced imitator produce new dimensions of love from the Savior of the world in his translations and revelations?

The Book of Mormon witnesses became my topic because I realized that many others would write about Joseph Smith. Yet one topic led inescapably to another. The basic question about Joseph Smith must be personality—in simple terms, whether he is honest and not deceived in reporting his incredible religious experiences. I began a book on his New York period, only to find that his family environment in New England became a book by itself. I started a small book profiling his marriage and family life, only to find that the subject required a large book and a dozen years for near-completion. Joseph Smith's private letters and personal writings are now available in the Dean C. Jessee edition, though several items included from Mark Hofmann are now questionable (for example, my tests indicate that the "treasure revelation" to Hyrum Smith in 1838 is spurious). Joseph Smith's speeches are reproduced from Nauvoo diaries in the Ehat and Cook edition. Published and unpublished sources on the Prophet portray a coherent personality—a youth predisposed by family background to seeking God and a true church; a young man willing to risk his life for the truth of his revelations; a maturing man occasionally displaying human anger when attacked but increasing in capacity for forbearance. The Prophet's life shows Christ-like generosity to family and his people, culminating as he labored to prepare them for his departure and died as their hostage. Almost any randomly selected pages of his personal writing show candor and religious sincerity. Joseph Smith well matches Christ's early apostles in native capacity, sincerity, and devotion to the Lord and his work. His forthright personal or dictated accounts of the First Vision all ring true in terms of his life and the simplicity of his words.

Some allege historical contradictions, though I see broad correlations that consistently support the Restoration. Technical problems in the First Vision accounts have satisfactory answers, but it is something of a myopic marvel that much ink flows today on the year of the vision or on minor variations in accounts, when the massive historical and theological issues support Joseph Smith on the message. History is not events, but events in perspective. The orthodox concept of Trinity emerged from a process of two centuries of ecclesiastical debate, not revelation. The resulting definition of the Nicene Council became the test of orthodoxy for Catholic and Protestant Christianity. The really big historical issue is that Joseph Smith claimed divine authority for rejecting this and other definitions, reporting that "the creeds were an abomination" to Christ and God. A study of Christian sources certainly vindicates Latter-day Saint teachings on the Godhead, apostasy, and the restoration of the organization and ordinances of the primitive church.

History becomes a weapon against the Church only when one loses sight of larger historical issues. Anti-Mormon literature has long traded on character assassination and trivia. Proving Joseph Smith's weaknesses does not invalidate his visions. The great revelations of God in the scriptures came either to Christ or to those much less perfect than he. The central question is the call and authority of any prophet, not his total saintliness, as the Bible record well attests. History is only as good as the integrity and care of its organizers, so if the facts seem to go against the Church, check the facts. My experience is that problems are unanswerable only for a time, so judgment sometimes needs to be suspended. History cannot always come up with immediate answers. I have a problem shelf, and I regularly take some off as solved as I put others on.

I have a negative testimony of anti-Mormon literature after decades of reading it to be well informed. It is boring and sterile to listen to professional complainers pour all information into a predetermined mold. One of the great religious stories of all time is there reduced to a series of supposed scandals in this shallow journalism. Since history is often used to shake faith, informed Latter-day Saints need to define the two main historical procedures. The first is gathering data, and validity is determined by what is contemporary, firsthand, reported without bias or remembered without distortion. In this first procedure there are fairly objective standards, though I find some trained Mormon scholars surprisingly sloppy about checking sources. But the second procedure in history brings most problems. After facts are determined, what generalizations or conclusions are to be drawn from them? All can agree that Joseph Smith told his First Vision in 1832, 1835, and 1838. A believer will see supplementing agreements, a determined critic will claim contradictions that invalidate the testimony, and a humanist will downplay the experience as only subjective anyway. They all agree on step one, identifying historical data, but radically differ in interpreting it, which is step two of the process. Lawyers constantly explain variance by their truism that "reasonable men may differ." So the discerning reader could well start with that slogan as a reminder that he should not be intimidated by the awesome terms "expert" or "historian." The student who gets his facts straight should make his own evaluation of what they mean. Indeed, Jesus and the prophets warn that we are responsible for making religious judgments humbly and carefully. President Hinckley well said in a general priesthood meeting in 1985 that the Church does not object to historical scrutiny when done with accuracy and balance. Those words summarize the two stages of quality history.

Science continues to probe earth and outer space, but what about inner space? The real nature of self remains at once the most important and the most elusive of questions. When Jesus lingered in poignant conversation after the Last Supper, he spoke reassuringly of being with the Father prior to the earth and returning soon to him. Removing barriers, he called his apostles "friends" and promised they would follow him. Nothing here suggests that humanity and divinity operate on different tracks of existence. Traditional Christianity proposes little about human origins except the hollow concept that we were created slightly before our earth life, which is followed by a static eternity of glorifying God or suffering some type of endless punishment. Christian common sense typically bypasses this simplistic scheme, but without divine basis for offering something better. Here modern scripture offers revealed knowledge of self that awakens many to a powerful recognition of their inner being.

Joseph Smith outlined our true past as individuals of dignity and accomplishment before coming into a world to be tested by life and to grow through that challenging process. A distant cousin to this idea is the concept of transmigration among Eastern religions, but it is surprising to read statistics in the West and find that nearly half those polled have a similar sense of prior existence. The pre-existence of mankind is plain in several early Christian sources, in ancient Judaism, and Western literature adds a sprinkling of insights. No doctrine reaches so deep into my inner being as this awareness of personal heritage. Knowing ancient parallels to the heavenly council recorded in the Book of Abraham, chapter three, and feeling the pronounced spiritual witness of its truth, I find the process of obtaining that book essentially irrelevant as a question of truth. Indeed, the expanded narrative about Abraham there also has striking parallels in historical Jewish sources. Evidently the papyri suggested the subject of Abraham to the Prophet, who then inquired and received revelation, his same method of "translation" of the Bible or of the seventh section of the Doctrine and Covenants. Whether or not this was the exact spiritual procedure, the result is highly impressive.

Mormonism likewise enhances the individual potential in the future, rescuing vital personalities from the obliteration assumed by skeptics or the constricted life of the saved or damned in schemes of the believer. The awe of discovery glows in Joseph Smith's opening words of Doctrine and Covenants 76, and this revelation on the future degrees of glory has an eternal scope worthy of an eternal Planner and Creator. A near lifetime has convinced me of unlimited possibilities and untapped powers, and I know of no other religious system that reaches into this developed sense of inner reality. I show why degrees of glory are an early Christian concept in my *Understanding Paul*, but here I am focusing on the insights of self-understanding. Of course such things are not measurable, but an inner sense of the elevated nature of human past and future is widely shared by highly intelligent people. They respond deeply to these doctrines as real, just as a developed sense of what is beautiful is widely shared in the arts and in nature. In both cases there is something less than objectivity but something more than subjectivity.

What is written by God's Spirit can be validated by God's Spirit. My testimony of the inspiration of the standard works is as strong as convictions about earthly knowledge, and it is constantly reaffirmed by marked peace and warmth within as these scriptures are studied. Joseph Smith outlines revelation as "pure intelligence flowing unto you" and "sudden strokes of ideas."[2] A reality in addition to sense perception, or truth in addition to logical proof, hardly needs defense. Scientific and historical methods parallel each other in reaching beyond data to find and interpret data. Slower analysis follows such creative thrusts, which are the moving forces of progress. Similarly, intelligence must include aesthetics. Music, art, and poetry fill such pervasive needs that I am emotionally starved without them. Beauty is truth in the sense that it extends actuality beyond physical senses and analytical logic. The whole person reaches God in his searching and renews this life-giving companionship through prayer. I testify that prayer brings the silent inflow of God's Spirit, insight into His purposes in my life and the lives of those in my circle of concern, and, at God's pleasure, answers of clarity in understanding and in events.

This spiritual knowledge is consistent with the world of intellect, though it transcends it. I value such knowledge beyond all facts, for it is the higher truth around which earthly facts can be meaningfully organized. The fields of human knowledge, for the most part, are not defined broadly enough to include spiritual perspective. Thus the experts in these fields often tend to ignore, reject, or even attack the concept of revelation and its content. After all, the field of history is practically defined as finding human explanations of events. Without contention, I must remember that the gospel is not on trial so much as the integrity of those who can honestly testify of it. Things are not much different in the professional world. In the final analysis, knowledge of any field is what one discovers or verifies without social pressure. Prizes, promotions, and associations of peers are often instruments to reward conformity under the name of respectable scholarship. I long ago learned that I would never speak with authority if I followed trends instead of firsthand sources. Just as there is no real knowledge without moral courage, there is no real religion without some form of martyrdom.

Moral responsibility is the central issue in every life, and Socrates is a superb non-scriptural example of undeviating intellectuality and unswerving accountability to the divine. His final "defense" is badly translated as the *Apology*, and there he insisted that he would not recant his probing ways to save his life. His mission of social criticism came from a "divine and spiritual" source: "this has been with me from childhood; a certain voice that comes to me" (*Apol.* 31 D). He modestly mentioned his unflinching performance in three dangerous battles for Athens. As he would not desert his assigned place as a soldier, he insisted, neither would he compromise a "divine" assignment to testify to Athens of its moral wrongs (*Apol.* 28 E). While not aspiring to any place in history, I have the same assignment. As a scholar I am trained to use scholarly methods and seek to use them honestly and with some degree of objectivity. But as a man touched by God's power I would be a coward to hide the inner knowledge of the divinity of Christ, of the Bible and modern scriptures, of Joseph Smith as a true prophet, and of the recognition of that spiritual power with succeeding prophets.

Peter showed his moral courage in martyrdom, and his first letter narrates the conduct on the cross of mankind's greatest moral model, showing how the writing of the New Testament was based on eyewitness experience with Jesus. At the outset of his second letter Peter also lists the main steps of growth after baptism. Here gospel knowing is clearly dependent on gospel living. The believer starts with faith and adds "virtue," with resulting knowledge, which is certainly the spiritual knowledge of the gospel, a testimony. Yet in Peter's progression, having a testimony is more a point of beginning than an end. For "knowledge" is followed by two qualities quite misleading in the King James Version: "temperance" and "patience." These terms in Greek simply mean "self-control" and "endurance," as a glance at most modern translations will show. If these are simple words, their application to life is challenging to the core and consumes decades. In summary, virtuous living precedes "knowledge," which then commits the convert to a lifetime of refining his virtues through trials and temptations. But such determined discipleship projects the believer beyond knowledge to companionship, for the final rewards of this ascending path are "godliness," followed by "brotherly kindness" and finally "charity." Thus self-control and endurance produce a Christ-like character, which advances one beyond knowledge to the use of the knowledge in eternal relationships, for Peter's final Greek words really mean "brotherhood" and "love," Christ's pinnacle principles.

A similar "ladder" of gospel progression is found in James, Paul, and less obviously John. I stress Peter's explanation because it so remarkably fits my personal growth. Thirty-five years ago I returned from an LDS mission, convinced that the gospel could be proved by the scriptures and the Spirit. I had assembled a missionary plan that solidly relied on Bible evidence for the Restoration. Looking back over a third of a century, I am impressed that few scriptures need modification in treatment, were I to give that missionary plan in lecture form today. I have since learned much about the limits of knowledge and time constraints on the learner. But careful study of Biblical languages has only confirmed my testimony that the scriptures solidly support the mission of Joseph Smith and the doctrines revealed to him.

Thus for me the gospel has successfully met three decades of testing, and in some measure, so have I. My spiritual knowledge still glows within, but I have learned by trial and error about lasting associations with God and His children. The intensity of my love for both is beyond words to express. My testimony is a key to commitment that means trying and trying again to be appropriately in harmony with God and loved ones. The resulting sense of wonder is remotely like my subdued amazement in college labs when experiments worked the way the textbooks claimed they would. Gospel living has supplemented my lifetime expansion of mind with a parallel expansion of soul. The ultimate knowledge of anything is experience with it, and using God's principles indeed brings the promised results of sustained joy.

A testimony gained must be maintained. A friend out of harmony with the Church once complained that he never learned anything in his Midwest sacrament meetings. But I have had students make the same complaint in a class where others said they were having the most exciting learning experience of their lives. Gospel education is infinitely rich and involves information, reason, revelation, and divine and human interrelationships. No one has perfect capacity in all these areas. So the uncommon gifts in common Saints can open doors to unmastered dimensions. The practical point here is that every Latter-day Saint is at a different level on the path to perfection, but all who are progressing share commitment and confidence in moving from the known to the unknown. A vital, applied faith is the principle behind spiritual growth. Lincoln, who struggled successfully for belief, shared this principle with a close friend who had known his earlier skepticism and laughed when he came upon the president lost in study of the Bible. This was the answer of a thoughtful leader who grew to become deeply committed to prayer and a steadfast sense of mission: "Take all of this book upon reason that you can, and the balance on faith, and you will live and die a happier and better man."[3]

Notes

1. *The Ensign*, May 1986, p. 42.
2. Andrew F. Ehat and Lyndon W. Cook, *The Words of Joseph Smith* (Provo, Utah: BYU Religious Studies Center, 1980), p. 5.
3. Joshua F. Speed, *Reminiscences of Abraham Lincoln* (Louisville: John P. Morton and Co., 1884), pp. 32-33.

22

Richard H. Cracroft

The Pattern Of Faith And Jolts Of Joy: Spiritual Surprises

Richard Cracroft, Professor of English at Brigham Young University, has served as a bishop, a stake president, and as President of the Zurich, Switzerland Mission. He earned B.A. and M.A. degrees at the University of Utah and a Ph.D. at the University of Wisconsin-Madison. Dr. Cracroft, who joined the BYU faculty in 1963, has served as Chairman of BYU's English Department and later as Dean of the College of Humanities. He and his wife, Janice Alger Cracroft, have three children. In the essay that follows, Brother Cracroft is frank about his many experiences with the Spirit—experiences that have frequently surprised, consistently given joy, and gradually taught him to recognize and follow a pattern of faith that he has found reliable and exhilarating.

I stood before them, at the end of a large *Bierstube* on an upper floor of the Munichholz Hotel in Steyr, Austria, enjoying once more the kind of spiritual surprise which has startled my life with refreshing frequency. "As all have not faith," I suppose the Lord has decided in my case, "let us give this man—and his kind—occasional jolts of joy. Otherwise, he'll never make it!"

So there I was, on a wintry Sunday morning in 1957, presenting a missionary discussion in my eight-month-old missionary German to a small group of Austrians in a cold and cluttered barroom carefully guarded by an Austrian plainclothes policeman ("plain clothes" meaning a slick leather trenchcoat, a slouch hat, and an unchanging expression).

Yet in the midst of this presentation on the need for a Savior in our lives, I was suddenly overwhelmed (not for the first time in those eight months) by the beauty of the plan I was outlining, by the wondrous nature of the Savior's role therein, and by the monumental significance of His role and that plan for me, my companion, and everyone in that room (including the cop), that city, Austria, and the entire world. Suddenly I transcended into the "O that I were an angel" or the "O, Jerusalem" experience and *felt* anew the thrill of what I had come to know as the Holy Spirit's workings on me—the welcome (but somehow different) chill up the spine; the fine, cold (but somehow different) sweat on my forehead; and the slight tremor of joy throughout my body. All of these signs affirmed to me that I was, at the moment, a testator of Eternal Truth, a witness for Jesus Christ. I thrilled.

Yet even as I looked at my minuscule "congregation" and saw the confirming Spirit working on each face (I'm not sure about the cop)—even then I was blessed with another affirming kind of testimony: suddenly I (or some part of me) was out of my body, at the back of the room, elevated in the corner, watching the whole event at a remove. I was looking at the backs of my friends; I was seeing *me* standing before that attentive group, while the other *me* in the rear corner was filled with a wondrous confirmation that what the young man was saying, in fervent but labored German, was true.

That other, somehow spiritually objective *me* was filled

with amazement at the changes which those truths had wrought upon that young man who, a year earlier, was struggling with himself, drifting, frustrated and purposeless, in and out of the gospel net. At that moment I realized Joy. And, like Enos, I knew that it was but a type of the joy which comes to every man and woman who, through the ministrations of the Holy Ghost, *realizes* Jesus Christ, and God, and the vision of the life of the Spirit.

Then, suddenly I was back in my earth-bound body, looking again through my own corporeal-spiritual eyes into the faces and hearts of the little congregation. And I knew, more than ever, that all of those truths which we encompass by the words, "The Gospel," were *really* true—true in a sense far beyond what I had hitherto comprehended; true in the sense of becoming, as my mission president, the late Jesse R. Curtis always said, "truer by the minute"; true in the sense that such truths are accessible by seeking unchanging patterns of faith which lead to knowledge and surprises of the Spirit—thrilling road signs on the course to eternal life.

II

So it has gone, since then, with me and the gospel and faith and life. Always endowed with a love for good books and for writing, I early opted for an English major (and was the only football player at Salt Lake City's East High School who joined the Pegasus [Literary] Club), a career as a teacher, and a lifetime of learning. This course was right, I felt, and I knew it was fun. Much later, I learned that such a course is termed "Intellectual," a label with which I never felt comfortable, implying as it seemed to that I was much brighter than I knew myself to be, and also implying an independence from God that I would ever shun.

Then I ran head-on into college—and into the company of brilliant young men (and a handful of teachers) who burningly disbelieved and who urged intellectual independence, themselves disdaining any spiritual dependence on God or His Church. They led me to taste the draughts of doubt (and a few other draughts, too). Amidst my own short-lived rebellion against Church and familial standards (which, it soon became apparent by my own guilt, had become *my* incontrovertible standards), I pondered life. My late-night thoughts were highly unoriginal self-catechisms regarding my own beliefs: Is there a Purpose in the Universe? Is this Purpose embodied in a God? Does this God or Purpose care about man? When we die, will we live again? If so, how? where? If we live again is there a judgment on our conduct during mortality? Is Jesus Christ truly what He is purported to be? Is prayer in His name listened to by Anyone? Would God or Christ really answer the prayers of individuals? Are prophets individuals who have received answers? Was Joseph Smith such a receptor? Is David O. McKay? (How I loved him!) I would then ponder the topics on which my friends could argue for hours: evolution, the historicity of Jesus of Nazareth, the personal weaknesses of Joseph Smith and other Church leaders, polygamy, the Mountain Meadows Massacre, the Blacks (in those days it was "the Negroes") and the Priesthood, the divinity of the Book of Mormon—and I was troubled by all of these topics. And so was everyone else I knew.

Night after night I would lie abed rehearsing this catechism, reviewing the arguments of my respected and articulate friends, their antitheses pounding in my ears. But, somehow, I kept on praying: each time, something within led me to conclude my vigil by kneeling in prayer. I would set aside my violations of my own standards, set aside my intellectual upheavals, and would pray to God just as I had been trained—for comfort, hope, and direction.

Amidst my follies, I also continued to attend Church meetings, where a wise bishop overlooked my hypocrisy (or, more simply and kindlier—*confusion*) and allowed me to become a senior ward teacher and a Sunday School teacher. I continued to perform both functions scrupulously, thereby keeping a fingernail grip on the outward Church, even as I was probing my inward beliefs. That same wise bishop urged but did not nag, set some tolerable and tolerant goals, and finally led me to see a course on which I would have to make some tentative decisions about my nightly catechism.

I decided that none of my questions could be decided by the intellect. I would have to opt for faith; and I soon realized that opting for faith was impossible without commitment. So I opted to test faith by living all of the commandments. I was amazed how soon I felt so very well about everything, and it was only a matter of days before I knew that I must also opt for the missionary experience.

I dreaded that experience, stretching out before me like a thirty-month sentence to Siberia. But I was also intrigued. I felt that a mission was, in fact, put up or shut up time for me, but also for the Lord. Frankly, I did not expect very much out of the missionary experience; but if faith precedes the miracle, I reasoned, I'd better see a miracle or two before long.

III

They came! I went to Austria and Switzerland, determined to place hard work on the altar. To my surprise, hard work led to increased faith; then, increasingly, to surprises of the Spirit, to promised miracles, as the Lord met the conditions of our bargain, "irrevocably decreed" as it had apparently been, "before the foundations of the world"—a bargain based in the pattern of faith, so simple, so true, and so available to everyone. My mission became a marvelous unfolding of my spirit, a time of discovering the patterns of joy.

I delighted to find that my companions and I could actually teach others the pattern. I soon saw the pattern I had just worked through repeated, with some variation, in the life of one of those we brought into the Church from that little group in Steyr, Austria (incidentally, most of the group in the *Bierstube* joined the Church within the following weeks).

Brother Karl, a leader in the Seventh-Day Adventist congregations in Upper Austria, first came to our attention when his wife, interested in our series of Tuesday lectures, invited us to meet him. Alert to the challenge, we armed ourselves with Sabbath-day scriptural references. Then, humble, fearful, and fasting, we rode our bikes to our meeting at his home. As we feared, our lesson on the Godhood was immediately challenged, and we allowed ourselves to be turned from our purpose to discussing the Sabbath. In the middle of the futile battle, however, a powerful inspiration struck my companion (whom I love today as I did then). He sent me, Doubting Dick, to my bicycle saddlebags to fetch the Plan of Salvation outline which I had carefully sketched on a roll of oilcloth. Since this was "my lesson," I began, now more fearful than ever, to teach those familiar concepts which we generally reserved until the second month of our visits. I wondered about my companion's inspiration.

But not for long. As I moved through the lesson, Brother Karl began to supply the supporting scriptures—even some we hadn't thought of. As I attempted to explain the various aspects of the Plan, he would gently interrupt and clarify the concepts to his wife and older children. And when I broached the need for vicarious baptism for the dead, he jumped to his feet, tears springing to his eyes, and loudly recited 1 Corinthians 15:29 ("Else what shall they do which are baptized for the dead..."). "I have studied for years," he cried, "to find out what this scripture meant, and now two young Americans make it crystal clear." Surprise: chill up the spine, cold sweat on the forehead, a body tremor. For all of us. Brother Karl was converted that evening and, with his wife, was baptized a month later.

I love him yet for the insights he taught me. One of us asked him in a later meeting how he had been able to overlook his strong feelings about the Sabbath. "I was faced by a larger, more comprehensive truth in which I had utmost faith," he said, "and I couldn't be bothered by lesser particulars." He knew that if he followed the grander truth, the other, lesser truths would all, somehow, fall into place. He had learned the pattern.

This spiritual surprise and the ensuing miracles also occurred in the life of Margarete, a sweet sixteen-year-old girl who also sat in that *Bierstube* on that long-ago morning. After a wonderful and profound conversion she joined the Church, and, through a series of inspired actions, was assisted in fleeing a terrible home environment to live among Church members in Switzerland. Just a few days later, she met a handsome young visitor from Germany who had joined the Church six months earlier and had chanced to come to Bern, Switzerland, for his vacation. They were married in the Swiss Temple two years later, have watched each of their children marry in the temple, and continue to live happily in Germany, where he serves as a bishop. The couple visited us recently, still rejoicing in their conversion and in each other, a joy which has also been renewed through a host of surprises of the Spirit. They know the pattern.

IV

I believe, at least in part, because I have watched the old patterns work in my life and in the lives of others. I believe because the patterns are testworthy. The individual makes a gesture towards belief and faith; the Spirit bears witness; the miracle follows; then the surprises of the Spirit crop up from time to time to remind the believer that though he or she is twenty or forty or sixty years out from Home, our Father will send a spark, a surprise, or a shock of recognition as if to say, "Here, my child, here is a whiff of truth, a thrill of remembrance, a tangible something to remind you—for a moment—that I'm here; that you're on course; that your feet are still treading, however imperfectly, the paths which will lead to joy in mortality and in eternity."

At least it has been so for me. I became an academic, a Professor, a Dean; I have learned the (in)appropriate skepticism; I have actively pursued *truth* (lower case), and frankly enjoyed the pursuit. But as an observer of others—not only as an academic but as a bishop and stake president, and now as a mission president—I have learned to my own satisfaction that the truths found in the historical record are secondary to the larger, comprehensive gospel *Truths* (upper case) found through faith—until those lesser truths find their larger, spiritual context. It is a matter of perspective, and I find more joy and satisfaction in the larger, vertical perspective than in the narrower, horizontal view.

For me the pattern has always followed the course it took one afternoon in 1967, in the stacks of the library at the

University of Wisconsin. I was pursuing a book through the aisles of bookshelves when, to my surprise, I found myself in the Mormon section, which I had not discovered in two years of intensive library work. I looked at a number of newer books, books which I had not read. Suddenly, a spiritual craving overwhelmed me and I sat down at a carrel, realizing that though I was "active" and "faithful," I had not made any real effort to study the gospel for over two years. I read hungrily all afternoon in the books I had found, then went home for a chat with my wife, confessing to her that I had allowed an embarrassing imbalance to develop in my life and had gradually shifted perspectives. I resolved to her that I would opt more strongly for the spiritual route, though I expressed concern that time and energy would be difficult to find, engaged as I was in completing my doctoral studies. Then another surprise (I shouldn't have been surprised by then—I knew the pattern): that Sunday, the bishop called me to be the new seminary teacher; I accepted, even before I learned there was a small but very welcome stipend. Suddenly I found myself, each weekday evening, spending from 10:30 p.m. until midnight studying the New Testament. It was a gift from the Lord, in answer to an enlivened faith, a gift which enabled me to regain my spiritual equipoise.

I have found, then, that even a slight gesture toward faith will beget opportunities to put one's life in harmony with God's pattern—regardless of mortal pressures. Indeed, every time I have opted to place faith above other matters, I have been almost instantly rewarded with spiritual surprises, with growth, with joy. I believe in the pattern: opting for faith soon begets change and growth and opportunity. It works; how can I not believe? How much more important is this joy than the spiritual bruisings which I inevitably receive through criticism of leadership, policies, programs—and fellow mortals. I find I must soon hasten back to the pattern to find spiritual growth and refreshment.

V

That spiritual manifestation which I experienced in

Austria in 1957 is a rich memory for me yet, but it has been a memory reinforced through many such surprises which have repeatedly affirmed to me that opting for faith back in 1956 was the right course to belief and testimony and increased faith. It is not a new option, of course. Rather, it is the timeless and proven way of the spiritual race, from Adam through Abraham and Moses, Isaiah and Jeremiah, from Jesus to Peter and John and Paul; it is the way of spiritual men from Joseph Smith to Brigham Young to David O. McKay, Spencer W. Kimball, and Ezra Taft Benson; it is the way for every one of us mortals who desires to have his or her name inscribed in the Lamb's Book of Life.

I am a common man, a scene-sweller at best. Yet even in my relatively insignificant ministry, tucked away in Provo, Utah, and Zurich, Switzerland, the Lord's will has been manifest and, with countless others who labor quietly in their ministries, I could present a rich catalogue of striking and wondrous surprises of the Spirit. A few weeks ago I was stopped on my way by a man who said, "That was quite a blessing you gave." He reminded me that four years before he had been given up for dead, with inoperable brain cancer; that I, who was then his stake president, had given him a blessing; that he had been cured—and had just then gotten around to telling me about it!

Again, he reminded me of the faith-pattern. I do not profess to have the gift of healing, but as I assess the list of persons whom I have blessed over several decades, I repeatedly find the old pattern of joyous surprise in which the Lord has reversed, abated, or slowed apparently mortal illnesses. I think of words which have crowded into my mouth at the bedside of several Saints certain to die, words which cry out against rational knowledge imparted by the doctor, words proclaiming healing or the promise of several more years of vigorous, productive life—and I wonder, but I no longer tremble, for the words are fulfilled.

I don't profess to know why He doesn't always heal, or why He often chooses to allow this young father or that mother or child to die while that one is spared, when to spare them all would seem merciful and just. I know only that we must "confess his hand in all things," understand our quaint perspective, and affirm that "blessed are the dead that die in the Lord" (D&C 63:49).

And I ponder the other surprises of the Spirit: the clear-cut instances of revelation I saw as stake president in selecting men to become bishops, manifestations so powerful that I could say "thus saith the Lord" in issuing those calls; or in selecting women to fill important callings in Relief Society, Primary, and the YWMIA—instances in which I could not take my mind or my pencil from a name on a list, a name I barely knew, until I resolved to issue the call; or instances in which it came clearly to me that the right name was not on the list. In one such case, I returned to fasting and prayer—with a deadline, only to hear my wife mention, five minutes before the deadline, the right person's name in an entirely different context, and receive the familiar chill up the spine and the confirmation I had sought. (Only to be told later that evening by the senior high councilor, while clearing the name, "Oh, I saw her in the store the other day and the Spirit said, 'There's the new president.' " "Why didn't you tell me?" I groused. "Why, the Lord's directing this stake; I knew you'd get the message soon enough.") So it went, time after time.

And I think of the intervention from beyond the grave: of the time when the recently deceased mother of a young missionary made her presence so powerfully known during the setting-apart that I finally had to acknowledge it in the blessing—and how the inactive father took me aside, pale and trembling, and said he had looked up and saw his deceased wife standing beside him. It made a difference in his life! And I think of the blessing of a believing but shattered alcoholic. Following the initial portion of the sealing blessing, his mother, also recently dead, literally took over the blessing. I was led to introduce her presence, to counsel the man to listen to the words of his mother—who spoke to him, through me, with all of the tender yet warning words she could pour from behind the veil. It was a humbling experience which my counselor and I will never forget.

These events are faithful realities. While they do not necessarily lead to belief, they affirm the pattern of faith, and they make vivid the actuality of the spiritual world. Collectively they overwhelm me and make it easy to believe such scriptural statements as "I beheld the heavens open....And I saw the Lord, and he stood before my face, and he talked with me, even as a man talketh one with another, face to face" (Moses 7:3-4); or to believe the experience in that wooded grove, that modern Mount of Transfiguration, in which Joseph Smith, Jr., says, "I saw a pillar of light exactly over my head, above the brightness of the sun, [and] I saw two Personages, whose brightness and glory defy all description, standing above me in the air. One of them spake unto me, calling me by name and said, pointing to the other — This is My Beloved Son. Hear Him!" (Joseph Smith—History 1:16-17).

VI

Truth and testimony have flooded the earth—but not many desire to wet their feet. "Give me evidence," they cry, overlooking the testimonies of thousands now dead who have left a record of their witness, or the witnesses of hundreds among us whose testimonies appear in print, who bear witness in meetings, who offer us accounts of their spiritual surprises. I believe these testimonies are true and faithful, for they spring from the great pattern, from faith, and, when they are listened to by the faithful, live afresh, for the Spirit transforms their words into Living Water. And the word flows forth—and always shall—the word which answers the questions of my youthful catechism (and everyone's): There is a God—I have learned it. Jesus of Nazareth is His Only Begotten in the flesh—I know it. The prophets of God speak and have spoken truth—the Spirit whispers it. Joseph Smith is a prophet of God—God declares it. The Book of Mormon is a true witness of Christ—Christ affirms it. The Church of Jesus Christ of Latter-day Saints continues as the "only true and living Church" with which our Lord is well pleased—He has spoken it.

It is for us, then, to rejoice, give thanks, and endure in faith and in gratitude for the pattern, for those flashes of

Truth which God in His grace grants His Saints. This witness, which has come through faith, is available to such as can be still, listen, and know that God is God and has all things in His sure hands, in which we must place ourselves, occasionally stirred by jolts of joy and faithfully awaiting the resolution.

Index